LIBERAL OPINIONS

LIBERAL OPINIONS

My Life in the Stream of History

William A. Norris

QUID PRO BOOKS

New Orleans, Louisiana

Published in 2016 by Quid Pro Books, in the series *Journeys and Memoirs.*

ISBN 978-1-61027-364-0 (pbk.)
ISBN 978-1-61027-363-3 (hbk.)
ISBN 978-1-61027-365-7 (eBook)

QUID PRO BOOKS
Quid Pro, LLC
5860 Citrus Blvd., Suite D-101
New Orleans, Louisiana 70123
www.quidprobooks.com

Publisher's Cataloging in Publication

Norris, William A.

    Liberal opinions : my life in the stream of history / William A. Norris; foreword by Edward Lazarus.

        p. cm. — (Journeys and memoirs)

1. Norris, William A., 1927—. 2. Judges—United States—Biography. 3. Lawyers—California—Biography. 4. Lawyers—United States—Biography. I. Title. II. Series.

KF 8745 .N31 A3 2016   341.32'84—dc20
Library of Congress Control Number: 2016948716   CIP

Front cover photograph, also found at page 242, © 1997 by Nathanson's Photography. Back cover photograph, also found at page 284, © 1999 by Lee Salem Photography. Photograph found at page 256 © 1991 by Alan Berliner. Photograph found at page 276 provided courtesy of Joe Negro. Used by permission. The author and publisher thank all those who have generously shared photographs for their contribution to this book.

*To Jane, with you I have written
the best chapters of my life.*

CONTENTS

FOREWORD

I have known Bill Norris for almost thirty years, since I began clerking for him in the summer of 1987. In that time, I have had the privilege to be his law clerk, mentee, colleague, and, most important to me, a friend to Bill and his family. Over those years, around the office or at Shabbat dinners at his house, Bill shared any number of stories from his youth, his time at Princeton and Stanford Law School, his career as one of Los Angeles' leading lawyers, his various roles serving the city and his adopted state of California, and his relationships with Justice William O. Douglas, Governors Pat and Jerry Brown, Bobby Kennedy, Warren Christopher, and other national figures. I was also lucky enough to be partial eye-witness to his deeply influential tenure on the U.S. Court of Appeals for the Ninth Circuit, where he quickly became a leading voice across an incredibly broad range of issues from civil rights (especially gay rights) to free speech, the death penalty, civil procedure, and, not least, corporate law, which is too rarely the strong suit of judges. And I was there to see Bill help expose Supreme Court nominee Robert Bork as a pretender to jurisprudential integrity as well as his important behind the scenes role in the nomination of then-Judge Anthony Kennedy to the Supreme Court.

Yet despite this long history with Bill, it wasn't until I read the manuscript for his memoir that I came to appreciate fully the rich panorama of Bill's singularly American story. The Horatio Alger elements jump off the page. Small town boy, son of immigrants, reared on the simple virtues of hard work and self-reliance, educated on the GI Bill, goes West with his bride and budding family to make his way in the world. He succeeds beyond imagination, one achievement piling on the next, by dint of a keen analytic mind and a zest for political and civic engagement.

But the tale told is more than just one of the American dream coming true. Bill's career embodied a unique feature of the American experiment —the engine of law, in the hands of brilliant, committed, and creative lawyers, to drive profound social change. He came of political age at the time of FDR's Four Freedoms speech that proclaimed a right to economic security and Hubert Humphrey's speech to the Democratic National Convention in 1948, urging the country to come out from under the "shadow of states' rights and into the sunshine of human rights." In and out of government, Bill relentlessly pursued those goals. He was ahead of his time, over and over again, on civil rights for African Americans, women, Native Americans, and gays, freedom of the press, gun control, education reform, health care. The list goes on. As a Judge, he did not engage in the pretense of serving merely an umpire calling balls and strikes; he used exacting legal logic to drive results consistent with the finest aspirations of the country that had bestowed opportunity on his parents and on him. Bill did not win (or has not yet won) every battle. With a different turn of luck, Bill might well have become a leading national political figure or a Supreme Court Justice. But he won more than his share and has left indelible marks from the acclaimed modern art museum he helped found in Los Angeles to the Supreme Court opinion affirming a right to gay marriage based on a theory of equality that he had championed more than two decades earlier.

If I have a complaint about Bill's memoir, it is the modesty with which he often presents his own role. In his insistence on extolling the brilliance of his colleagues and law clerks (thank you my friend), Bill dramatically undersells his own fearsome and tireless intelligence. It is true that, with generous spirit, he often propelled junior lawyers into senior roles and drew eagerly on the thinking of the young recruits to the Norris brigade. For Bill, this was as much a part of mentorship as the lifelong career advice he has given dozens of us. But make no mistake. Bill led from the front with a relentless perfectionism. He would demand rewrite after rewrite to the point of infuriation, and sometimes beyond. If that did not do the trick, he would push you off the computer and rewrite himself. He was in search of extreme clarity of thought and expression, an impregnability of argument. He expected equally of himself and those around him— and over time we absorbed that expectation for ourselves in one of the great gifts of the relationship.

Another of Bill's remarkable traits is his unquenchable optimism in a cynical age. In the time I have known him, Bill has been appreciative of the past but also un-nostalgic, firmly convinced that his latest endeavor or whatever chapter comes next will be at least as enjoyable and fulfilling as the last. He has certainly achieved great happiness now, enjoying life with his great love, Jane, surrounded by beloved children and grandchildren, proud of his extended clan of former colleagues and clerks, who have gone on to great success in the judiciary, academia, government, private practice, non-profit, and business.

I remember well my first phone conversation with Bill—my interview for a clerkship in his Chambers. At the end, sight unseen, he hired me with a single phrase: "Pack your tennis racquet." He made the decision on pure instinct, the same instinct that led Stanford Professor George Osborne to advise him after a grilling in his first year class—"Trust your gut." That gut led Bill to a fascinating and important life that I am so deeply grateful to have intersected. It is well chronicled here.

EDWARD LAZARUS

Washington, D.C.
June 2016

"My clerkship with Justice Douglas was tremendously important. He told me, Christopher, get out into the stream of history and see what happens."

Warren Christopher

LIBERAL OPINIONS

William A. Norris

PROLOGUE:
ECHOES OF AN EARLY DECISION

I received the call from one of my last law clerks, Tobias Wolff, the morning of December 22, 2010. He had just left the ceremony at the Department of the Interior in Washington, D.C., and his voice shook with emotion as he described what he had witnessed. Tobias was one of the honored guests when President Obama signed the repeal of the odious piece of legislation known as "Don't Ask, Don't Tell," in which courageous and patriotic men and women in the military had been forced for decades to deny their basic identities because they wanted to serve our country. The repeal was so important, Obama said, "For we are not a nation that says, 'don't ask, don't tell.' We are a nation that says, 'Out of many, we are one.'"

Tobias painted the whole scene for me. The congressional leaders who surrounded the president as he signed, the presence of the Chairman of the Joint Chiefs of Staff, Mike Mullen, and the Attorney General, Eric Holder, the audience that was filled with those who, like Tobias, had worked to make this day possible. He told me the story that Obama had recounted about a soldier during the brutal Battle of the Bulge in World War II, when Patton's Third Army was attacked on a narrow trail.

During that battle, a private named Lloyd Corwin fell into a ravine and would have died, had Andy Lee, a fellow soldier, not risked his own life to save him. These were men of my generation, who served in uniform in World War II like two of my older brothers. Forty years later, Corwin, with grown children of his own, met Andy for a reunion. Andy told him that he was gay. By 2010 both men were dead, but Corwin's son was in the audience that day and heard the president say, "Lloyd knew what mattered. He knew what had kept him alive; what made it possible for him to come home and start a family and live the rest of his life. It was his friend."

Tobias had been the chief advisor to the Obama campaign on LGBT issues and wrote the campaign's position statement on the repeal of the Don't Ask, Don't Tell policy. When the President took office, Tobias had been involved in some very high-level discussions about repealing the statute, and when the president announced in the State of the Union that this was a priority, he convened a working group that wound up including Tobias as a key player. Tobias knew that I had been working on the issue of gay rights since he was just a child. During his clerkship interview with me, we had a deep discussion about this pernicious law, whose very *purpose* was to force people to live a lie, to pretend that their true selves do not really exist. In that respect, the Don't Ask, Don't Tell policy was sui generis; it was completely unique. It was also evil.

The repeal took longer than I had thought it would, but I knew that the law could never stand the test of time. In 1997, right after I retired as a federal judge, the national gay rights organization LAMBDA awarded me their prestigious Liberty Award. It was a well-attended affair held at the Beverly Wilshire Hotel. Los Angeles Mayor Richard Riordan introduced me, saying, "When Bill and I were in Princeton together, 'diversity' meant having a roommate from Texas." He got a big laugh.

It was one of my first speeches after I left the bench and, as I put it then, "reclaimed my First Amendment rights." And on October 16, 1997, I did so with a vengeance, about a subject that was very important to me. I began by invoking the Civil Rights movement and recalling President Bill Clinton's recent visit to Arkansas when he joined the governor Mike Huckabee in deploring the racist legacy of Orval Faubus and his refusal to permit the desegregation of the Little Rock schools. President Clinton was, of course, responsible for Don't Ask, Don't Tell.

I drew the parallel between civil rights for African Americans and civil rights for gay men and lesbians, which I called "the most intractable civil rights issue of the nineties." I focused on Don't Ask, Don't Tell, which had been the rule of the land since 1994 and called it "evil, just as the racism of Governor Faubus was evil. Indeed, I will make a prediction tonight," I said. The room was packed and silent as a cathedral. "I predict that Don't Ask, Don't Tell will not long stand the test of time. The policy is so wrong-headed that its demise will come sooner than its supporters may think. Yes, I predict that Don't Ask, Don't Tell will soon be laid to rest in our national cemetery of shame, alongside other discriminatory actions that stain our national heritage." I called on President Clinton to "admit his mistake of judgment and renounce Don't Ask, Don't Tell policy before it becomes a permanent stain on his legacy."

He never did.

Fourteen years after my speech, when the statue was finally successfully repealed, the Obama Administration held the signing ceremony in the Department of the Interior, and Tobias was in the front row.

Crying.

It was his handsome image—a single tear sliding down his right cheek —that appeared in magazines and newspapers all over the country. Tobias later told me he figured that photographers "love seeing a grown man cry." If there had been photographers present during my call with Tobias while he told me about the ceremony, they could have taken pictures of two grown men crying. I too felt powerful emotions overwhelm me, fueled by memories of the long fight for a particular battle for justice, equality, and civil rights that had been one of my toughest and proudest moments as a judge. Tobias had been a leader in fighting that battle, bringing his formidable intellect into a conflict that went to the heart of his identity as a homosexual man. For me, the battle went to the heart of my identity as a heterosexual man who believes in simple justice. One of the great privileges of being a federal judge is the occasional opportunity to actually perform justice on an issue that may not be easily, much less universally, appreciated.

I had such an opportunity in 1987, in a case concerning an African American homosexual man named Sergeant Perry J. Watkins—a clerk who had served in the United States Army for fourteen years with distinction, but was not permitted to reenlist. It was my most celebrated case, or, for some folks, the most horrendous opinion I ever wrote. Put very simply, my argument was that sexual orientation, like the color of one's skin, was fixed at birth. One of the greatest victories in the Civil Rights movement was to point out that statutes that distinguish between blacks and whites violate the Equal Protection Clause of the Constitution. I expanded this argument to include homosexuals, in a ruling that was a bombshell. I will share the details of the Watkins case later in this story, but when Tobias called me that historic morning of the signing ceremony of the repeal of Don't Ask, Don't Tell, he said, "You played a role in making this possible. I will never be able to express my gratitude."

In looking back, I suppose that I have played a role, sometimes big, sometimes small, in making a few things possible. And that is the story that I am about to tell. In many ways, telling this story is my way of trying to express my gratitude to so many people who helped me along the way.

And it all began in 1927, in Turtle Creek, Pennsylvania.

William Albert Norris, age 3

PART I

HOW A KID FROM TURTLE CREEK PA BECAME A PRINCETON GRADUATE

"None of us got where we are solely by pulling ourselves up by our bootstraps. We got here because somebody—a parent, a teacher, an Ivy League crony or a few nuns—bent down and helped us pick up our boots."

Thurgood Marshall

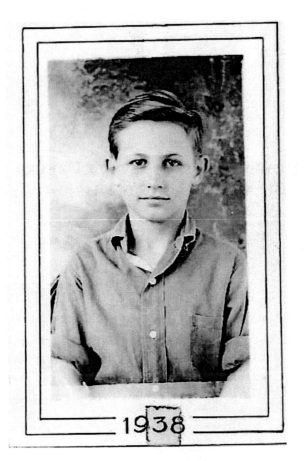

1938

Bill Norris, age 11

1

THE BOY FROM TURTLE CREEK

I have lived most of my life in California. Or maybe I should put it another way: I have lived most of my *lives* in California.

The end of World War II brought me to California as a young Navy pharmacy mate in San Diego where I met my first wife, who eventually became the mother of my four children. I went to Princeton on the GI Bill and returned to California to attend law school at Stanford. I practiced law in Los Angeles for over forty years. During those years, I worked in politics and public service. I even ran for the office of California's Attorney General. (And lost, but that comes later.) For seventeen years, I served as a judge on the Ninth Circuit Court of Appeals. I mentored quite a few brilliant, young lawyers who went on to make their own mark in the country. As its Founding President, I played a leading role in the creation of L.A.'s Museum of Contemporary Art (MOCA).

California not only provided the backdrop of my professional life, it was the place where all the most important pieces of my adult family life played out. Most of my four children and four step-children all consider California their home. I married three women from California, but it is not surprising, I suppose, that my great love, and death-do-us-part partner in life, Jane Jelenko, is like me, a California transplant, though her roots are back in New York. She understands intuitively that when folks assume that California was the single most formative experience of my life, I would have to disagree. I think that all I became, all I accomplished, and most important, all the most central and vital values of my life—fairness, equality, unapologetic liberalism, a commitment to civil rights and civil liberties—were formed in Turtle Creek, Pennsylvania. I have often spoken about the promises of liberty and fairness that lie at the center of our legal heritage. For me, the seeds of those promises were planted in Turtle Creek.

If you travel about twelve miles southeast from the tall buildings and wonderful universities and great ball fields of Pittsburgh, Pennsylvania, you will reach my old hometown. Turtle Creek is sometimes referred to as a "suburb" of Pittsburgh, but in fact it's a borough in Alleghany County, distinct enough to have its own census and its own very unique character. Those of us who came from there liked to pronounce it, "Turtle Crik," referring to the tributary of the 130-mile Monongahela River that gave our town its name.

It is an old settlement. One of the local myths was that Turtle Creek Valley was named for "Little Turtle," or Chief Michikinikwa, who was a Miami Nation war chief in the 1790's. In fact, I found out only recently that the place was most likely named by the Indians because of the abundance of turtles that thrived in the creek. I had to laugh because when I lived there, actual turtles in Turtle Creek were nowhere to be found. It was one of the most polluted streams in the county and even the subject of a Congressional committee investigation.

Somehow the place thrived. In the 1900s, George Westinghouse made Turtle Creek Valley the site of two big factories. Three different railroads converged in that little canyon, including the old Pennsylvania Railroad. The Westinghouse plants, the railroads and the old steel mills provided a livelihood to many of the 4000 families, including mine, who lived there.

Before Gene Kelly became a movie star, his sister lived in Turtle Creek and directed the dancing in my high school's annual minstrel show in which I once performed. Then there was Leon Hart, one of the greatest football players of all time who played eight seasons with the Detroit Lions. That they were our most famous celebrities probably says a lot about the modesty of the place and the people.

Like many parts of America during the Depression, my small community was marked by an appreciation for the importance of family and the value of hard work, education and personal responsibility.

From the 1920's to the 1940's, my parents, my three brothers, two sisters and I just considered Turtle Creek our home. And we loved it.

2

COMING TO AMERICA

Many of the families had lived in Turtle Creek for generations but others of us were the children of recent immigrants. There were Irish and Italian and Polish families who, like immigrants throughout American history, had been lured to the United States by the promise of making a much better, more prosperous, life. For those who were drawn to Turtle Creek, the Westinghouse plants were powerful magnets.

My parents' stories mirrored those of many immigrants in the early twentieth century. My father's name was George Norris and he was born in Liverpool, England in 1893. Florence Clive was my mother's maiden name and she was born in Manchester in the same year. Along with millions of other immigrants, my parents' first experience of the United States was disembarking at Ellis Island.

My mother arrived first. To describe the hardship of her early life is to take a chapter out of a novel by Dickens. She spent her first four years in a small cottage outside of Manchester, and her father would bale hay from their property and make extra money by transporting furniture and household goods in his horse drawn cart. My mother's memories of that time of a modest but intact family life were cloudy. She was such a small child, the youngest of four girls, during those brief calm family days. On Christmas Day, when my mother was four years old, her mother died giving birth to the only boy in the family. This tragic anniversary always made that holiday a somber one for her and for our family. My mother would say that after her mother died, her father "just went to pieces," overwhelmed by the responsibility for the four girls and infant boy.

Since he was unable to care for his young brood, the children were all dispersed to different aunts. My mother, raised by an aunt who already had three children of her own, felt close to the family. She lived and went

9

to school in Newton Heath, a poor, densely industrialized suburb of Manchester that is now probably most famous as the home of the Manchester United Football Club. But it is rough and run-down, disadvantaged and polluted, and one can only imagine what it was like in the beginning of the twentieth century.

My mother liked to point out the paradox of her educational life. Like all children then, she was required to take a proficiency exam after a certain grade level. She was told that because she had done so well, she no longer had to go to school. Her formal education stopped when she was eleven years old. Her story was certainly not exceptional; child labor was a fact of life for most people at that time. Children were one more mouth to feed so therefore needed to contribute to the family. At the age of eleven-and-a-half, before she even reached puberty, my mother left school for work in the spinning mills of Manchester.

Manchester is known as the first industrial town in England and its cotton mills were one of its first industries. The mills were occupational safety nightmares. Steam and cotton fiber filled the air in the crammed spaces, where hundreds of workers labored for only five dollars a week.

With their small hands, children were valuable employees in the mills. As a small child working in the spinning mills, my mother was in charge of four looms, large machines that demanded far more from her physically than she was able to give. The mill was unbearably hot so she had to wear a little white shift with bloomers underneath. The workers started the day at six in the morning and went home at five in the afternoon. Every week she was given an envelope that contained her pay, but she was never allowed to open it. She gave it directly to her aunt who then would give her a shilling for the week.

Not surprisingly, she became very ill, although it was never clear exactly with what. When referring to her illness she always said that she "took a paralysis" and completely lost muscle function. She was bedridden for eight or nine months in her aunt's home. After that she returned to work, but this time in the weaving sheds, which were apparently less stressful on a young body. After a few years of relative stability, her beloved aunt and her family left Manchester to follow her aunt's prosperous older brother to Turtle Creek, Pennsylvania, in the United States. My mother was once more abandoned; at fourteen, too young to live independently, she was sent to another aunt's home.

This one had no children of her own and had little interest in them and only reluctantly agreed to take care of her. My mother said, "She was very wicked with us, very strict." Among the many privations was an almost pathological level of control over my mother's social life. I have a picture of my mother at seventeen, and she was a lovely girl with wide set eyes, softly curling hair, and a sweet but intelligent face. Her aunt made it clear that there would be absolutely no gentleman callers until my mother was nearly out of her teenage years. My mother was miserable. She continued to work and returned to her new home, which was a cold and forbidding place. What a contrast her life was to that contained in the letters that she received from her aunt in Turtle Creek. The new and wonderful life in American described in those letters foreshadowed how much my mother would like it there.

But life in England went on. Finally, she was allowed to date. She went out with one young man, but he was easy to dismiss after she laid eyes on another, handsome George Norris who worked as a copy boy for the *Manchester Evening Chronicle*. She knew that he was "the one" and he remained her one and only until she was widowed at the age of 87. She died at ninety-eight.

As a copy boy, my father would ride his bicycle and accompany a reporter to cover a story such as a fire. The reporter would write down some of the facts, maybe even interview a bystander, then hand his notes to my father who would jump on his bike and pedal back to the newspaper office. It was a wonderful introduction to the world of journalism for him and it got into his blood. He learned to take shorthand and to type, knowing that one day, he too would be writing the stories.

My parents dated for about two years and married at St. Ann's Church in Newton Heath, on July 29, 1914, when they were both twenty-one years old. How strange it is to look back and realize what a momentous week in history surrounded the day of my parents wedding. On July 28, the Archduke Franz Ferdinand was murdered in Sarajevo and within the following week, like dominos tumbling down one after the other, Germany declared war first on Russia, then on France, Britain in response declared war on Germany, and the United States declared its neutrality. All of a sudden the reliable order of the civilized world was falling apart.

I am not sure why my father did not immediately enlist, but he never did. The young couple lived with his parents. My mother would say that she and my father established a small shop selling "bits of this and bits of that." One evening, when my father returned from his job at the paper, my mother announced that she was going to America to see what it was like and visit her aunt. Her mother-in-law was astonished at her new daughter-in-law's grand plans, but my father was a sensible man and knew already that trying to hold my mother back when she was determined to do something was a mistake. He agreed that she could go and said that he would follow her as soon as he could. A few weeks later, my father and her sister took her to the port in Liverpool and waved goodbye as she embarked on the *Orduna*, with 27 pounds sterling in her pocket and a one-way ticket. Her courage wavered a bit as she stood on the deck waving to her new husband and to her sister. "What have I done?" she thought, as tears streamed down her face.

She left on February 3. The day after she set sail, the Germans expanded the war into the seas and prepared to attack British ships. The *Orduna* was well underway when a German submarine stopped the boat. The Captain of the *Orduna* replaced the British flag with an American one, saving the lives of the passengers and crew.

My mother was miserably sick for the entire nine-day journey and was cared for by a woman to whom she became intensely attached. When they disembarked at Ellis Island, the woman shepherded her through the early encounters with the immigration authorities. They asked my mother if she was pregnant and she indignantly replied that she was absolutely not!

In fact, she *was* pregnant. Her first-born-to-be was her passenger during that voyage to America.

This story is not just part of my own family lore, but is also part of a bigger national immigration record preserved at the Ellis Island Museum. In the late 1990's when my wife, Jane, took our son David on a tour of the museum, she picked up a phone to listen to the oral history recording of those who had disembarked there. One of the voices sounded strangely familiar to her. She looked at the names of the recorded voices and saw the name: Florence Norris, 1915.

Jane called me immediately in L.A. to say that we had to travel together to New York because there was a special exhibit that I simply had to see. Some months later, Jane and I went to Ellis Island and entered the vast and beautiful museum that memorializes the millions who traveled from all over the world to create a new future in the United States. The feeling of what it must have been like, a vast warehouse of humanity, remains. Jane led me to an upstairs exhibit area where I picked up a headphone and listened to the voices of those who had made the passage.

I was unprepared for my mother's lilting, British accented voice—a voice I had not heard since her death several years before—as she recounted the adventure that began on the *Orduna* in early February of 1915 and led to her arrival in Ellis Island. She described the noise and the throngs of people and how frightening the whole scene was to her younger self, who was so far away from anything resembling home. They had no food or water and she carried her blankets with her because she knew that Turtle Creek was colder than she was used to. Everyone pushed her as she made her way through immigration, and shrill cries of weeping little children seemed never to stop.

I stood there looking at Jane, listening to my mother. I was at this time already retired as a federal judge. But listening to my mother transported me to a distant past and I was struck by the courage and the strength and the bloody-mindedness that it took for my mother to get on that boat and come to the United States. And I felt a kind of gratitude that I had never experienced before.

Wedding photograph of George and Florence Norris, 1914

3

FAMILY LIFE

My mother set out to find her aunt's home in Turtle Creek, Pennsylvania. But she took the wrong train, so in the freezing cold her aunt was waiting at one station while my mother arrived at the other one. Finally, she found her way to her new home in America. She must have been awestruck by her aunt's large house in Turtle Creek with three bedrooms and two bathrooms, a big living room, dining room and kitchen.

My father arrived a few months later, sailing on the famously tragic *Lusitania* on what must have been one of its final safe passages across the Atlantic. As we all learned in high school, on May 7, 1915 the Germans made good on their threat to attack passenger vessels and sank the *Lusitania* with American passengers aboard, thus creating a huge diplomatic crisis in the war. But my father was safe. When my father first arrived, he had a tough time finding a job, but a friend of my mother's uncle managed to pull a few strings at the Westinghouse factory—a place the locals always referred to as "the Westinghouse"—and my father's first job in the United States was for the princely wage of 20 cents an hour. My mother's pregnancy made work out of the question for her. So with a wife and a new family on the way, my father took the factory job, even though it was not the journalism career that he loved.

He had only been at the factory for about six weeks when he complained of a terrible sore throat. But this was not an ordinary sore throat, especially in the time before antibiotics. His fever spiked, his joints swelled, and he could barely move. My father was desperately ill with rheumatic fever. In the upstairs bedroom his life teetered on the edge, and downstairs, my mother gave birth to my brother George. Rheumatic fever inflames the heart, joints and central nervous system so sometimes it is accompanied by crazy behavior—crying or jerky movements or even wild

15

laughter. My father must have exhibited some of this because a doctor came in one Sunday morning, put his hand on my mother's shoulder and said, "Lassie, I'm sorry but you are going to lose your husband. He's absolutely out of control."

Fortunately, her uncle took matters into his own hands and summoned members of the British lodge, a social group of British ex-pats who lived in the Turtle Creek area. They brought in a different doctor who suggested that my father be transported to Braddock, a town that was a couple of towns away from Turtle Creek. Of course there were no cars or buses available, so somehow they managed to get my father on a streetcar that took him to the doctor who saved his life. About a week after his treatment, my father was able to move and slowly he regained his strength. Remarkably, he was hired by the Westinghouse again, this time to inspect the munitions shells needed by the British Army for the war in Europe. With increased compensation, life began to change for my parents.

They rented a small house and with their new independence they started to grow their family, having six children over fifteen years. My oldest brother George soon got a younger brother, Lloyd and then Jack, whom we all called Spratt, was born. Then came Laverne, me and Dorothy.

I always felt, however, that the day of my birth marked me for a particular destiny. No. I wasn't born on September 17, the date when the Constitution was signed in 1787. I believed that mine was the destiny of a passionate baseball fan, because I was born on August 30, 1927, and every baseball fan worthy of claiming that title knows that this was almost one month to the day before Babe Ruth hit his sixtieth home run. This momentous one was against the Washington Senators and created a record that held for thirty-four years. So I always felt proud to have been born in 1927, as if my birth during that important year gave me a special connection to The Great Bambino.

Two years later, the Great Depression hit.

* * *

There were two basic facts of life for the six kids in the Norris family: We were always very independent and we always worked.

By the time that I was born in 1927, my father had left the Westinghouse factory. He had been fired for writing articles in support of the union. The good news was that this allowed him to return to journalism, his true love. He became both the editor and advertising manager of the *Turtle Creek Independent*, the local weekly that covered the towns of

Turtle Creek, East Pittsburgh, Wolftown, Wilmerding, East McKeesport, Forest Hills, Pitcairn, Trafford, Wall and Chalfant. The paper was founded in 1912 and was published until 1976. My father managed its advertising and edited its stories from 1922 to 1944.

Adult supervision was not a very big part of our lives. The fifteen years that separated the oldest child from the youngest meant that when I was growing up, George and Lloyd and later Spratt were already out of the house. I interacted mostly with my friends rather than siblings. Family meals were holiday affairs. In most aspects of daily life, we fended for ourselves. No parental hovering over homework assignments for us. I was closest in age to Laverne, who was an incredibly popular girl, so I enjoyed basking in the reflected glow of her success. Spratt would sometimes buy me a Coke at Hoffman's drugstore, which was the hangout he had with his buddies. I cannot really remember any family fights, except for the time that the two girls "borrowed" my new sled and crashed it. Everyone worried about the girls' injuries and no one but me cared about my poor ruined sled.

We were good kids, surrounded by friends with whom we enjoyed all kinds of unsupervised fun. But we were responsible and hard working. That is not to boast, but just to point out the reality; we all grew up with a vigorous sense of personal responsibility. We worked hard in school and at any job we could possibly get. There was no question that we needed to contribute most of our earnings for the general welfare of our family so we did. The Depression was devastating for our community, as it was for the whole country.

Perhaps one reason that we were all such upright kids was because of the standard set by my oldest brother George. There was no kindergarten in Turtle Creek, and when I began first grade, my teacher Miss Morgan still remembered my brother George from when he was in first grade twelve years before. "Oh," she said, "*You* must be George's little brother." This was shorthand for the fact that she had very high expectations for me. After all, she had already educated two of George's other little brothers and sister, and they had all lived up to her high standards and George's exemplary first grade performance.

The year that I started first grade, George graduated from Turtle Creek High School, got married, and soon became a conductor on the Pennsylvania Railroad from New York to Washington. I often think about the timing of our lives. George graduated in 1933, during the bleakest period of the Depression. There was absolutely no way that he could possibly have gone to college at that time.

But George was such an intelligent man. I always have believed that had our positions been reversed, had he been number five and I number one, there is no question that he would have become a judge (or a senator, or even higher office) and I would have been the conductor on the railroad. Not going to college was never a source of resentment or regret for him, but I have always been struck by what a loss it was for our country to have a whole generation of brilliant young men and women denied a college education because they could not afford it. George enjoyed a happy life, but what did our country lose with his more limited role? George was gifted as a writer and a thinker and was a charismatic boy. He had a magnetism and ease with folks that made people gravitate to him. He also set a standard for the rest of us that we may not have consciously aspired to, but emulated nonetheless. The only thing that stood in the way of George and monumental success was missing out on a college education.

Two years after George was born, Lloyd appeared. He was another bright hard working young man and excelled in math. On one of our family vacations to Cheat Lake in West Virginia, Lloyd fished me out of the water after I had wandered in too deep. I was unconscious, but survived—my big brother had saved my life. But once more, a Norris son started work right out of high school as college was out of the question in those days. Lloyd was a drill press operator in the Westinghouse. Jack was the next child, born a few years after Lloyd. For some reason, we liked to call him Spratt. Even though our parents showed no preferences among the six of us, my mother had a soft spot for her Jackie. After he graduated he too started working at the Westinghouse plant.

Laverne was three years older than I, so we intersected in our schooling more than I did with my brothers. She was one of those girls who seemed to have it all: she was beautiful, an A-student, a cheerleader for the football team, and broke through the glass ceiling in the marching band by becoming Turtle Creek High School's first female drum majorette. She eventually became a stewardess with Pan American Airlines. I have a picture of her looking stunning in her uniform standing in front of one of her planes. She moved up the ranks of the company and traveled the world, especially Latin America. She loved Cuba and mastered Spanish. Dorothy was the baby of the family, six years behind her sister and three years behind me. She had a very different life from the rest of us Turtle "Crikkers" because our parents decided to move to Miami in the summer of 1944 when she began her freshman year in high school.

But so much had happened to our family before that move.

I had four Norris predecessors in the Turtle Creek School system, but I think I managed to make my own mark. Looking back on those early years in school, I can only summon a few vivid memories. One of the first was my star turn as Jack Frost in the first grade Christmas play—a big challenge. This was difficult for me because my talents did not include an ability to memorize lines. I always struggled with rote memorization throughout my life.

Then, in fourth grade, there was Miss Lyons, a tough, very stern, fourth grade teacher who was also the principal. Those were the golden years of diagramming sentences, which is the lost art of deconstructing a sentence and learning how it all fits together. Looking back, I think that some of the precision in my legal writing came from the fourth grade when Miss Lyons insisted that we diagram nearly every sentence we encountered. I took to it as if I had been born understanding subjects and predicates, subjective complements and gerunds. I became so confident in my ability, that I even debated Miss Lyons about some of her grammatical decisions regarding a tangled participial phrase.

I realized two things when arguing with Miss Lyons about how to diagram particularly complex sentences: First, I was good at pulling apart a sentence, and second, I was good at arguing. Decades later as a lawyer and then as a judge, both talents served me well.

I suppose that part of my relish in debate came from a keen sense of competition. We were a competitive bunch, as anyone who played cards in our house could attest. But sports were also a big part of our lives. My mother was an avid Pittsburgh Pirates baseball fan. My ambition when I was growing up was to replace Arky Vaughan as shortstop for the Pirates. He was the first and only player to hit two home runs in one All-Star Game. When baseball games sprang up in our neighborhood I would always play shortstop. Sometimes, when we were especially lucky, we would go to Forbes Field in Pittsburgh on Boys' Day and get in for free. I even got to meet the legendary shortstop Honus Wagner in the flesh. He played an astonishing twenty-one seasons during his career from 1897 to 1917, so when I met him he had already retired. But it didn't matter. He was a legend.

When I was twelve years old, I first met a man who was going to have a formidable influence on my early educational life. Dr. A. Nelson Adelman was the new superintendent of schools in Turtle Creek. He was young and full of ambitions for our school district, which was underperforming for college matriculation for all the reasons that school districts in economically strapped areas sent few kids on to college.

I was an eighth grade graduate and keenly anticipating my move into the big leagues at Turtle Creek High where I would go through the rite of passage known as Freshman Year in High School. Alas, this was not meant to be. Doc Adelman changed the format. Ninth grade was moved from the first year of High School back to an additional year of Junior High.

Layman Allen was one of my closest friends in school and remained so throughout our lives. We were both high achievers academically and with our friends were in open revolt over the change in the high school line up. We got into all sorts of mischief.

While the details are lost in the mists of time, I do know that we were perceived as the ring-leaders of this insurrection and hauled into Adelman's office to face the consequences. I did not want my father to know anything about it. I never had to be disciplined by him and did not want him to be disappointed in me. Immediately, I began to plead my case. If he would keep this little incident between us, I suggested, I would get straight A's from then on. This was exactly the leverage Doc Adelman wanted. He agreed to avoid involving my father in the whole matter, and I was relieved enough to keep my word, even though I was still stung by the fact that the mythic days of high school were one more endless year away.

It was also about this time that I started working in any job that I could find. It was just a part of life for all of us. First I peddled magazines door to door. This was the golden age of magazine journalism and I was responsible for selling some of the great ones—*Liberty, Women's Home Companion, Colliers* were all part of my portfolio. One summer I worked fulltime in a wallpaper and paint store and learned the useful arts of trimming wallpaper and schlepping paint. Once I made a list of all the jobs I have held in my life; my children and Jane were astonished as they went through the dozens of entries.

My favorite jobs when I was growing up always had something to do with my father and the *Independent*. I started writing for him, mostly obituaries, or articles that gave our readers the "who, what, when, where and why" of borough council meetings. My favorite beat, though, was covering high school sports. I loved reporting the news and loved turning my reporting into stories and writing about people and events to inform my readers. Early on, like so many of the guys in the newspaper, I was a hunt and peck typist. That stopped when I was a sophomore in high school and I learned touch typing. This was not as uncomplicated as it might seem.

In September 1941, Layman and I thought that we were pretty clever young high school sophomores. We didn't expect to go to college but the Westinghouse factory floor had no appeal for us. We would much rather work in the plant's office building, wear clean shirts, and flirt with the cute girls who worked as secretaries. So we signed up for the commercial track to learn typing and shorthand and enjoy being the only two guys in classes filled with smart, pretty girls!

This all was going according to plan for a couple of months until Miss Chilcote, a biology teacher, took an interest in the two of us. One lab day when we were busy dissecting something, Miss Chilcote asked us to step into the hall.

"What other classes are you boys taking?" she asked.

Layman and I looked at each other. Somehow we knew this would not end well. We told her we were taking English and Biology and Secretarial courses.

I can still remember how her face darkened with anger. She literally grabbed Layman's left ear and my right one and marched us down the hall into the principal's office. Half the males in our high school at that time would drop out before graduation to earn some money in the factory. And I think that Miss Chilcote was not going to permit two of her smartest young men to stay in school as slackers. Our principal looked up with some dismay as she walked through the door. My sense was that he was as intimidated by her as we were. "*What kind of school are you running?*" she asked. She did not raise her voice but every single word cut through the silence of the office as if it were a drill. Within days, Layman and I were out of the steno pool and into the tougher academic courses. Ultimately the two of us graduated first and second in our class, thanks in no small part to Miss Chilcote.

But we sure learned how to type.

Fortunately, our move into more academic courses did not create too much of a drag on our social lives. I had a girlfriend named Iris Moroney from another township, just on the outskirts of Turtle Creek. Because of the distance and my work obligations, I didn't see her much after school. But Iris was my girl, despite the fact that she was not able to join me at the weekly dances at the town bank.

Our town had one bank and on the second floor was a big hall. Every Tuesday night we would all gather there, school friends, but also young people from the community. My sister Laverne and my big brother Lloyd's girlfriend Leda gave me a few dance lessons at home. As the melodies of "In the Mood" or "Moonlight Serenade" would play on the record player, we would all be dancing our hearts out. The songs that were played at each dance would be divided into dance cycles of two slow pieces and one jitterbug. I had lots of friends but when the eighth cycle came up, Aggie Woods, my favorite dancing partner, and I would always manage to find each other and dance together. I was not the best dancer, but I just loved it. I still do.

These were the formative years in Turtle Creek. My family was in the background, agreeable and supportive, but for me the fundamental organizing principle of my life involved being out in the world. Going to school, dancing on Tuesdays, playing all the sports I could manage, working at the paper or at the railroad or at the paint store or any place else. My days were packed with activities, some that engaged me intellectually, some physically, some socially, and always there were the ones that contributed some money to the family. The specific activities of course changed over time, but this basic template has stayed with me for eighty-seven years: work hard, stay busy, stay engaged, make some kind of contribution to your community.

And it all began in Turtle Creek.

4

A TIME OF WAR

I was only five years old when Franklin Roosevelt was elected president and eighteen years old when he died in 1945, so after my parents, he was the single most influential adult in my growing up. There were few homes in Turtle Creek that did not have a picture of Roosevelt hanging someplace in the house, usually near the radio, and ours was no exception.

I am not one for hero worship. My respect and affection for Roosevelt was predicated on completely rational thought. I continue to cherish his liberalism, his assertion in word and deed of the importance of government's responsibility for bettering the individual lives of its citizens, and the masterful way he transformed a country that was desperate into one that had hope. His values and his example were the foundation of my own efforts in public service.

We listened to many "Fireside Chats" and other speeches from Roosevelt on our radio, but his 1944 State of the Union Message influenced me for the rest of my life. I was a junior in High School then. The war was still going on and I was at home with my sisters and parents. At 9:00 that evening, all over our town, all over Pennsylvania, all over the United States, families were gathered around their radios to listen to our president give his State of the Union address. The war had been going on for three years and many families, the Norrises included, had young men in combat. Things were looking bleaker for the Germans but D-Day was still six months away.

I am not sure what we expected to hear, but what he said that night was profound. He covered some of the usual and important topics of the day. But then he went into a completely unanticipated direction. He acknowledged that our republic had grown strong under our constitutional rights to life and liberty. He went on to say, however, that these political rights had proved inadequate to the pursuit of happiness because "true individual freedom cannot exist without economic security and independence."

In that remarkable—some would say radical—speech, Roosevelt embraced what he called a second Bill of Rights. This Bill of Rights would include the right to adequate medical care, the right to a good education and the right of every family to decent housing. He declared economic rights to be as fundamental as our constitutionally protected political and civil rights. I was just a teenager at the time and knew very little about the Constitution. But the speech left a mark on my subconscious, as it resonated powerfully with my own sense of right and wrong. Later, these were convictions that defined my approach to the law and to public service throughout my career.

Even then, I was very aware of the inequities in our country and not just the economic ones. There was only one African American in our class and I remember her so very well. Her name was Lucille Bagley and she was a member of one of the very few African American families in Turtle Creek. One day, while Layman and I were still in the girls' class polishing our shorthand and typing, our teacher explained to the girls what they could expect after graduation, specifically the jobs that they could get at the Westinghouse office building near the big factory.

He made it clear, however, that he was not talking to *all* the girls. He then singled out Lucille and told her quite pointedly that she could not expect to ever work at the Westinghouse offices. If she wanted an office job she would have to go elsewhere. He seemed to think he was doing her a favor with his honesty. I was shocked by what I was hearing. I had never before experienced such racism and it struck a nerve in me that nearly propelled me from my seat to slug him. I also know that I was reacting as much to the content of what he was saying, the terrible realities of segregation, as I was to his public humiliation of Lucille. For me, that marked the beginning of my personal crusade for civil rights, and while Roosevelt was not explicitly referring to discrimination against minorities, implicit in his State of the Union was a commitment to equality and fairness for all people. And that commitment became a core value for me as well.

There was another winter night I recall when some of us were gathered around the radio: December 7, 1941. My brother John, who my mother called Jackie and the rest of us called Spratt, was still living at home and we shared a bedroom. We all had heard that Pearl Harbor had been attacked, but what did that mean? Was America going to war? Again, we gathered in the living room to hear Roosevelt speak. He called it a "day that will live in infamy" and all of a sudden, history seemed to have become something very personal. We were actually living in the midst of an important moment in history.

Christmas was a few weeks later and since that holiday was never a big celebration in our house, because my mother associated it with the death of her mother, she threw all her celebratory energy into New Year's Eve. Every year the Norrises would have a New Year's Eve party, featuring some seriously competitive card playing. Despite the grave news of Pearl Harbor, the party went forward. Spratt brought four or five of his buddies home that New Year's Eve and told us that they were going to enlist in a few days. We were all with our President and willing to serve. I felt my own frustration at only being fourteen and much too young to get in the mix.

Lloyd did not enlist, but was drafted into the Navy after Spratt was already in Texas for basic training in the Army Air Forces. Since George worked on the railroad, and the railroads were considered to be part of our national security, his war effort was on the home front.

Spratt wanted to fly airplanes, but because he did not have 20-20 vision he worked as an aircraft mechanic. He began his training far away in Texas. On the way to his next post, he came through Pittsburgh, and the family raced up to see him. Then he was moved to Fort Dix, New Jersey, which was the big Army and Air Force base south of Trenton. We wanted to take advantage of seeing him once more before he left for England, so my parents, sisters and I drove down in the family car to see him off. Once we were there we had no idea where to find him! During this time of war, the base was simply an overwhelming place, teeming with soldiers. Finally, somehow, we managed to track him down and have a few hours with him.

In England, when the big bombers came back from raids on Europe, he would check the engines and make sure they would be flightworthy for yet another mission. Every once in a while a letter would arrive from Spratt and it would be like a national holiday in our house. Our mother was especially relieved to think that her Jackie was safe.

May 17, 1943 was a beautiful day, the week following Mother's Day. On that day, we received a telegram from the War Department. It began with agonizing succinctness: "The Secretary of War desires me to express his deep regret..." and then went on to say that Spratt had been reported missing in action since the first of May in the skies over France. "If further details or other information are received," the telegram concluded, "You will be promptly notified."

Soon we were notified. John-Jack-Jackie-Spratt Norris was dead.

Years later my brother Lloyd did some detective work and found out the details. Spratt was a member of the 364th bomber squad and was on a mission in a B-17, which was shot down near Auray, a small town in northwestern France. There were ten crewmen aboard and Spratt had managed to talk his way into being a tail gunner. He never told us. He wanted to spare all of us, but especially our mother, the anguish of worry. His plane was at about 30,000 feet when it caught fire. The crew was told to exit and one of them recalled that as he prepared to jump, the radioman was fighting the fire. The plane exploded. Six of the men were killed, but the pilot, co-pilot, navigator and, miraculously, the radioman survived. Two of the survivors became POWs and two escaped with the help of the French underground.

Spratt was not so lucky.

I am not sure how his remains were found, but they were and he was brought back to Turtle Creek and buried in the military section at Church Hill Cemetery. We were all devastated.

And yet our sorrow, like that of so many families who lost sons in the war, was subsumed in the larger story of tragedy and redemption in that global struggle. This is nowhere more poignantly illustrated than in St Paul's Cathedral in London, where a shrine was created to commemorate and memorialize the American soldiers who died in battle, defending a country far from their own shores. The chapel was dedicated on July 4, 1951. Britain was still suffering the effects of the devastation of the war, but nonetheless, they came up with the funds to honor the 28,000 Americans who had died over there.

Jane and I visited the chapel several years ago when we were in London. We walked into the cavernous, historic cathedral in which every space contained echoes of history. Then we turned east and entered the American Chapel, which was the site that had been destroyed by bombs during the war. In this sacred space, a semi-circular apse was created, and on the stained glass windows insignia representing the forty-eight states of the Union from which men had served, surround a depiction of the service and suffering of a soldier in terms of the life of Christ. The altar was placed between two soaring pillars. One could imagine how many American families who had lost a son or a daughter in the war might have come to pay their respects here.

In one part of the chapel is a 473-page red book with gold engraving. The cover is inscribed with the dates, 1941-1945, and in it 28,000 names are contained of the American dead. There were twelve Norrises in the book, but we could easily find Spratt. Between Norris H.M. and Norris K.A. was Norris J.D. Sgt. U.S.A.A.F. The solemnity and the grace of the chapel were greatly comforting, as was the beauty of knowing that within a cathedral that had dominated the London skyline since 1697, where kings and queens were crowned and buried, royal weddings were held, prime ministers and archbishops lay in state, and quiet worship and public spectacle had existed for hundreds of years, there was a small place honoring my brother and others who gave their lives during that war. There is something moving to me knowing that in the country of my parents' birth, my brother's name has secured a small space on its soil.

So with tens of thousands of other American parents, my parents buried a son. I don't know how others grieved but mine were made of stern stock and never showed any real public expression of emotion. Whatever grief they felt, they certainly did not share with us or anyone else.

Companions Pallbearers For Sergeant John Norris

Soldier to Be Buried on Saturday from Turtle Creek Church; Was Killed in 1943

TURTLE CREEK — The six men who entered the armed forces with him shortly after Pearl Harbor will carry Sergeant John Norris to his final resting place in the soldiers' plot in Churchill Cemetery Saturday afternoon.

The former Turtle Creek soldier will be buried from the Evangelical and Reformed (Old Brick) Church following services at 1:30 o'clock. The body will lie in state at the church one hour before services, at which Judge Samuel Weiss, of Common Pleas Court, will deliver the eulogy.

Sergeant Norris, who was 23 when he lost his life in Europe, on May 17, 1943, was an aerial gunner on a bomber. Known familiarly as "Sprat," he graduated from Turtle Creek High School with the class of 1938.

Surviving are his parents, Mr. and Mrs. George Norris, formerly of Turtle Creek, now of Miami, Fla., two sisters, Laverne and Dorothy and three brothers, Lloyd, George and William.

Pallbearers at the funeral will be John Kerr, Forrest Bethune, Jr., Albert Samuels, Robert Felt, Robert Speelman and Armand Zemarel. Other members of the "Huffman Wolves," an unchartered social organization to which

SGT. JOHN NORRIS

"Sprat" belonged, will participate in the service.

Friends are being received at the Quinlan Funeral Home, Shaw avenue, until one hour before services.

Bill Norris, graduation from high school, 1945

5

ON MY OWN

My parents had decided to move to Miami just before my senior year in high school. The climate there was much better for my father, whose asthma had gotten severe. Laverne and Dorothy were prepared to go with them, but I was very reluctant because it would mean giving up Senior Year at Turtle Creek High School.

Everything was going so well in Turtle Creek. I had been elected President of the Junior Class, I had a serious girlfriend, and I loved going to the dances with my close circle of friends. I was in charge of my life. If there were any way to stay in Turtle Creek with my parents' agreement, I was determined to find it. But I needed to have a plan.

The first order of business was to find a place to stay and a close second was finding a job to replace the one I had working with my dad. I applied for a job at a newspaper in neighboring Wilmerding that was similar to the *Turtle Creek Independent* and got it. I worked out a deal with a classmate named Bill Porter. He and his mother and sister lived in an apartment over a little grocery store. Bill suggested that I could live with them during our senior year in an extra room they had. I talked to his mother about it and offered to pay ten or fifteen dollars a week.

With these two deals in hand, I convinced my parents that I could manage staying behind. Even so, on the day of their departure for Miami, my bags were packed and it was unclear whether I would join them or not. I gulped hard and saw them off.

I settled quite happily into the Porter household. Mrs. Porter was a real Rosie the Riveter, working on the floor at the Westinghouse factory. She worked the swing shift from about four in the afternoon to midnight. Bill and his sister Esther and I would improvise our meals during the week. On weekends Mrs. Porter would cook for us and bake us pies. I couldn't ask her to do my laundry, so I would carry a laundry bag with me when I rode the street car on the way to my newspaper job in Wilmerding and drop it off with my Aunt Dolly, my mother's sister. She would have it ready for me to pick up for my return trip to Turtle Creek.

Miss Chilcote's intervention in our academic lives in sophomore year helped Layman and me to change our academic trajectory, but Doc Adelman never lost sight of the two of us. He appreciated the fact that there was a fair bit of talent in the Turtle Creek school system but that few kids went on to college. He seemed to think that Layman and I might be destined for bigger things; we shouldn't be planning to work in the Westinghouse plant but to go to college and get a real education.

I had so many bylines by that time, writing a sports column for the Wilmerding paper, that journalism seemed an obvious profession. But as we got to know each other a bit better, Doc Adelman suggested that a life in politics would be a great option for me. Start in local politics, then run for Congress, perhaps, then who knows what might be in store. Perhaps becoming the first Pennsylvania governor to hail from Turtle Creek. But first I needed to think seriously about going to college and he encouraged me to go to a college with a good journalism program.

I was doing well in school and managed to make a little money with an additional job at a Pittsburgh newspaper where I covered Wall Street. I even tried my hand at hard manual labor (a job made possible by the labor shortage during the war), picking up the talus from the railway beds. But I lasted on that job for only one day.

At Christmas time, much to the delight of both our mothers, my brother George made it possible for my girlfriend Iris and me to take the train down to Miami to visit my family. Naturally we stopped in Baltimore to visit him. That train ride exposed me to shocking, segregated parts of America, where the external image of calm could not conceal terrible racial injustice. Iris was a great swimmer and we lounged at the beach and returned with deep suntans. Our bold trip together was the talk of our classmates.

There was never campaigning for student government in Turtle Creek High School. I was elected class president again in Senior year without having to persuade anyone. As president I was chair of the student council as well. I only gradually realized that my classmates had a confidence in me that I am not sure I quite understood. In the Turtle Creek High School Yearbook of 1945, the year we graduated, on the page with the student officers, the class wrote, "We all honor WILLIAM NORRIS because he has done so much for us. He is really one swell kid and to him we take off our lid." I was voted the best student and Layman was voted the "Most original boy."

One of the other yearbook sections was "The Crystal Ball," where our classmates predicted where the senior class would end up in the future. One column was labeled "Today" and there all our names appeared. The column next to it was labeled "Tomorrow" and there were the predictions. Layman's future was a very accurate prediction; he was going to be a "lawyer." Next to my name was "President of the United States." In some ways, I think that all my life I have tried to live up to that vote of confidence from my classmates.

The presidency of the United States may have been completely out of reach but college no longer was, again, thanks to Doc Adelman. He and I spent a fair bit of time looking at schools with good journalism programs and decided that Wisconsin was the place to go. He managed to persuade the University of Wisconsin to give me in-state tuition, which saved me a lot of money. So my immediate future after graduation was clear: I would go to college and study journalism.

I was the valedictorian on graduation day, and Layman, my friend and academic peer, was the salutatorian. My mother came up from Miami to see me graduate, and I could tell that she was proud. She and my father had barely finished elementary school in England, yet her children were all high school graduates, and I was even college bound.

Right after graduation I headed off to the University of Wisconsin in Madison and dove into my classes that summer semester. I took a full load with History, English, Spanish and Zoology. I only had to pay in state tuition, which was a relief, but I worked in the cafeteria in the girls' dormitory, serving food to earn some spending money. This began a solitary period in my life. After all my friends in high school, it was strange to not know anyone: no girls to date, no guys to hang out with, no dances. I concentrated on my studies and on work and aced everything—except Zoology.

At the end of the summer of 1945, the war was over, but I knew that since I had just turned eighteen that August, Uncle Sam would probably tap me on the shoulder and ask me to serve. I beat him to the punch and went down to Milwaukee and enlisted in the Navy. Initially, I thought that I would become a pilot, but when I heard that this would require a four-year commitment I said, "I will pass on that, thank you." I became a hospital corpsman instead.

Before I reported for duty in the Navy, I went to Miami and lived with my parents for a few months, of course working on one job or another. My sisters Dorothy and Laverne were in Miami and we spent some time together until the Navy summoned me to go to San Diego for boot camp in November, 1945.

Bill Norris during his Navy service, San Diego

Basic Training is no picnic, of course, but for me the worst part was not the pushups or the running, not the dirt, nor having someone barking orders at me. What I hated more than anything else was target practice. I knew that nothing good came from guns and an awful lot that was not good came from them.

After boot camp I took the medical skills test and was assigned to the U.S. Naval Hospital in Balboa Park. I was trained as a pharmacist's mate third class and worked at the hospital taking care of sailors who were returning from the Pacific. Fortunately, as a hospital corpsman I was far away from anything more to do with those damn guns.

Then I heard about a job opening that was irresistible. The hospital published a little newspaper, the guy in charge had shipped out, and they were looking for someone to take it over. I could not imagine my good luck! This was just the kind of work I loved, and I certainly was more experienced than most other young men in the hospital. Even at eighteen, I had over six years of experience in the newspaper business. They accepted me and I did everything from writing the articles to coming up with snappy headlines to figuring out the layout. Once a week I went downtown to a local printer to get it published.

Sometimes, I would get materials, including cartoons, from Navy headquarters that had been sent to all the bases for their newspapers. One of the cartoons went something like this. There was a brand new recruit standing near a commanding officer and the officer said, "Young man, you haven't saluted me!" In the next frame the recruit asked, "Well, what's your job?" In the next frame the glowering commanding officer said, "I am the base commander!" In the final frame the new recruit said, "Oh! That sounds like a heck of a good job! Don't mess it up!"

This seemed a pretty innocent cartoon to me, but *not* to my commanding officer. My captain had to approve my work and usually things were just fine. But when he saw that cartoon in the base newspaper, he was livid. He warned me that if I published anything like that again, he would fire me. I managed to incur his wrath again and he made good on his threat. He gave me a captain's mast which meant that I was restricted to the base for a while.

This restriction severely cut into my social life in San Diego. I had started attending the YWCA Saturday night dances for young servicemen to meet young ladies in a highly chaperoned setting. No sailors over twenty-one were permitted access to the innocent high school girls at the Y, but since I was just eighteen, I was more than welcomed. I set my sights on Kitty Horn, the best dancer in the room. She was every bit as good as my dance partners back in Turtle Creek. We hit it off and became regulars—until my captain put the kibosh on my leaving the base. When the captain's mast was lifted, Kitty and I resumed our dancing partnership. I also resumed my duties at the hospital.

Coincidentally, Layman Allen, my old sidekick from Turtle Creek, also was in the Navy. He was stationed in San Francisco at the time in the radar program and we would exchange letters. In one of them, he said that there was someone in his program who was an alum from Princeton University. This alum urged Layman to apply and Layman thought that I should as well.

I replied, "*Where's Princeton?*" Nonetheless, I agreed to meet Layman at the Victoria Hotel in Santa Barbara, midway between our two bases, on Easter weekend 1946, to discuss this Princeton idea. Meanwhile, I decided to do some investigating of my own. A navy buddy who worked in the hospital was the son of a United States Congressman. I figured if anyone would know about Princeton he would, so I asked him about it. "Do you know anyone who has gone to Princeton?" he asked. I said no and admitted that I did not even know where it was. He replied, "Well, if you don't know someone who has gone there, you can give up. You will never get in. Forget about it." I reported this to Layman who was undeterred. So we both applied.

But our boldness was for naught.

This was the problem: The University would not even consider applications from enlisted men who were still on active duty. But later, the news came from Washington that all enlisted men who did not have a certain service ending date would be discharged in August. When I heard that, I wrote Princeton again and asked, in effect, "How about now?" I assumed I would be discharged in August in time to enter the freshman class at Princeton in September.

I waited to hear back with bated breath. Then on one day, I received two communications. One was a letter in a thick, official envelope from the Department of the Navy in Washington, D.C., announcing that all pharmacist mates were essential to the Navy and any discharge notices did not apply to us because we were needed to care for the sailors returning from the Pacific. On the very same day my father received a telegram for me in Miami. The telegram was momentous. "Congratulations," it said. "You have been admitted to Princeton for the fall term." I had been admitted to Princeton but I was still stuck in the Navy.

That was probably the most dramatic day of my life thus far.

I told my father about my predicament. I discovered later that he sold his old Buick and used the money to come up to Washington all the way from Miami to lobby his government on my behalf. He began knocking on doors in the Pentagon and the Navy Department, even congressmen's offices in the Capitol, trying to persuade anyone who would listen that his son needed to be released from his military service. He got into Princeton University for crying out loud! My father was such a wonderful man. I was incredibly touched when I heard what he had done.

I continued to serve until the Navy finally discharged me in the spring of 1947. Still dressed in my Navy pea coat, I found my way to Princeton and went directly to the admissions office. When I told the woman at the front desk who I was, she began to laugh. "I am sure that Mr. Edwards, the Director of Admissions, would love to see you," she said. I asked her what was so funny. She told me that their file on me was unlike any other they had ever seen. When I met Mr. Edwards I asked if I could be admitted for the fall term. He shook his head, smiling, and said that they couldn't do that just yet, since they had not sent out the acceptance letters for the incoming class. But I left with the warm feeling that everything was going to be fine.

Back in Miami, my parents gave me a small Royal typewriter for a combined welcome home, congratulations on Princeton and happy birthday gift. When I set off for college in September, I had my Navy pea coat to keep me warm during the cold winters. I had the GI Bill for tuition, my books and a monthly stipend. And I had my great friend Layman Allen to boot. I was the first Norris kid to go to college. And that college was Princeton University.

By the way, it's in New Jersey.

Bill and Kitty Norris: wedding party at the Princeton Chapel

Left to right: Kitty's Uncle Henry and Aunt Irene, Kitty and Bill, Bill's mother, Dorothy and brother George, Leda and brother Lloyd

6

PRINCETON

When Layman Allen and I showed up at Princeton in September of 1947, courtesy of the GI Bill, we were in a state of shock. Here we were, the academic stars of Turtle Creek High School, but tiny, irrelevant, pipsqueaks in the august halls of a university that had just celebrated its 200th birthday in 1946. With its sweeping lawns and ivy covered stone buildings, not to mention the Nobel prize winners and United States Presidents among its former students and current faculty, the University just exuded world class intellectual power unlike anything we had ever imagined, much less actually seen.

Armed with my Navy-issue pea coat and my precious Royal typewriter, I was ready, or as ready as I ever would be, to face the new world. And what a world it was! For all the celebrated history and incredible resources, what made Princeton great for me were my fellow students. I had never encountered such well-educated young men in my life (women were several decades in the future). Most had studied at superb private prep schools such as Phillips Exeter and Choate. We found them to be quite daunting to say the least. They had already studied Latin and Greek, calculus, literature, and history that seemed at the graduate student level, not high school.

As Layman and I marveled at our new classmates, we concluded that either we had no business being there because we did not know anything, or that the brilliant prep school guys did not need to be there because they already knew everything! Of course, both were wrong. By the middle of the second year, we public school guys had caught up.

Even though we might not have known a Latin declension from a hole in the ground, we did have our own very important realm of expertise from growing up in Turtle Creek, an expertise that was not taught in these elite schools. We knew *people*. From Turtle Creek and from our experiences in the Navy, we understood what life was like for all sorts of people. We had a much better feeling for the bigger world, the one that was not cossetted by privilege and economic security. And because of that, we possessed a different kind of confidence and independence about moving around in all sorts of situations. We were genuinely comfortable not only with who we were, but also with the world outside the ivied halls of Princeton.

So we unpacked the few things that we had, I set up my typewriter on my desk, and we settled into our rooms at Dodd Hall, where we soon realized that we hit the jackpot in roommates. Perhaps it was providential, perhaps Princeton had some unique insight, but it was our good fortune to have drawn Donald Stokes as our roommate. In freshman year, he gave us another, very special edge.

From an old Quaker family in Philadelphia, a graduate of the Germantown Friends School, Don was simply an intellectual giant. Learned in all the subjects, able to connect concepts and ideas that were way beyond our reach, Don made Layman and me feel as if we had won the intellectual lottery. We did not have just another freshman as our roommate; we had someone with a mind like that of a fully formed professor.

Except we *did* have another freshman as our roommate and that was what made Don so remarkable. His combination of intellect and pedigree gave him an excuse to be insufferable, but instead he was one of the nicest, warmest, funniest and most caring men I have ever known. He studied political science, but he could have studied anything and been a star. Our initial shyness immediately gave way to a "Three Musketeers" camaraderie. Actually, we became the four musketeers, because our fourth roommate was Pete Spruance. We became known as the only room on campus with four Democrats!

Layman and I, like millions of other returning service men, could never have attended a great university like Princeton had it not been for the GI Bill. During the summer before my senior year, on June 22, 1944, President Roosevelt signed a momentous piece of legislation that was formally called the Serviceman's Readjustment Act of 1944, but quickly became known as the GI Bill of Rights. That bill gave service men and women options that they never could have dreamed of in the past: low interest mortgages, loans to small businesses, and the incredible possibility of college tuition, room and board, books and a small stipend.

The number of veterans who flocked to take advantage of the college tuition astonished those who crafted the GI Bill. They probably assumed that small business or home loans would be what interested most veterans, but by 1956, over 2.2 million veterans had used the GI Bill to attend college. What was especially interesting was that the vast majority of them went to the top thirty-eight schools in the country—from large state universities to smaller private colleges to the Ivy League. The GI Bill was pivotal in shaping, indeed in transforming, these returning GI's lives. And we never forgot what it did for us. The GI Bill became a touchstone, not unlike the civil rights era or Vietnam for later generations.

It certainly was one for me and for Layman. Princeton educated quite a few veterans, but by the time we arrived, our class was by no means the largest one. The classes of 1948 and 1949 had lots of vets, fewer in the class of 1951, which was ours. The GI bill paid for tuition and books, and we received a monthly stipend of about $90.00. Was it enough? No. Obviously neither my family nor Layman's were in any position to provide financial support. In that way we were unusual at Princeton, even among the vets.

A sociology professor of ours once tried to illustrate to our sociology class some sense of the inherent privilege of Princeton students and said, "I am sure that *all* of you are getting *some* financial help from your family." It was a moment of truth for me. I did not want to advertise my situation, or score some points. On the other hand, he needed to know that his stereotypes were not always true. I shyly put up my hand and he called on me. "Actually, professor," I said. "I'm not getting a dime from my family."

Not only did the GI Bill provide educations to people for whom it would have been out of reach, in doing so it played an important role in democratizing this country in unprecedented ways. As a child of the Roosevelt era, I have always had very strong views of the role of the federal government in many aspects of life, and especially in higher education. Our country cannot afford to shortchange children of great ability and I need look no further than my oldest brother George. He had a good life as a railroad conductor, but he was underutilized in that job. How many future scientists, political leaders, potentially great minds had no shot at college?

The luck of being born when I was made all the difference for me. In personal terms the GI bill opened the doors to Princeton and Princeton opened the doors period. If you do well at a school like Princeton, your opportunities are boundless.

As soon as I got settled, signed up for classes, and figured out my way around the beautiful Gothic campus, I looked for a job (of course). I learned that there was a great institution at Princeton known as the University Press Club. Founded in 1900 by undergraduates who wanted to be journalists, they figured out that they could become stringers for newspapers and wire services around the country. They wrote and reported stories from Princeton, and some newspapers were likely to use them. Or maybe they could find a professor who could give a good quotation and then that could be contributed to a bigger story. Initially a slot in the press club was sold to the highest bidder, but that did not last long. Soon you had to interview to become a member and that is the way it was when I was there.

The Press Club selected four freshmen to become members and then we were each assigned to a particular newspaper or wire service as a stringer. There were all sorts of papers with whom the Press Club had a relationship: The *Philadelphia Inquirer,* the *New Jersey Star Ledger,* the *Daily Trentonian,* even the wire services like the Associated Press or United Press International. The pinnacle of success, the slot that was always snagged by a senior, was to report for the *New York Times.*

Because I was already so experienced as a journalist, the competition was pretty easy for me and I found myself working there. My first year I was a stringer for the *Daily Trentonian* and they paid me for every piece they took. Fortunately, they took a few of my pieces and that was exactly what I needed to keep myself going.

The first year sailed by. I was working hard and studying hard and feeling absolutely exhilarated by where I was and what I was doing. Sometimes, Layman and I would head up to Trenton and go to dances. The people we met at those dances didn't even know where Choate or Philips Exeter was and couldn't have cared less. They knew how to have fun and boy did they know how to dance! We discovered a terrific Saturday night dance at an Italian lodge and had a wonderful time. Just as in Turtle Creek.

At times, I hopped on the train at Princeton Junction. I would ask the conductor if he knew my brother, George Norris. I loved the reaction when I told them that I was George's little brother. "*You* are related to George!?" they would ask and refuse to take my ticket. And then launch into what a great guy he was, what an absolutely wonderful person he was, what a leader and killer poker player he was. I just basked in the reflected glory.

One Sunday, after visiting George and his family in Baltimore, I planned to hitchhike back to school. The weather was terrible—pouring rain and a blustery wind. George piled his wife and children and me into the car to at least take me to a major road where I might have a better shot at getting picked up. The rain never did let up, we drove and drove in search of that perfect hitchhiking spot, until finally George drove me all the way back to school. George was my guardian angel when I was a student, sometimes when he could spare it, he would even slip me a little spending money.

When the school year ended, I hitchhiked back out to California. I needed to make some serious money over the summer to help out for the rest of the year. Kitty, whom I had met at the dances when I was in the Navy, threw me a much-needed lifeline. She corresponded with me and told me that her brother-in-law could get me a well-paying job in a tuna factory in San Diego. Kitty and I had become good friends and it turned out that there was a room I could use in her family's home.

I will never forget the experience of working in that tuna factory. My job was to get the fish out of the barrels and arrange them for processing by the women workers on the assembly line. I loved flirting with the young—even the not so young—women there, even though they spoke Spanish and my language skills were minimal at best. We would pantomime and laugh and sometimes I could hear them gossiping about me. Of all the jobs I have had, and I have had a quite a few, these women created the most fun for me.

On the other hand, it was also the most offensive. When I got on the bus to head back to Kitty's house, no matter how crowded the bus was, people gave me a very wide berth. If I ever wanted to know what it was like to be a leper in the Middle Ages, I found out that summer. I felt as if I smelled like tuna all the time—it was as if it had gotten into my pores. Even if I showered for an hour I couldn't rid myself of the horrible stench. It was awful but lucrative. And over that summer, Kitty and I had a wonderful time. We got very close and her parents were like family to me.

Each year at Princeton, Layman and I became a little more confident. I was getting better and better assignments from the University Press Club for better and better newspapers. During the spring of our sophomore year, Don Stokes suggested that we join him in declaring the Woodrow Wilson School of Public and International Affairs as our major for Junior and Senior years.

The Woodrow Wilson School is a unique, interdisciplinary program within the university that is designed to prepare upper classmen in the field of public policy. The school of public policy was founded in 1930, and in 1948 it was named after our 28th President, Princeton alum and former Princeton University President, Woodrow Wilson. When I say it was interdisciplinary, I am not exaggerating. We took economics, sociology, history, politics, some of us even took physics and biochemistry. The whole idea behind the school was to develop future leaders in public policy.

In the Woodrow Wilson School, we were divided into three groups. One professor was assigned to each group and each group was assigned a specific public policy issue to study. In our case, Don Stokes was the chairman of our group, and we had three vice chairmen. The faculty member stepped aside and let us grapple with whatever issue we had been assigned. One of our policy challenges in junior year was "Balancing New Jersey's Budget" and my piece of that issue was to focus on the relationship between the state of New Jersey and the United States government, and how that financial relationship unfolded in terms of balancing the budget.

I immersed myself in the subject. I went to Trenton to review records and interview both experts and government bureaucrats. I even went to Washington, D.C., thanks to George, and looked at records there. I was responsible for both a written report and an oral presentation, in which I had to field questions from my entire group. It was a rigorous and fascinating exercise, and I learned so much about budgets, about defending research and about public presentations.

Meanwhile, I was contacted by two Princeton alums—Dan Coyle and Don Stewart—who ran a local Princeton weekly newspaper. They were about twelve years older than I, made their lives in their beloved Princeton, and founded a little weekly newspaper called *Town Topics*. It was Princeton's version of the *Turtle Creek Independent,* and of course I grew up working for that paper. I worked for them doing exactly what I had done for my father: covering lots of local events as well as peddling advertising to the local merchants. It provided a nice cushion for me and later for Kitty and me. This great experience complemented my work at the University Press Club. My future was pretty clear: I was going to be a journalist after graduating from Princeton University.

Distance did not fray the connection between Kitty and me. In some ways, it may have made it stronger. In the summer between my sophomore and junior years, before I was to start in the Woodrow Wilson School, I invited Kitty to come east this time and we would stay with my family in Miami. While we were there, she decided to become a court reporter and learned how to do the swift typing required for that job. At the end of the summer, I asked Kitty to come up to Princeton with me. Kitty told me that she received a letter from her mother in San Diego urging her not to do this. Then she received a letter from her father saying he supported her decision and had intervened with her mother. He told her that Kitty needed to experience different places and become more independent.

Layman was also very involved with a young woman who also moved to Princeton, so she and Kitty shared a small apartment together. Kitty was a secretary at the Educational Testing Service, and we spent as much time as we could together, which probably was not that much given how hard I was working. Then Layman proposed to his girlfriend, Chris, and she accepted! Kitty moved in with a group of other girls, and we started talking seriously about getting married, which we did in June before our senior year.

We married in the Princeton chapel and it was a very simple, very nice event. My mother came up from Miami, and my brothers George and Lloyd and their families attended as did many of our friends. I wore my one suit—a hand-me-down from Lloyd—and Kitty wore a suit as well. Don Stokes' family had a little cottage in the Pocono Mountains and they let us go there for our honeymoon. Through Kitty's wonderful resourcefulness— she spoke to someone who knew someone who needed someone to house sit for them—when we returned to Princeton as husband and wife, we were able to settle into a big, lovely home on Nassau Street as house- sitters for a family that was travelling for the summer. Kitty went back to work at the Educational Testing Service. I went back to work for the Princeton weekly newspaper. I even got to play softball on a local team. It was a glorious summer, free of financial worries.

Senior year brought some major changes in my life. We moved from the great house on Nassau Street into veterans' housing off-campus. By November, Kitty was pregnant. The GI Bill support had run out. Along with my working for the *Town Topics*, as the president of the University Press Club, I landed the prestigious assignment of stringer for the *New York Times*. I recently looked at the University Press Club website and read this passage describing the years I worked there:

> The post-War world in which the Press Club resumed work was a different place. The power of the atom had been unlocked, and Princeton proved to be an epicenter of the new atomic age. Albert Einstein, who had landed in Princeton before the war, abjured the bomb and began preaching pacifism. With a photo- genic mane of God-like white hair, Einstein became Princeton's most enduring, and endearing, figure. In 1947 Einstein was joined at Princeton's Institute for Advanced Study by Manhat- tan Project director J. Robert Oppenheimer. Four years later Princeton became the home of one of the nation's leading nu- clear research facilities, the Princeton Plasma Physics Lab.[*]

How fascinating to see this description of a time I remember so vividly. One of my most thrilling assignments was to interview Einstein. The Hebrew University of Jerusalem gave Einstein an honorary degree, and since he was not able to go to Israel to receive it, they brought the mountain to Mohammed—so to speak—and organized the presentation in

---

[*] http://www.universitypressclub.com/about/history

Princeton, which I covered for the *New York Times*. I went to interview him at his home and met this iconic figure, so easily caricatured with his crazy hair, a salt and pepper coat buttoned up to his chin, baggy pants, a pair of loafers, of course with no socks. He was the picture of the absent minded genius and he opened his front door and invited me in. I met him and interviewed him and gave the quotes to the pool reporters. I had arrived in the Major Leagues as a reporter. The Princeton student newspaper reported that I saw my future in journalism.

But life has a funny way of changing your plans.

My turning point came when one of my professors encouraged me to sign up for the absolutely legendary Alpheus T. Mason's Constitutional Law Interpretation class. Alpheus Mason was both a scholar of Jurisprudence and a great judicial biographer who had written books on Louis Brandeis and Harlan Fiske Stone that were erudite in the extreme but also surprisingly popular. His book on Brandeis was published in 1947 and had been on the bestseller lists for months, selling an astonishing 50,000 copies. Mason first arrived in Princeton in 1925, when he was only 26, so even though he was 51 when I studied with him, he seemed like an institution. I had absolutely *no* interest in the law. I had *no* interest in that class. I did not care if it was the hardest class in the Princeton curriculum—which incidentally had been its reputation. The most important factor was my complete and utter lack of curiosity about the Constitution or the law.

Alpheus T. Mason changed my life.

I fell in love with the Constitution. I can still remember the moment of reading, really reading and permitting the implications of Article III of that powerful document to hit home. The first sentence stopped me cold: "The judicial power of the United States, shall be vested in one Supreme Court, and in such inferior courts as the Congress may from time to time ordain and establish." It all seemed simple and straightforward until one ponders the enormity of its implications. What *was* judicial power? I thought. What were its limits? How can it be contained or most responsibly expressed? How does an individual, with individual quirks and points of view, manage to transcend intellectual limitations to exercise jurisprudence for society?

Part of the class consisted of Mason's lectures. The other part was small group discussions that were moderated by a preceptor who was, in our case, a young professor named Bill Beaney. I suppose that my engagement with the material revealed something about my talents and interests, because Beaney decided that I should become a lawyer and he would not rest until I took the LSAT's. I had no interest in taking them. I was writing my senior thesis on the American Medical Association for the

Wilson School. I was working long hours at the Press Club, both as a reporter and as its president. I was married and I had my regular course-work to maintain. I was becoming a policy wonk at the Woodrow Wilson School and had thoughts of moving to Washington where policy wonks go to heaven.

"Just take the LSAT's," Beaney said. "Don't even study for them. Just take them."

So I did.

I do not remember what the results were but Beaney insisted that I apply to law school.

"I don't want to go to law school," I said. "I don't know any lawyers; I don't know anything about the law. I don't know anything about law firms."

If this was not sufficiently persuasive, I had a final point that I was sure would get him off my back. "And I am *not* interested!"

It did not get him off my back. So I went home and talked to Kitty about it. "Maybe I should apply to law school," I told her. "I think that I may be as smart as the guys who go to law school." She was surprised since she had expected that we would be heading to Washington for a government job. She asked me, "How are we going to eat?" But she was always supportive of me and I proceeded to apply to two law schools, one in the East and the other in the West: Yale and Stanford.

I did not exactly forget about my law school applications, but they receded to the back of my mind as my senior thesis demanded an enormous amount of intellectual energy and time. I was so absorbed in it, and knew how important the project was, that I even resigned as a stringer for the *New York Times*. I still have the letter I received from Carl Purcell, the suburban editor of the paper with whom I worked. It was dated February 25, 1951.

> Dear Bill,
>
> Your regret at having to leave your association with the New York Times is shared by everyone here who has had anything to do with you and your work. We have found you highly compe-tent and reliable in every sense. You were always "on the ball." I cannot recall any occasion when you did not give a good ac-count of yourself.... We have been most happy in our dealings with you, Bill, and sincerely regret that you have to write that thesis. We wish you success in that and in anything else you do, and we are sure you will have it.

Of course I regretted it too! But I also needed to keep clear about my priorities and writing my thesis filled up my entire field of vision. Looking back, I am both impressed and depressed by my prescience. The title of my thesis was "The American Medical Association and Health Insurance." Harry Truman had proposed a national health insurance plan and I was all for it. Growing up in Turtle Creek I had seen how devastating an illness in a family could be, and the lack of universal health insurance was something that really bothered me. I immersed myself in trying to understand how a well-financed interest group could destroy a policy that was good for so many people in the country.

My research took me back to the nineteenth century, when there was great enthusiasm about some form of public health insurance, but even then the states' rights advocates rejected the notion of any kind of federal policy. I went through old issues of the Journal of the American Medical Association to find out what happened. For 132 pages (every one of which were typed by Kitty), I developed my thesis and explored this vexing problem in American politics and society. I think that I may have been the only student to have had a comic book in the appendix of my thesis. It was a piece of AMA propaganda to "educate" kids (and their parents) about their point of view. The comic book was called "The Sad Case of Waiting Room Willie," and the main character is a sad sack, kind of Emmett Kelly clown, the victim of Truman's health insurance plan. I knew that these comic books were in every doctor's waiting room in the country.

In the spring, I received two envelopes: one from Stanford and one from Yale. I had been admitted to both, and then it was just a question of who was going to give me more money. I called Stanford and told them that I needed more money and the person with whom I spoke asked why I wanted to go to Stanford. "Because I want to take a trip!" I told him laughing. After some back and forth between Yale and Stanford, I went to the school that was the highest bidder.

I graduated Phi Beta Kappa in June of 1951, and it was time to say goodbye to my dear comrades, Don and Layman. We weren't sentimental guys. I think that we just took for granted the fact that we were separating in geography only and we were destined to be friends for life, which of course we were. Don went off to Yale where he would get a Ph.D. in political science and embark on a brilliant academic career. Layman was heading to Harvard for a Master's degree in public policy, but like me, he also eventually turned to the law.

He made the choice I did not and went to Yale Law School. For the last fifty years he has been a professor at the University of Michigan School of Law. He developed the use of mathematical logic to analyze legal relations and later the use of artificial intelligence in expert systems that help attorneys interpret complex and ambiguous legal texts. It sounds arcane, but the practicality of Turtle Creek has never left him. He devised games to teach school children about logic, mathematics and law. The most famous of these, WFF'N PROOF and Equations, are used nationwide and are the basis for national scholastic tournaments for elementary and secondary school students. Miss Chilcote and Doc Adelman little knew where their good deeds would lead.

Once more, Kitty arranged for us to rent the house on Nassau Street, this time not just for the two of us but for our new family, and not for the whole summer, but just a couple of months. Our daughter Barbara was born in July, and in an old Ford that Don Stokes and I had bought together, Kitty, Barbara and I, accompanied by one of Kitty's nieces from San Diego who arrived to help out, piled our things in the car and headed down to Baltimore so that big brother George could check out the car. George took one look at the jalopy and set to work on it so that it would make it all the way to California. We were finally on our way, buoyed by our excitement and by the four brand new tires, courtesy of George Norris.

PART II

BECOMING A LAWYER

*"Security is not the meaning of my life.
Great opportunities are worth the risk."*

Shirley Hufstedler

7

SURVIVING IN STANFORD LAW SCHOOL

With my new Princeton diploma for the class of 1951 in the trunk, Kitty, two-month old Barbara, Kitty's niece, and I left the ivy-covered buildings of one of the oldest schools in the United States, and with a brief detour to Baltimore, drove 2,938 miles and arrived at a place that was gleaming and modern and pristine. The contrast could not have been more striking, and indeed everything at the law school was brand new.

Kitty and I moved into our new home in the housing set aside for married veterans, and our social life revolved around the couple that lived next door, Leo and Jean Biegenzahn. Like us, they had a baby, and so Kitty and Jean became inseparable. Leo would play an important role in coming to my rescue financially, and indeed physically, but that comes later.

When I arrived as a One-L, Stanford Law School's gleaming, modern, new home, the Outer Quadrangle was only one year old. I was about to spend a lot of my time over the next three years in that huge five-story building that had two large lecture halls, a three-story library and a warren of rooms and offices. Even the *Stanford Law Review* was relatively new; it was only first published in 1948. Two future justices of the Supreme Court of the United States, William Rehnquist and Sandra Day O'Connor, were in their third year when I was a One-L.

Carl Spaeth, the dean of the Law School, was a relatively young man in his mid-forties. A former Rhodes Scholar and only thirty-nine when he was made dean of Stanford in 1946, he was one of the people in charge of its great expansion during those years. He had worked in the State Department during the War and was a man of enormous intellectual breadth.

51

Stanford Law maintained small classes so there were only about three hundred of us there. The school was just recovering from World War II, when its enrollment had dropped down to fewer than thirty students. Those must have been difficult times, but one would not have noticed from the impression the school made that August day in 1951. Since its founding, it had been committed to a very diverse student body. No more gentleman's club for me. Stanford not only admitted women, but Hispanic and Asian students as well. This all seems easy to take for granted today, but at the time it was very unusual.

I can look back on the history of this great school, its distinguished alums, all the important learning that took place there, but for me, my memories of Stanford are dominated by the incredible financial insecurity of our time there. Even though Stanford gave me a scholarship and a stipend, it was not enough to support my young family. Those years were the most difficult times in my life, bar none.

When I was in Princeton I had figured things out in ways that were very consistent with my identity as a young journalist. With the happy combination of the University Press Club and *Town Topics*, not to mention the enormous help from the GI Bill, my personal and financial life were well-organized. When Kitty and I were married, we had her salary from the Educational Testing Service as well. We were frugal but we were comfortable.

But at Stanford I had to scramble. I could not get any of the kind of work that was within my wheelhouse. Job options in journalism, even if they existed, were for undergraduates and not for law students. I was desperate to find anything that could pay the bills. During football season I found out that they needed people to sell concessions, to walk up and down the aisles hocking peanuts or whatever we were selling at the time. My job was peddling some sticky orange colored beverage to the crowds— hardly the most remunerative line of work for a man with a family to support. When Christmas that first year came around, I drove Kitty and Barbara in that old Ford down to San Diego for the holiday. While they celebrated with the family, I worked as a mailman during the Christmas rush.

As we were preparing to return to Palo Alto, we realized that we were broke—down to our last fifty cents. Forget about buying notebooks for my classes, we needed to have some food in the refrigerator. Kitty's Father slipped me a twenty-dollar bill for the trip home; I later learned that Kitty's Mom did the same thing for her. When we got back to Stanford, what we found in the mail was a miracle. Dan and Don who owned *Town Topics* in Princeton sent me a bonus check for *five hundred dollars!* It looked like a million bucks to me and gave us some much-needed relief during a terrible time. But even five hundred dollars in 1952 could only go so far. Our first year was a blur of work and anxiety. Near the end of it a classmate of mine named Bill Hagen worked in a car dealership and managed to get me a job there selling used cars.

I turned out to be a star in the used car business. But it was not enough.

My close friend and neighbor Leo Biegenzhan, a big, strong guy, had a job at the local VA psychiatric hospital. Knowing about my worries, he suggested that as a veteran and someone who had worked in the Navy hospital I might have a shot at a job there. When I went for an interview, they thought that I was too small and could not handle the large and potentially violent guys in the wards. Leo stood up for me and said that even though I was physically small, I was one of those tough, wiry guys who could handle anything. We were on the graveyard shift, starting work at midnight and working until eight in the morning. Most of the time, if the patients behaved themselves, we would sit in two big chairs and study.

But this was a ward in a mental institution, and we were not surrounded by peacefully sleeping patients. They were troubled men, and when their troubles became even more agonizing, they could be completely unpredictable. Part of our job included getting them up in the morning and through breakfast before we could leave. One morning, a little dull from the lack of sleep, I stood there organizing one patient for his breakfast. I did not realize that behind me an enormous guy had propelled himself over a table to attack another patient and I was in the way. Fortunately, Leo saw it happening and wrestled him to the ground. When I heard the racket behind me, I helped Leo get him into the tub that we used to calm the guys down when they were out of control. I don't know if I would be here today if it weren't for Leo. This patient was huge, and fueled by his own demons, he was ready to clobber me.

Then we went off to class.

I am not sure when I slept, but I must have. And Kitty was pregnant again. Our son Don—named after Donald Stokes—was born in January 1953. I simply could not miss a day of work at the used car lot that day, so Bill Hagen was pressed into action to bring Kitty and the baby home. When they got there, they had no key to enter the house, so Bill had to break a window and crawl in.

During my second year, with a wife and two children to support, I got so desperate that I considered dropping out of Stanford and looked at the federal government again for a secure job. I came up with a plan: we could move to Washington, I would work for the government and attend Georgetown Law School at night to finish my degree. I took the Civil Service exam. The results were circulated among various agencies and then they would make some offers. I got a few offers and I could see some possibilities open up before me, mainly the possibility of being relieved of the terrible financial pressures.

I made an appointment with the Dean Spaeth to tell him about my plan to withdraw from Stanford. I told him that I was going to leave at the end of the quarter, head to Washington, D.C. for a government job and financial security, and then finish my law school education at Georgetown. I assured him that this had nothing to do with how much I liked Stanford, but that it was strictly a practical decision.

Dean Spaeth did not give up easily. The next thing that I knew, I heard from Phil Neal, who later went on to become the dean of the law school at the University of Chicago. He had recruited me to go to Stanford when I was still at Princeton. I described my situation: family responsibilities, the jobs at the VA and at the car dealership, my classes at law school and the relentless, constant money worries. He listened carefully and then said that they wanted me to stay at Stanford and would figure out a way of making that possible so I could quit these peripheral jobs and work on my studies.

"You are going to be on the *Law Review*," he said. "You will be working on your classes; we will give you more money but you will have to stop selling cars."

"Not a chance," I responded. I was really hitting my stride as a car salesman in the Mountain View Chrysler Plymouth dealership, right out on Route 101. I would go down in the evening and have the whole used car lot to myself. When there were no customers, I would study. Sundays were the best, because I was there all day and customers tended to like to buy cars on a Sunday afternoon. Phil Neal and I went back and forth and arrived at a compromise: I would give it all up—except for Sundays.

And one day, Phil Neal walked into the dealership in search of a new car. It was the only new car I ever sold—I got him a good deal!

In the first year I had taken all the required courses and studied hard. I was immersed in legal reasoning, legal institutions and the close analysis of judicial decisions. We went through the time honored elements of a legal education in that first year: Torts, Legal Research and Writing, Civil Procedure I, Contracts, Criminal Law, Constitutional Law, Property and Federal Litigation. Having established that foundation, the second and third years opened up more choices for coursework. We could focus, for example, on Business and Commercial Law, Civil Procedure and Litigation, Public Policy, Constitutional Law and Labor Law. I cannot begin to remember all the classes that I took.

I was getting a tremendous education, but what has really stuck with me from those days was that I learned about myself: what mattered to me and how my mind worked. Much of the education during the first year was in the classic law school Socratic method, where we would sit in large lecture halls and be called on indiscriminately by professors. Professor George Osborne was an elderly and distinguished man, a legend at Stanford who arrived there in 1923. A brilliant professor, he seemed old even though he was only 59 when he taught our class. He was able to nail you on the slightest slip of your argument in the midst of a grilling. To say he was intimidating was an understatement. His mission in life was to strike the fear of the law into the students, and he succeeded. This was a profession that required tough, rigorous minds, and you had better get serious about it.

There were about eighty or ninety students in the class, and he would hone in on one student at a time until he finally moved on to the next victim. One day, when I was the subject of his ruthless interrogation, he really had me on the defensive. One tough question after another came at me as if I were an intellectual punching bag against a heavyweight champion. I was having a hell of a time trying to come up with the answer to the final question and he let me go.

He started walking down the aisle looking for his next victim and while he was surveying the field, out of nowhere, I answered the question by beginning, "I don't know why, but my gut tells me..." something or other. "That's all I have to say," I finished. He whirled around and gave me a sharp look. Had I been disrespectful? Maybe fancy Stanford University students do not use terms like "my gut tells me?" Maybe when he had turned his back, I was dismissed and needed to keep my thoughts to myself?

Then I heard him say, "You stick with that gut." And he moved on to challenge another student.

"You stick with that gut." I never heard him say that again but it stuck with me for the rest of my life. These five words gave me a lot of confidence because they meant that as important as book learning was, good instincts might be even more important. I had always thought that I was out of place at law school, that my true vocation should have been as a policy wonk and journalist. I thought that I was *really* meant for that. And yet a man like Osborne, who had trained literally thousands of law students at Stanford and Harvard and certainly did not throw around compliments with any kind of freedom, encouraged me to stick with my gut. Perhaps, I began to think, that meant I was in the right place and had an intuitive talent for the law that could serve me well. The ensuing years only proved him right, not only in some of my arguments or approaches to untangling complicated legal problems, but also in finding talented young lawyers to work in our firm or as law clerks when I was a judge. I could see beyond their impressive resumes and recognize that they might have something difficult to pinpoint but essential for the job.

All the exams from the first year took place at the very end of the school year, but Professor Osborne wanted to go on sabbatical, so he was given permission to give his final exam at the end of the second quarter. It was the only grade that any of us got before the end of the year. Happily, I was invited to join forces with two friends to study for the exam. The grades were posted on a big bulletin board in the main hall and there was a buzz all over the law school. "Who is this guy Norris?" Wondering what had happened, I looked at the board and discovered that for the second time in the history of the law school someone had gotten an A+ in Osborne's class.

And that someone was me.

That moment was a kind of a turning point for me. I thought to myself, "Well, I guess I'm not so bad at this."

As the years at Stanford passed, especially after the middle of my second year when some of the financial worries were alleviated, I became close to a group of wonderful friends who all came onto the *Stanford Law Review* together. It was a great group of guys, including Vic Palmieri, Frank Farella and Dick St. Johns. (Incidentally, Leo Biegenzahn was also an outstanding student, but always the iconoclast, he had no interest in the Law Review.)

I was not insulted at all when they did little to disguise their shock when they discovered that I was number two in the class. They knew that I was smart, because everyone at Stanford was smart, and I did have that A plus. But I was so exhausted from work for so much of the time, I am sure that I did not appear to be a leading intellectual light.

The person who *was* the leading intellectual light, and the clear number one, was Ted Finman, a very quiet, modest, but extremely bright man, a real legal scholar. We all agreed that Ted would be the President of the Law Review. I was number two in the class and was named the Executive Editor. This was a perfect allocation of our talents and interests. I was no legal scholar, had no interest in the abstract and intellectualized approach to the work. I liked to engage in the problems of the law, and I liked to work with words and with other writers. So we had a very harmonious working relationship. But for some reason, Ted did not submit the article he was working on by the end of the year, so he decided to push back his graduation for another year. Ted became first in his class the following year and went on to a life-long career as a distinguished law professor at Wisconsin Law School. So I became first in our class by default; I always said that I was first, but with an asterisk.

At the end of my third year was another turning point. Kitty was caring for our two small children and we were managing to stay afloat financially. Finally, it was time to figure out what we were going to do.

Stanford often had students who went on to clerk for the great Supreme Court Justice William O. Douglas. He was assigned to be "Circuit Justice" for the Ninth Circuit and his practice was to ask every law school in that large area—which extended from Arizona to Hawaii—to nominate someone for a clerkship with him. One of his former law clerks, Sam Sparrow, a lawyer in Oakland, would interview the candidates and make a recommendation to Douglas. Now as number one in my class, I was the Stanford choice for the spot.

To prepare for the interview, I met with Dean Spaeth and asked him for advice on how to handle it. I will always remember his words: "Just be yourself." Armed with that sage advice, I went to Sam Sparrow's office in Oakland for the interview. As I was preparing to leave, he said, "I'm a little hesitant to do this, Bill. Still, I have to tell you that I have only one more interview to do, but I am fairly certain that the job is yours."

I was pretty pleased, but I live by the bird in the hand philosophy and was not exactly celebrating my new job as a clerk to a Supreme Court Justice.

After Sam conducted his last interview, he called me and explained that he could not make an offer to me after all. His last interviewee was a young man named Harvey Grossman, the nominee of UCLA Law School, which was a fairly young law school at the time. Harvey Grossman had all A's. "No one else ever had all A's from law school," Sam said, "Including you!"

He was very nice about it but told me that he would not feel comfortable extending the offer to me because UCLA had to be seen as equal to Stanford in its legal education, both schools being part of the enormous Ninth Circuit area. He did not want to appear to be making a judgment on the school rather than on the student. As it turns out, Harvey Grossman became a good friend of mine later in my life. As for now, he was just a name, a straight-A student and Justice Douglas' new law clerk. I was not crushed by the decision; there were many other opportunities to be a lawyer. Besides, I never expected a kid like me from Turtle Creek would become a Supreme Court law clerk.

8

MY FIRST JOB AS A LAWYER

We were now a family of four and school was officially a thing of the past for me. I was a young man, on the cusp of turning twenty-seven, with degrees from two great schools and what everyone would have said was a promising future. But what did that future mean for Bill Norris? One thing that it certainly meant was getting a job in my new profession. Even though it looked like clerking for a Supreme Court Justice was not meant to be, I had many other options to work through.

In the summer of 1954, America was in a period of tremendous postwar growth and stability. Images of perfect, prosperous, white, all-American families seemed to be everywhere. In some ways, Kitty and I and our friends were the embodiment of that image.

There was another America, the African American America. Segregation was a fact of life. In the fall of 1954, when I was working in my first job with a small law firm named Northcutt Ely, Kitty and I and our family arrived in Washington, D.C., which was still a segregated city. Our nation's capital had separate entrances in department stores, separate restrooms and separate drinking fountains for Black people and White people. The seismic changes wrought by the *Brown v. Board of Education* decision that had been handed down by the Supreme Court on May 17, 1954—just around the time of my graduation—had not yet revealed themselves in the facts of daily life. The decision did demonstrate the power of the courts to right the wrongs of centuries. I thought of my African American classmate Lucille Bagley in Turtle Creek and wondered what she might have been thinking on that momentous day.

The communist witch hunting of Joseph McCarthy had ruined the lives of many progressives, and throughout the spring, as we were studying and working hard, the Army-McCarthy hearings were being conducted on television. There was a small television in the apartment that Kitty and I rented. (Don especially liked the television; Kitty remembers him running around our apartment wearing a cape and pretending to be Superman.) We watched some of the hearings, as did Americans all over the country. On our flickering, black and white television screen, we could see the Wisconsin Senator demeaning and defaming innocent people—ruining lives.

Two professions that were meaningful to me—journalism and the law—came together to defeat that horrible bully. The legendary journalist Edward R Murrow in his program *See It Now* confronted him in March, and the gradual unraveling of McCarthy's power began. In June, just after my graduation, the great lawyer Joseph Welch effectively put an end to his tyranny with his simple eloquence: "Have you, at long last, no decency?" McCarthy's once terrible power crumbled in the face of justice and integrity.

This was the background of our lives back then. But as with so many young people who were launching a new phase of their adult lives, what was going on in the bigger world could not engage my attention as much as the decisions I had to make for my future and the future of my family.

Northcutt Ely recruited me out of Stanford, and I had accepted his offer. He had a small law firm, based in Washington, D.C., specializing in natural resource issues. The principal reason that I was drawn to his firm was because he was working on one of the biggest, most important cases in the country, which involved the mighty 1,450 mile Colorado River. Someone once said that Colorado River is considered one of the "most controlled, controversial and litigated rivers in the world," and during my first job, I would experience firsthand the reality of that observation.

Though my job would ultimately take me to D.C., Kitty, the two kids and I went to Los Angeles for the summer where I would get myself up to speed on the Colorado River case and study for the bar exam. I was paid the princely sum of $400 a month and somehow we managed to rent a small furnished house. While many of my peers were obsessively studying for the bar exam, my circumstances made me immune to the contagious nature of those powerful anxieties. I thought to myself, "Wait a minute. They told me at Stanford that I'm pretty good. Why do I have to go off and study so much?" I was definitely not going to pay for some bar prep class. I had better things to do with my money and my time. I took out a few of my old notebooks from law school, went through them, went to the testing site, took the exam and passed it. Not very dramatic but that was the way it was.

After our summer in Los Angeles, Kitty—who was now pregnant with Kim—Barbara, Don and I moved to Washington, D.C., to the home office of the firm. It was the lightest move imaginable: no furniture, just our clothes and our kids. And rather than drive thousands of miles in the old Ford, we flew across the country, courtesy of Northcutt Ely, from Los Angeles to National Airport in D.C. I had been to Washington before when I was in high school, but as we came in for a landing, I enjoyed my first bird's eye view of the Capitol, the Washington Monument, the Lincoln Memorial and the Potomac River. Once there, I took the D.C. bar exam and also passed that one.

Northcutt Ely had a special expertise in water in the West, and he was appointed as special assistant attorney general of California to represent the state in its long running and incredibly complicated interstate dispute over the Colorado River. In the Colorado River litigation, emotional, practical and dramatic public policy issues converged. This was a massive litigation that would eventually go to the Supreme Court, last eleven years and cost five million dollars—which was a lot of money back then!

I learned that the basic conflict in the case involved how much of the Colorado River's precious water each state was going to have. This river served the water needs of nearly 40 million people in the southwestern United States, and California, with its incredible population growth, was determined to secure its piece. It was boom times in California, and its population expansion was viewed with nervousness and suspicion by all the other states, especially Arizona. Therein was the problem.

The Colorado River snakes through seven states in the west: Colorado, Arizona, Nevada, California and Utah in the U.S., as well as Baja California and Sonora in Mexico. It also drains water through its tributaries from significant parts of Wyoming and New Mexico. Each state wanted a part of the flow of the great river, and the tug of war had been going on for decades. In 1922 delegates from the Colorado River basin states met in New Mexico and worked out an agreement. They had initially thought that the water could be given to each state individually, but the technical problems in actually figuring out each state's fair share made that almost impossible. Instead, they all agreed that the best option would be to divide the river into its Upper and Lower Basins, give equal shares to each basin, and the states within each basin would have access to that share of the water.

This arrangement worked well when water was abundant. But there was not always enough water to go around, and that caused constant problems with the agreement. Arizona, with its vast deserts and its desperate need for water, became the state that created the most conflict from the very beginning of the agreement. Realizing that they would be competing with booming California for the precious water allotted to the Lower Basin, Arizona refused to ratify the compact even after signing it. Finally, in 1944, Arizona ratified the compact, but that still did not resolve the basic dispute between California and Arizona about river use. In 1952

Arizona sued California and asked the Supreme Court to take the apportionment of the water out of the states' hands and decide it in the court. And that led to the case *Arizona v. California*, which was my introduction to working as a real lawyer.

Of course, I was a tiny cog in a gigantic machine. The case had already been going on for two years before I joined; it would continue for another nine after I left. To appreciate the scope of those involved consider the official Supreme Court document on the case, which lists: "Messrs. Edmund G. Brown, Atty. Gen., Northcutt Ely, Robert L. McCarty and Prentiss Moore, Asst. Attys. Gen., and Gilbert F. Nelson, George M. Treister, Irving Jaffe and Robert Sterling Wolf, Deputy Attys. Gen., for defendant State of California." The Supreme Court appointed one of the best lawyers of his generation—Simon Rifkind—to be the Special Master of the case.

Rifkind was asked by the Supreme Court to help sort out all the complexities involved in the dispute and there were many. I attended his first hearing for the lawyers of the various states in Phoenix and was struck by the rather diminutive bearing of this giant in the law. He could not have been more than 5'5" and around 140 pounds, and he wore horn-rimmed glasses that only magnified his blue eyes. His focus, brilliance and intellectual agility were striking.

My year with Northcutt Ely was important for two very personal reasons. The first was that it was during the Colorado River dispute that I first met Edmund G. "Pat" Brown, who was then the Attorney General of California. At one point during the meeting in Arizona, he asked me to draft a speech for him to deliver to the participants, emphasizing California's interests in water. I was astonished that he would even have noticed me, much less trusted me to write something. Naturally I did my best and turned it around as quickly as possible. He was pleased and delivered the statement, which became part of the public record on the dispute. This was the beginning of a relationship that would play an enormously important role in my life.

Pat Brown embodies, in many ways, the overall significance of that experience for me, because here I was in the great nexus of law and public policy. As I have often said, I never intended to become a lawyer. My destiny, I had thought, was in the world of public policy for which the Woodrow Wilson School prepared me. Working that year in the midst of the Colorado River dispute, I was immersed in a critical public policy issue with people who excelled in the field. Pat Brown was the Attorney General of California and was fully engaged in protecting the water rights of the state's citizens, something that would affect their lives every single day.

The second personal reason for the importance of that year had to do with my ever-expanding family. Kitty was pregnant during this time. We were living in Alexandria, Virginia, and I was commuting every day to our offices on K Street in Washington. One of my Stanford professors, Charlie Corker, was also working on the Colorado River case. Kitty was pretty far along in her pregnancy, and Charlie and I once talked about names for the new member of my family. He said that the best name would be Justiciable Northcutt Norris. Kitty just roared with laughter when I told her that idea.

Needless to say, that was not the name we chose. But in another way, the Colorado River litigation actually was responsible for Kim's name! I attended a Congressional hearing about the dispute on Capitol Hill and a young woman named Kim was testifying. I cannot remember what she was talking about or what her professional standing was, but I remember being very impressed with her intelligence and poise. I also thought that she had a great name. When I came back and suggested that name to Kitty, she agreed. Kim was born on April 21, 1955, and was welcomed by her older brother and sister as young siblings always welcome a new arrival: with delight and a heavy dose of suspicion. Curiously, Pat Brown, who was then the attorney general of California, was also born on April 21, almost fifty years before our Kim.

The months in Washington flew by. I was working hard, occasionally traveling for the case. Sometimes I would take the family to Baltimore to visit with my brother George and his family. It was a settled, interesting and comfortable life. Then, in the spring of 1955, I received a telegram from the office of Supreme Court Justice William O. Douglas. It was an offer to be the law clerk to Justice Douglas starting in the Fall term.

I could not believe it! To be plucked from private practice was very unusual. I cannot imagine any young lawyer turning down such an opportunity no matter where they were, and I certainly was not going to— nor was Northcutt Ely. He was delighted with my news and eager to do anything that he could to accommodate my plans. The Supreme Court term begins the first Monday in October, but I needed to be there earlier to get up to speed on the work.

Clerking for a United States Supreme Court Justice is the highest honor that any recent graduate can receive. I have noticed a special bond exists with those of us who have had this experience of clerking at the Supreme Court. We are a kind of a secret society, or elite club with no walls. At the time I never considered the implications for my career. I simply could not believe that I would have the opportunity to serve, to learn, to see the workings of the highest court in the land, from inside its chambers.

Of course I said yes.

Justice William O. Douglas

9

JUSTICE WILLIAM O. DOUGLAS

I will never forget the first day of my clerkship.

I was driving an eight-year-old, two-door Chevy that my brother George—who helped me in so many different ways over the years—had found for me. It was the summer so the city was empty and oppressive with the heat and humidity that earned Washington the status of a diplomatic hardship post. I cannot say that I cared at all. With no air conditioning in the Chevy, I drove that clunker down Independence Avenue, windows wide open, past lots of government buildings, feeling excited and nervous and just a little overwhelmed that I would soon be working for one of the greatest Justices in the United States Supreme Court.

I looked up at the Capitol building and even though I had lived in Washington for a year, it was as if I were seeing it with a different set of eyes. The geography of Washington is defined by the three branches of government: The White House is set apart, 1.6 miles away from Congress and the Supreme Court, but in that small separation the genius of our Founding Fathers is contained. I felt that sense of history in a new way the day I was to begin my own work within the corridors of power. Immediately after the Capitol, I turned left onto First Street, NE, and there it was—the Supreme Court.

The impressive marble building had a timeless Athenian grandeur that belied the fact that it had only been built in 1935. With its eight magisterial Corinthian columns and "Equal Justice for All" engraved just under the pediment, the building takes up almost the entire city block. When you face the building, on the left is the statue of the Contemplation of Justice—a woman—and on the right is the male Authority of Law. The front doors are bronze and huge and while I did not walk through them that first day—those of us who worked there had a separate entrance—they added to the incredibly solemn and inspiring impression that the building makes.

I had been told to go to a separate entrance in the parking lot that was below the building, and the security people would let me in. They not only let me in, they practically saluted me, *not* the treatment to which I was accustomed. It made me feel as if I was a kind of imposter! Didn't they know I was just Bill Norris, the youngest son of George and Florence Norris from Turtle Creek, PA? I gulped, collected myself, parked the car and found my way up the back entrance and into the main corridor, to what is known as the Great Hall.

Justice Douglas was one of the four legal giants who were appointed by my hero, Franklin Delano Roosevelt. As history has shown, these four men—Felix Frankfurter, Hugo Black, Robert Jackson and William O. Douglas—were among the greatest justices ever to serve. William O. Douglas was one of the youngest justices when he was appointed—only forty years old—and served for the longest time in the history of the court. He was there for thirty-six years, a period that would involve some of the most momentous decisions in the Supreme Court's history in a career that spanned from President Franklin Delano Roosevelt to President Gerald Ford. He participated in the decision concerning the internment of citizens during World War II, as well as *Brown v. Board of Education*, *New York Times v. Sullivan*, and the *Griswold* case that redefined the whole notion of privacy as envisioned in the Constitution.

In the book *Scorpions*, which chronicles the clash of personalities and the power of conflicting judicial philosophies among these New Deal justices, lawyer and historian Noah Feldman writes, "Assessments of Douglas as a justice are deeply divided between those who consider him arbitrary and outrageous, and those who judge him the most advanced proponent of liberal principle ever to sit on the court: again, there is truth in both propositions."[*]

For me, he was a great man.

But I had not yet met him!

Justice Douglas was not in his chambers when I arrived that day—in fact he was on vacation in Washington State—but Harvey Grossman, the UCLA straight-A student who got the job before me, was still there along with two secretaries. The ratio of justices' secretaries to law clerks was already a bit unusual because other justices had one secretary and two clerks whereas Douglas had the reverse. I was to learn that Justice

---

[*] Noah Feldman, *Scorpions* (New York: Twelve Hachette Book Group 2010), p. 173.

Douglas would never do anything according to some set of unwritten rules, especially those that might be cherished by the other justices. The independence of mind that characterized so many of his greatest decisions had its down side in his relationships; he had a chaotic personal life and robust conflicts with the other Justices. He was a loner by nature but also a man who had a passion for politics, which was a point of connection between us. By the time I came along, any aspirations for the Presidency that may have once occupied him were over.

He was also a pragmatist. One reason that he had two secretaries was because he was not just a Supreme Court Justice but also an author of popular books—eventually he would write twelve of them and some of them were best sellers on topics ranging from legal questions like liberty, to books on nature, the Himalaya mountains, the Soviet Union, and the West. He became a writer partly because he had a great and voracious intellect and an amazing fluidity and facility with words, but also because he had very expensive alimony payments. The two secretaries were there to type up the drafts of his books, and I soon found out that doing a little literary research would also become part of my job.

When I came to clerk for him he was recently married to his second wife, Mercedes Davidson, who was much younger than he was. He was a relatively happy man, compared to other more tumultuous times of his life and that was good for me.

Harvey Grossman greeted me in Douglas' office. He had already served his year and was getting ready to move on, but stuck around so he could give me the two-week crash course on how to be Justice Douglas's clerk. Harvey explained that the clerks for each Justice would have the responsibility to read all of the petitions for certiorari—and there were hundreds, maybe even thousands at the time. (Petitions for certiorari are the most common way cases reach the Supreme Court.) In all the other chambers, because there were usually two clerks, they would divide them up. Chief Justice Earl Warren had three law clerks, because he had additional duties

Being the only Douglas clerk, however, meant that I had to read every cert petition. And then I would have to type up a little summary of the case and make a one-word recommendation at the bottom of it. Normally, it would be no more than one page, single spaced, and then "grant" or "denied." The Court grants only a small fraction of cert petitions.

Secondly, the Justices are briefed by their clerks on the cases scheduled for oral argument. I would have to read the lawyers' briefs and again write a memorandum for the Justice. That task was not such a big deal, with neither the same large volume of work, nor the pressure to get a yes or no question right. Preparing Douglas for oral arguments was not a major part of the job because, I learned, he *never* asked any questions during argument. He had a very inquisitive mind, but reserved his inquiry for discussion with his law clerk (me) and with his fellow Justices in conference.

During oral argument, he would take his place in the great courtroom, and while the back and forth among the lawyers and the Justices was going on he would appear to be paying no attention, sometimes he might even be writing an opinion on a different case. Occasionally, he would send notes back to me in chambers, requesting some research on a point he was writing about. I would send back my reply to the bench. I recall one instance when I quoted a well-known legal writer and the Justice wrote back a terse response, "I don't get my law from X."

In the next phase after argument, the Justices would meet in conference to discuss the cases. My role was to prepare my Justice for discussion with his colleagues as needed.

Finally, one of the Justices was assigned the role of writing the opinion, whether for the majority or the dissent. Normally, the law clerks were those who provided the first draft. I was put on notice well before I arrived at the Supreme Court that Justice Douglas was the one Justice who wrote all of his own opinions and that I was not to worry about drafting for him. Harvey explained what that meant. Justice Douglas would just take the briefs and start writing—not typing—his opinions in long hand and hand them to the secretaries who would type them up. Once the draft was typed up, it was my responsibility to read it carefully and make sure everything that was written was accurate and that there were no holes in the argument.

This was the basic job description—if there is any such thing—but really learning the job required being with Justice Douglas and that was an intimidating prospect. He did not have a great reputation for being a caring mentor to his clerks, or even for liking them very much. Harvey told me that he may be very gruff and brusque at times but that I would learn a lot. It was common knowledge—and I am still not sure if this is apocryphal or not—that he had once referred to law clerks as "the lowest form of human life."*

It's not as if he had warm feelings for many people around the Court— and the feeling was mutual. But Douglas and Justice Felix Frankfurter had a special dislike for each other. They were like a couple of kids scrapping in the sandbox. The clerks were not allowed in the conference room, of course, but sometimes we could be out in the corridor, standing in those

---

* Feldman, *Scorpions*, p. 431.

marble halls that echoed even when one whispered. When Douglas and Frankfurter were yelling at each other in the conference room, their voices seemed to get amplified in the hall. On his way back from a conference, still energized and angry, Douglas would stop to give me a report, relishing the points he made over "Frankfurter!"

Douglas was a great outdoorsman and loved to go hiking, especially out West. Part of the lore surrounding him included a story from a time he went horseback riding on a mountain trail in Washington State. The horse reared at one point and Douglas got thrown off. He fell badly—actually he could have died tumbling down that incline—broke twenty-three ribs and had a concussion. When word got around the Court that "Douglas fell off a cliff!" One of the law clerks famously asked, "Where was Frankfurter?"

So this is the world that I was entering that summer of 1955. After Harvey left, I got to know the other Supreme Court clerks and made friendships that lasted a lifetime. One of them was Justice Stanley Reed's clerk Rod Hills, who was a year behind me at Stanford. It was nice to see a familiar face because we had gotten to know each other on the *Law Review*. Curiously, even though Justice Reed studied law at the University of Virginia, he never received a law degree! He passed the bar, however, and had been Roosevelt's solicitor general before becoming a Supreme Court Justice.

As I did, Rod reported for duty during the summer of '55. One day, during Douglas's summer vacation, Rod came into my office in the chambers and said that Justice Reed and Justice Clark wanted to play golf at the Congressional Country Club in Maryland. Justice Reed said to his clerk, "Rod, could you get a fourth? We want you to go play golf with us." So he came and got me, and the four of us headed off to the exclusive Congressional Country Club in Bethesda, Maryland.

I was not a very experienced golfer at the time, but had played a little. When I was twelve or thirteen, one of my many jobs was as a caddy at the local public course. Hardly the elegance and manicured lawns of Congressional Country Club! Our memorable foursome was Justice Stanley Reed, Justice Tom C. Clark, Rod Hills—who later became chairman of the FCC under Reagan—and me. Sometimes I played a little golf with the other clerks who were there during the summer, then returned to Justice Douglas' empty chambers and used his bathroom, which included a shower, before I went back to work.

I cannot remember exactly when I met Bill Douglas in the flesh, but at some point in September he arrived in his Chambers. He was a good-looking guy, a vigorous fifty-seven years old at the time, and he was very personable with me, which I discovered was unusual for him. In some ways we had two important things in common. He grew up in Yakima, Washington, the son of a minister, and his father died when Bill was five years old. So the family, which never had much money, became really poor and scraped by just trying to survive.

Bill learned early on that he had to work and contribute to the family. He had almost as many jobs as I did, especially when he went to Whitman College in Walla Walla, Washington. He did not sell cars or work in a VA hospital, as I had at Stanford, but he did work as a janitor in an office building and a clerk in a jewelry store. And, he worked as a waiter, or a "hasher," in a fraternity as I had at the University of Wisconsin! It's not as if we shared hard luck stories—far from it, neither one of us discussed these things—but on some level those experiences defined both of us in very significant ways.

He was also passionately interested in politics and the way public policy affects daily life. At one point he nurtured the dream of becoming president. He had been considered by Roosevelt as his running mate in 1944, but was aced out by Harry Truman, who got the nomination and rose to the presidency with FDR's death. I wonder what thoughts ran through Douglas' mind at that historic moment. Not that I ever had presidential ambitions—despite the Turtle Creek High School Year Book Looking Glass Predictions—but later on, when I returned to California, political life was like oxygen for me.

Douglas was a committed early environmentalist. The year before I became his law clerk, he was outraged that there were plans to turn the C&O Canal into a highway and organized a hike along its 180 miles to protest the plan. He got a lot of headlines—he loved being in the spotlight—and the area was turned not into a freeway but into a national park. There is a William O. Douglas Wilderness Area in Washington State, which was the result of his efforts to preserve the Cougar Lakes there.

For whatever reason, we worked well together. If I had any complaint at all, it was that he simply had no concept of the sheer volume of work he was expecting from a single law clerk. He was oblivious to the work-load. I would have a deadline because the cert memos would have to be ready by the next day. Then he would send me across the street to the Library of Congress to do some research for a book or a speech that he was writing— and he wrote a lot of books and made a lot of speeches. Sometimes, I even had to read the book he was working on and provide some further research. I have always been a hard worker, but the hours at the Supreme Court were unreal, and Douglas seemed to have absolutely no interest in the fact that I had a wife and three young children at home.

But that did not mean that he could not be gracious and thoughtful to me. One day my oldest brother George brought our father and one of his daughters to the Supreme Court to see where I worked and to bask in a little bit of familial pride. Justice Douglas very kindly welcomed my father and brother and niece into his chambers, and they all spoke a little while. Then I showed my family to the gallery to observe the Justices as they heard the arguments of that day. My niece Nancy Hanna got worried that they did not seem to be listening to the lawyer's arguments. George explained that this was kind of a public presentation for the record and that the Justices already knew all the facts from papers that were prepared by people like me. It was a memorable day for all of us.

The most important part of my job was to determine whether or not Justice Douglas was citing a case properly. He was the opinion writer, but I realized that he had a practice of taking a paragraph or several couple of sentences out of his opinion and stapling it to a different page where it might have greater relevance. I would write a commentary, or maybe a revision of a paragraph or even a page, and I would bring my inserts to his desk when he summoned me. I would sit across from him and hand him each neatly typed page one at a time as I explained my comments. And it worked! He would read what I had written and without saying a word he would either throw my work into the waste paper basket or talk about it, or, the best moment of all, he would read it and say, "Staple it to the draft!"

Brown v. Board of Education, one of the most important cases of all time, had been decided the year before, but its shock waves continued throughout the docket during my clerkship year. We had a number of cases involving the application of *Brown* as precedent beyond the sphere of public education, for example, swimming pool segregation in Alabama, or segregation in some university in Georgia. There were dispensed with quickly by citing *Brown*.

There was a very important case the year that I clerked that would figure very prominently in a later chapter of my life and, indeed, in the country's history. The case was *Bolling v. Sharpe* and it focused on segregation not in some Southern backwater, but in the nation's capital. Washington was always a hybrid city—as President Kennedy once observed, it was a city of "Southern efficiency and Northern charm." But in fact, it was a very Southern city, especially in terms of its treatment of its large African American population. I was astonished to see the segregation that appeared to be part of daily life there. It was only a matter of time after *Brown* before this situation would be challenged. In *Bolling* it was.

But the significance of the decision was not restricted to the citizens of the District of Columbia in 1957. As it turns out, the legal reasoning in the *Bolling v. Sharpe* decision became crucially important in 1987.

But that comes later.

Amidst all this activity, the Colorado River Case appeared on my desk! The case was pending before the United States Supreme Court, and sometimes the Court would have to decide some minor procedural matter. So suddenly I received some papers on the Colorado River litigation that looked very familiar. It was the first time that conflict of interest presented itself to me. There was nothing complicated about it at all, and I will never understand why lawyers can get themselves tangled up in conflicts when the decision is so very clear. I went right into Justice Douglas office and said, "I don't think I should be involved here." He said, "Just bring me the papers. No big deal."

And that was that.

When I was clerking for Justice Douglas, James "Scotty" Reston, the powerful Washington Bureau Chief of the *New York Times*, and a man who regularly consorted with power, had a brief discussion with Justice Douglas about the paper's Supreme Court coverage. Justice Douglas did not think it would be proper for him to have a relationship with Reston, but I could act almost as his proxy. He told me to talk to Reston very openly and suggest some possible new approaches the *Times* might attempt.

I could not imagine how anyone could really understand the inner workings of the Court, the details of what went on there, without some education in law school. When I spoke with Mr. Reston, I suggested that the *New York Times* might send a reporter to law school and he would then be in a better position to do the job. Reston seemed to think that this was good advice, since in 1956, their young reporter Anthony Lewis took a leave from the paper to attend Harvard Law School on a Neiman Fellowship to study law, "with special reference to the Supreme Court."

It was also a year when new, important friendships for life were formed. This did not happen over lunch in the special law clerk lunchroom because as Douglas' only clerk, I would usually eat lunch at my desk. The eighteen of us rarely got together as a group, but on occasion there was a more formal gathering when distinguished speakers would address our group in the lunchroom. Andrew Kaufmann, who became a professor at Harvard Law School, was a Frankfurter clerk who remained to work for him a second year. Despite the profound and legendary disagreements between our respective Justices, Andy and I became great pals.

One tradition in the Court was that every Justice would have lunch with the clerks at least once during the term. I recall a specific occasion when Felix Frankfurter came to have lunch with us. We all sat around a big table in the lunchroom, and the Justice began by going around the room and asking each clerk to pose a question to him. He did not say a word; he just listened to all eighteen questions. He then proceeded to group them into categories, talk about them, remembering which clerk asked which question, and then he answered each question. It was a remarkable performance.

At one point, one of the clerks disagreed with Frankfurter about a footnote in a particular case that had occurred years ago. Bob Hamilton did not work for Frankfurter, but for Justice Tom Clark. Hamilton was a brilliant academic type, who eventually became a law professor at University of Texas. Frankfurter and Hamilton were in disagreement over that footnote, what it said and what it meant. Bob Hamilton would not back down. He was very understated, very modest, but determined.

Finally, Frankfurter wanted to settle the matter and turned to Andy Kaufman and said, "Andy, go up and get Volume X of the *U.S. Reports.*" There was a stony silence in that room, and everyone was wondering how this dispute was going to turn out. Andy returned with that volume of the *U.S. Reports* and you could tell immediately, just from the look on his face, what the outcome was going to be. Frankfurter took the volume, went to the footnote and started reading it with a stony expression on his face. Everyone knew that Bob Hamilton was right and the great Felix Frankfurter was wrong! I could not resist telling that story to Justice Douglas who savored the punch line and howled with laughter.

I think of those of us sitting around that lunch table that day and am grateful for the friendships that endured. Wayne Barnett was another Harvard Law School graduate and a Justice Harlan clerk. He ended up as a tax scholar and eventually was on the faculty at Stanford and then on the faculty of the University of Washington Law School. He married a wonderful artist named Jackie Marx whom he met during the summer of '55 when law clerks had a lot more freedom. She worked with some U.S. senator or congressman and eventually a relationship blossomed between them.

But this was not easy for Wayne. "Wayne, why don't you marry that woman?" I would ask him. And he would reply immediately, "Oh, I couldn't!" He was a poor boy from Las Vegas, who was so smart and confident and Jackie was quite an upper class young woman from a very wealthy family. He said, "Bill, I'd feel uncomfortable doing that. I want to be the breadwinner of the family." I thought he was nuts. "Aw, c'mon, Wayne," I would say. "Forget it! You obviously just love this woman. Go ahead and marry her, then worry about the money." And finally, he married her and they have been very happy together. I would frequently visit them up in Seattle whenever I sat there to hear arguments for the Ninth Circuit.

There were others who would go on to play significant roles in my life: Julian Burke, who clerked for Stanley Reed, and I ended up practicing law together in Los Angeles; John Nolan, who also clerked for Tom Clark, remained in Washington as a major lawyer at Steptoe & Johnson. We later were involved in Democratic politics together and were co-moderators of some Aspen Institute Executive programs because of our common love of public policy and a little skiing on the side. Bob Cole who clerked for Sherman Minton, joined the law faculty at Boalt Hall at Berkeley and remained there. I performed his marriage ceremony to Professor Eleanor Swift, a colleague of Bob's at Berkeley.

Occasionally we had the opportunity to spend some time with other Justices and my favorite was the charming and incredibly warm Chief Justice, Earl Warren. He seemed genuinely interested in the law clerks. He would sometimes visit with Bill Douglas and knowing that he and I were both from California, he would stop and chat with me and even inquire about Kitty and my family.

In the end, though, my major relationship for that year was with the brilliant, irascible, visionary legal genius William O. Douglas. I think he really liked me and I liked him. I also liked the way he treated me. He was tough, he was respectful, he was fair and in an utterly unsentimental way, he was surprisingly gentle with me. I heard some feedback that he thought I was pretty good and over that year I also spent time with him outside of the Supreme Court. He would take me hiking along his precious Chesapeake and Ohio Canal, along the Potomac. Later, when I was a lawyer living in Pasadena, when he would be in town, he would invite me to go hiking with him in the San Gabriel Mountains near my home.

We would hike on the trail and I would listen to his thoughts about the environment, about privacy and about the role of the judiciary. We would have discussions about "judicial activism." Douglas, to my mind, took a straightforward, realistic approach. He used to go crazy when he was accused of "judicial activism" when the very nature of the job is to make a decision. To that end, everyone is a judicial activist. His best definition of judicial activism was "an opinion that you don't agree with."

There are things that you learn very consciously, and there are things that you learn as if by osmosis. I think that during my year with Justice Douglas I learned that there are decisions that must be made that go against the prevailing pressures, in which the law is decided and then the rest of society needs to catch up. He also "trusted his gut," another approach we had in common.

And then, to my utter amazement, the year was over. I needed to look for another job and Kitty and I both wanted to move back to California. When I asked Douglas for a little time to go out to the West Coast to interview with some law firms he encouraged me to make the trip. I took some time off and met with some firms both in Los Angeles and the Bay Area. There was one small problem: I had no idea what kind of law I wanted to practice. This was not exactly the highly focused career path that many young lawyers may follow.

By this time, Warren Christopher had taken an interest in me. He was five years ahead of me at Stanford Law School and five years ahead of me as a clerk to Justice Douglas. When it came time for me to choose a law firm, Chris began recruiting me to join his firm, which was O'Melveny and Myers.

I did not know about law firms, I did not know about the practice of law, but—trusting my gut again—I instinctively knew that I wanted to be in a relatively small firm, rather than a large firm. I told Chris I thought his firm was too big for me and I wanted to look elsewhere. Instead of trying to persuade me that I was wrong and should work with him, Chris understood and said, "You want a small firm? I'm going to send you to one of my colleagues from law school." Bob Taylor was now a leader in a very small law firm at the time and it was called Tuttle & Taylor. When I was in Los Angeles I met with Bob Taylor and his partner Ed Tuttle. Again, Chris was right. This was the kind of firm where I would fit.

My relationship with Douglas did not end there. As a lawyer, I would go back to Washington, and he would frequently invite me to have lunch with him in his chambers. When I ran for Attorney General in California, Douglas was *very* interested and always wanted me to report how it was going, his own interest in politics and mine converging.

On my last day as a clerk for the Supreme Court, I said goodbye and thank you to the secretaries, to some of my fellow clerks who were still around, to any Justice who was still there. Douglas had already gone West for his annual summer vacation. And I had already put Kitty and the three kids on the flight to Los Angeles, courtesy of Tuttle & Taylor. Those were the years when people who were not passengers could still get on the planes before they took off, to settle family members for the flight. When it was time for the takeoff, my three-year-old son Don looked up at me and said, "Dad, you better get off the plane." I did so I could do my final task as Justice Douglas' clerk. As Harvey had done for me, I remained for a few weeks to orient the new clerk, William Cohen.

But now it was time to leave. I walked down the marble halls, re-membering vividly how intimidating it all was when I arrived a year before. I got in my now nine-year-old Chevy, pulled out of the parking lot, gave the attendant a warm smile, and turned right on First Street NE and right on Independence Avenue to head home. I needed to pack my bags and meet my family and start my new life in California.

PART III

PRIVATE PRACTICE AND PUBLIC SERVICE

*"Few will have the greatness to bend history itself; but
each of us can work to change a small portion of
events, and in the total of all those acts will be
written the history of this generation."*

Robert F. Kennedy

Bill and Kitty Norris: family photograph, circa 1956,
with children Barbara (left), Don and Kim

10

LEARNING LITIGATION AT TUTTLE & TAYLOR

Monday, August 6, 1956, was one of the most important days of my life. It was my first day of work at Tuttle & Taylor, which was to remain my professional home for the next twenty-four years. It was also the day that I caught my first glimpse of the insider's view of California Democratic politics. Warren Christopher suggested that I go with him to the California chapter of the Adlai Stevenson for President headquarters in Los Angeles. We did not stay long, and it was only a glimpse, but being there and seeing the energy of the Democratic Party in California's political life connected me once more with the Woodrow Wilson School and my love of politics.

Kitty and I had found a nice place to live in Pasadena. At last we had a permanent residence for our three young children: Barbara who was five, Don who was three and Kim who was a year-and-a-half. We had good neighbors, good schools, and a yard in which the kids could play and Kitty could, at last, garden. We had moved around so much she could never plant any annuals with the thought that she might actually see them bloom year after year. But we now owned a house! And she began to make it our permanent home.

I drove downtown to my new office on Fifth Street facing Pershing Square to report for duty at Tuttle & Taylor. There were only four lawyers including me—Bob Taylor, Ed Tuttle and Merlin Call, who had been one year ahead of me at Stanford—but none of them were litigators. Ed Tuttle was a native Californian and had attended Caltech as a young man and USC law school. He was of a slightly different generation—a shade older than the rest of us—and had practiced with another firm for several years, where his client base included California's agricultural cooperatives. In 1952, the California Fruit Growers Association, the orange cooperative that had been around since 1925, changed its name to the Sunkist

79

Growers, Inc. And it was at that point that Ed, who had been working with the Fruit Growers Association in another firm, took Sunkist as a client and set up his own shop. Ed Tuttle's business acumen meant that he understood how to represent our clients' concerns not just from a legal perspective but also with their business interests in mind. This was one of the reasons that even when he split off from his larger firm, the orange and avocado cooperatives stayed with him. Bob Taylor was only four years older than I and a native Californian. He practiced in San Francisco for a little while and then moved to Los Angeles where Ed Tuttle had already established his small, specialized, boutique firm. By 1953 he was a partner (things moved quickly in those days) and by 1954 the firm's name was changed to include his.

One can look at an orange or an avocado in the supermarket and have absolutely no notion of the incredible amounts of money and litigation that were involved in every aspect of the existence of that fruit, from growing it to getting it to market. So for Ed, the work with the cooperatives offered a substantial practice and gave him enough stability to branch out on his own, which he did. Then he brought in Bob Taylor and, three years later, me.

I was open for anything when I arrived, twenty-nine years old, a father of three, and someone who did not want to specialize in a single area of the law. I would always concentrate on whatever assignment I took on and then would zero in on the next one. This is a talent that I seem to have, an ability to focus intently on a single subject and then switch my focus, just as intently, to another. I did not emerge from law school, or from my clerkship, with a burning desire to become the world's leading expert in corporate law, or First Amendment law, or civil procedures. Just give me a project and a deadline, and set me loose!

And that is exactly what they did. Bob Taylor immediately put me to work on a major transaction involving the heirs of an old man who had recently died. He explained to me that this was not just your ordinary wills and estates kind of work because the elderly man really had not left much of an estate. What he did leave to his heirs was an interest in the oil, gas and minerals that lay underneath a large tract of land in northwestern New Mexico. A rancher owned the surface rights to the land, but that is not where its true value lay. The real money was below the surface, in what the dearly departed believed was a massive deposit of untapped oil. It turns out that he was wrong, but that came later. What was down below was even more valuable.

This was my first case and it was a doozy. It consumed my life for the next four or five months. There were five or six heirs and Bob Taylor was in the midst of negotiating an agreement between them and the Kerr-

McGee Oil Company who had tremendous interest in those rights. We then worked with Kerr-McGee against the rancher and Phillips Petroleum, the oil company that associated itself with the rancher. Kerr-McGee was a huge Oklahoma oil company that was established in 1929 and had a whole arsenal of legal firepower. The case was very complex. Our side had to take on the rancher who owned the surface rights to the property and who claimed that he had some rights to what lay below as well.

When I stepped in, litigation had already begun in federal court in Albuquerque, because clearly there was going to be some money to be made somewhere. Bob apparently had confidence in me that I did not exactly have in myself, because as I worked on the case over the next few weeks, I became more and more convinced that I did not know anything. I did not know anything about mineral rights. I did not know anything about corporate fights. And I had never taken a deposition before in my life.

Before I knew it, I was traveling to Albuquerque to listen to the depositions that were being taken by experienced lawyers for the two major oil companies. I would go to the deposition and sit there, absorbing the brilliance of some of Albuquerque's finest attorneys. Slowly it began to dawn on me that these honorable members of the bar, both from Albuquerque and from the oil companies, were just not all that good. They missed lapses in the story, they did not follow up when a follow up question could have resolved so much. And the questions themselves often did not lead anywhere substantive. Before I knew it, *I* was taking depositions. It was on-the-job training. But what became apparent was that this was not a fight that involved oil; this was a fight that involved one of the largest uranium deposits in the continental United States.

The case clipped along rather quickly, and after a few months it finally arrived at the point of summary judgment—where each party can ask the court for a decision in its favor before going to the time and expense of a full trial. Both parties were going to enter petitions for summary judgment. I was going to prepare the motion for our side, suggesting to the court that there was no need at all for a trial because there were no more fact issues to resolve and the merits of the case were so lopsided in our favor. There was only one minor problem: I did not know how to prepare a motion for summary judgment.

I told Bob about my summary judgment disability and confessed, "I think I need a little help." He said to me, "Well look, one of my classmates by the name of Shirley Hufstedler is now operating out of her home. She's had a baby, so she's freelancing." He said he would give Shirley a call and we would work out something so that she could come in on a contract basis.

Shirley Hufstedler became one of the most legendary women in the law. She was in the Stanford class two years before Justice Sandra Day O'Connor. But I do not think many people doubt that if a Democrat had been President instead of Ronald Reagan, Shirley Hufstedler would have been the first woman appointed to the Supreme Court. She eventually became a lifelong friend and trusted confidante.

I had never met her before, but went to her home where she was caring for her baby and her garden, as well as keeping completely up to speed on her legal work. I received the best tutorial on how to prepare a motion for summary judgment that anyone could have had. At summary judgment, the judge decides whether the case actually presents a factual dispute and, accordingly, whether a case should proceed to trial. Are there genuine issues of material fact that are unresolved? If there are not and the law is in its favor, the moving party is entitled to judgment as a matter of law.

What I learned during my time with Shirley was about the practical and strategic significance of the distinction between legal and factual issues. At summary judgment, the court is tasked with assessing the factual record—which is completely developed by the time summary judgment motions are filed—to see if there are any disputed issues of fact. It's one of the few times in the civil context that a judge is really delving into the factual record, although ostensibly only to see if there is a "dispute." Normally any kind of fact-finding is in the purview of the jury.

Shirley showed me how the best summary judgment orders lay out the facts and legal standards for the claims at issue and then clearly explain why, as a matter of law, those facts entitle the moving party to judgment. Opinions like that are easiest for the parties to understand, and they are also clearest for the appeals courts to read and assess. Shirley and I went through every detail of the case and she saw the significance of some points that I had entirely missed (but never would again!). The money involved was astronomical. There may not have been oil, but there was a phenomenal deposit of uranium valued at $50 million dollars—that would be about half a billion today.

It was touch and go. The trial date was approaching, and this is the period of time when both parties are trying to avoid the very expensive, often protracted and usually unpredictable experience of a trial. The clock was ticking. Our trial date was only weeks away and we seemed to have reached an impasse. Phillips Petroleum offered a settlement that I had thought was actually very good for everyone involved. My clients were not rich people. Under the terms of this settlement, they would have been taken care of for a few generations. But they said no.

This is where I learned a very important lesson about the way that negotiations, the law and rational thinking are only part of what is involved in these kinds of transactions. The other part, a crucial element, is the swirl of irrational emotions. The back and forth during a deposition can bring out very strong and uncomfortable feelings in the persons who are being deposed. The need to explain a point of view when being barraged by leading questions can make even the toughest character feel vulnerable and then furious when the deposition is concluded.

When I advised the family, suggesting that Phillips' offer was advantageous to them, they refused to settle because "They accused our father of fraud!" Thus the emotional immediately became the financial. But in the end both sides agreed to settle the case.

Now that my first case was behind me, I felt comfortable broadening my focus to include additional activities. Several months before, on my first day of work, Warren Christopher had taken me straight to the state campaign headquarters of Adlai Stevenson and introduced me to Fred Dutton. Fred had served on the first editorial board of the Stanford Law Review with Chris, Shirley Hufstedler and Bob Taylor. His varied and very significant political career began as southern California campaign manager for Adlai Stevenson's 1956 presidential campaign. Afterwards, he signed on with Edmund G. "Pat" Brown's campaign for governor and later served as his chief of staff.

No Democrat had a prayer of defeating Eisenhower in 1956, but still a few of them had hope, and the tall, cerebral Stevenson was the leader of the pack. He had been a hero of mine from his first run in 1952. Fred Dutton spoke to me about getting involved in the Stevenson campaign. I had never participated in any political campaign before—even my election as class president for Turtle Creek High School happened without campaigning—and while I was pleased to catch a glimpse of the inside of this world, I knew that my focus at that moment had to be on earning my stripes as a lawyer. But it would not be long before I would jump into the political fray.

As we all know, Adlai Stevenson lost the race and Eisenhower once more was our President. But what was most important was that out of the Stevenson campaign arose a grassroots statewide organization called the California Democratic Council. Though not part of the official party, it was very well organized by volunteers. This is where I found my political home in my very own assembly district in Pasadena. When I arrived, I was privileged to meet one of the most gifted guides on California politics—an extraordinary woman, who was the granddaughter of William Jennings Bryan. Her name was Rudd Brown.

11

A LOT OF BALLS IN THE AIR

Our success with the uranium case in New Mexico marked the beginning of a new, expansive period for Tuttle & Taylor and a very expansive period for me in my professional and political life in California. After the uranium case, I think it became clear that I had a talent for litigation and it suited my cast of mind and competitive instincts. Since there was no litigation department in the firm, all of a sudden I was it! Gradually, we began to accumulate a few clients and a few successes that were actually disproportionate to the size and initial visibility of our young firm. Clients and successes have a tendency to multiply in the law as in most professions.

I was working hard for Tuttle & Taylor and eventually started recruiting some top talent, but in my spare time, I was up to my ears in politics. Not national politics, my world was retail politics on the local level. My new home was the Pasadena chapter of the California Democratic Council, and the two leaders of my law firm, who were thoroughbred Republicans, were completely supportive of my political pursuits. I was so rigorously compartmentalized, I never permitted my political activities to in any way appear in my professional world.

Adlai Stevenson's first run for president inspired a few young future politicians like Alan Cranston, who became a U.S. Senator, and George Miller, who became a Congressman, to start organizing the far flung California supporters of Stevenson into a loosely affiliated network of "Stevenson Clubs." They realized that even if a Democratic President was not in the cards, it was still possible to mobilize that talent and political commitment into other aspects of electoral politics, both on the national and state level. They were especially interested in reclaiming the governorship in Sacramento, which they thought had been held by the Republicans for too long.

In 1953, after Stevenson's first defeat, they created the California Democratic Council, or the CDC, a one of a kind organization of Democratic state politics. I learned about it during the second Stevenson campaign and was impressed with the volunteers that they had managed to assemble. This was the kind of organization that offered me immersion in California state politics and an opportunity to participate in a meaningful way. Fred Dutton suggested that I get involved in my own assembly district in Pasadena, where we were living. Eventually, I also started attending their annual state conventions, which usually took place in Fresno.

Off-year elections, while dull nationally, can be exciting on a state and local level. The one in 1958 was fascinating. First of all, Pat Brown decided to run for governor. He had proved his ability to win statewide office by securing the Attorney General position both in 1950 and in 1954, and that was unusual, because at the time he was the only Democrat to win statewide office. He took this as a sign that perhaps he could win the Governor's seat against Republican Senator Bill Knowland of Oakland. His instincts were good: he was elected governor by a million vote margin.

Chris was very involved in Brown's campaign and I participated only marginally because of my other obligations. I became the deputy campaign manager for Rudd Brown, who was the Democratic nominee for the U.S. House of Representatives from the 21st District, which covered the northern two-thirds of Los Angeles County, including Pasadena and Sierra Madre to the east and Burbank and the San Fernando Valley to the west. She was running against Edgar W. Hiestand, the Republican incumbent who had held office since 1953. He was the epitome of a California Republican businessman and politician: perpetually middle aged, with wire-rimmed glasses, a bow tie, and a firm unyielding expression on his face.

In contrast, Rudd Brown was an absolute dynamo. She was thirty-seven years old, charismatic, intelligent, attractive and completely the master of the issues in her district. The contrast between Brown and Hiestand oddly foreshadowed the contrast that we saw two years later in the match between young, attractive, visionary Jack Kennedy and the tight, hidebound Republican standard-bearer Richard Nixon.

Rudd Brown was an absolute natural in the political world and came by it honestly. She was the granddaughter of the great, though three times failed, presidential candidate William Jennings Bryan. Her mother, Ruth Bryan Owen Rhode, had represented a Florida district in Congress and served as minister to Denmark. Rudd remembered being a young girl and campaigning with her mother when she ran for Congress in 1928. There she learned firsthand the bare-knuckled world of politics. She also was with her mother in 1936 as she made a multi-state tour campaigning for Roosevelt.

Rudd moved to California in 1951 with her husband, Harrison Brown, who was a very famous geophysicist at Caltech. Rudd was not content to be a housewife, she had lived all over the world by that time and was fascinated by politics. She became involved in Adlai Stevenson's first presidential campaign in 1952, where she met some of the key players in California's Democratic political world and eventually became one of them. In one article about her, she remembered her time working with Stevenson: "As I listened to his speeches I finally said, 'I've got to do something about this,' and I went down to the local headquarters. I soon found they were able to occupy all my waking hours.'" She was appointed to the Democratic State Central Committee in 1954, and in 1956 was named the head of the Southern California Women's delegation for the national convention. Her advice to women: "Act like a lady. Think like a man. Work like a dog."

In other words, she was a pro—she had the connections and the drive that were necessary in the grueling world of retail politics to defeat a powerful incumbent. Helen MacGregor, her campaign manager, took me under her wing and made me the deputy campaign manager. It was such an exciting race, one that most people never dreamed could be close because this was such a traditionally Republican district. But by the time Election Day rolled around, we were neck-and-neck. In fact, for twenty-four hours we actually thought she had won! But when the final votes were tallied, Hiestand had 51.9%.

For me, however, the whole experience was a very big win. My colleagues at Tuttle & Taylor, despite their Republican loyalties, completely supported my Democratic political adventures. Things were changing in California in 1958. Pat Brown swept into office. Warren Christopher and Fred Dutton had both been very involved in Brown's campaign and both went to Sacramento with him. Dutton was his chief-of-staff and remained there, while Chris stayed as a senior advisor for a while and then returned to O'Melveny. To have a visible Democrat in a small law office was not a bad thing at that time.

I became a bit more visible in 1960, when Rudd asked me to be her campaign manager. This was a thrilling year to be a Democrat in California: the convention that nominated John F. Kennedy was in Los Angeles, and even though I was not a delegate, it was the first presidential convention that I had ever attended. To have it in my hometown made the experience especially exciting, since I could watch the behind the scenes politics unfold in my own back yard.

The convention took place from the 11th to the 15th of July, and while Kennedy was a favorite, a few weeks before the convention both Adlai Stevenson and Lyndon Johnson threw their hats into the ring. California loved Adlai, but he had already lost twice and the catch phrase in the delegation was that we needed a "fresh face." Johnson did not have nearly the appeal of Stevenson. When Kennedy challenged Johnson to a televised debate and Johnson accepted, Kennedy was the clear winner. Nonetheless, Johnson was such a politically powerful figure, and presented enough of a challenge despite his late entry, that Bobby Kennedy worked the convention floor intensely, making sure that his brother had all the delegates needed to win.

As we all know, he did.

Rudd and I hoped that this time around all the lessons learned from the previous campaign could be applied and we would have a winner. As her campaign manager, I was able to bring in some people to help, and I had a friend who was a brilliant lawyer, a graduate from Stanford a few years younger than I, who became my issues director for the campaign. He did research, got us prepared, wrote speeches, seemed to be very much on the top of his game—and ours. And of course, he was a brilliant Stanford-trained lawyer. If *he* could not get the job done, no one could.

There was only one small problem. Our brilliant research director somehow did not manage to find a crucial element of our opponent's biography: he was a member, in very good standing, of the John Birch Society. Somehow we did not know that. And it would have been a very useful bit of opposition research to have deployed during the campaign, since by that time, the John Birch Society had lost some of its previous luster.

Election night that November was euphoric and depressing: John F. Kennedy defeated Richard Nixon in an incredible squeaker, winning 49.7 percent over Nixon's 49.6 percent, a margin of only 0.17 percent. In California, Nixon won but by an unusually narrow margin—he had 50.1 percent of the vote to Kennedy's 49.55 percent. But ours was not a close race at all: Hiestand won decisively with 58.4 percent of the vote, over our 41.6—a terrible disappointment. In 1962 Hiestand finally was redistricted into the far Western part of the old 21st District which was much more Democratic. But that was too late for us.

Politics always combines elation and chagrin, but it was still wonderful to be able to manage a campaign and continue with my law practice at Tuttle & Taylor. I found I wanted the complex, rich life of victories and defeats, law and politics, public service and pursuit of my profession. I was beginning to have a lot of balls in the air.

Rudd Brown with volunteer Barbara Norris, 1960

J. Keith Mann

12

AT LEAST I DIDN'T MISS MY FLIGHT

By 1961, my practice at Tuttle & Taylor was expanding and I had a number of different clients who were taking up quite a bit of my time. Gradually we grew: first one new lawyer, then a few more, appeared in our firm. I kept in touch with Stanford and made sure to track some of the promising graduates, trying to get them to consider working at our small, but increasingly prestigious firm. Often I succeeded.

We had become a traditional American family. I would head out to work every morning, and Kitty would take care of our brood. Our children, who were smack dab in the middle of the baby boom generation, were thriving in Pasadena, and Don was now thoroughly outnumbered by girls with the arrival of Alison in 1959. Kitty was a fantastic mother, and we had a very busy life, with friends and family and lots of professional and political activity. On those evenings when I came home at a decent hour, Kitty made sure that we had a drink together in some peace and quiet before our family dinner. In retrospect, the first few months of our dazzling new President's term marked a period of calm, and a kind of innocence, that was forever lost for all of us with his murder.

That does not mean that things were uncomplicated in 1961. President Kennedy had only been in the White House for less than two months when he faced a domestic crisis. The flight engineers of six major airlines—Pan American, Eastern, American, National, Flying Tigers and United—went on strike. Their strike had nothing to do with their wages; a jurisdictional issue caused this one. Put simply, the flight engineers did not want to have their union become part of the airline pilot union.

In the late fifties, each of the airlines individually negotiated a collective bargaining agreement with the Flight Engineers' International Association. The 1957 agreement lasted for three years and was to be reopened in June of 1960. Each side wanted changes in wages, hours, rules and working conditions, a standard labor relations negotiation. But the circumstances for the airlines had changed a great deal during the fifties with the introduction of jets as commercial aircraft.

The jets were designed with three seats in the cockpit, and that third seat was where the conflict was located: trained pilots—who were represented by the Airline Pilots' Association—wanted a pilot in the seat, while the flight engineers believed that this was the seat that their members should occupy. The flight engineers struck individual airlines over this issue in the fifties: United in 1955, Eastern in 1958 and Continental in 1959. When Eastern was grounded, the airline accommodated both unions: a four-person crew was the selected option; though costly, both the flight engineer and a third pilot would be seated in the cockpit. But the four-person crew did not become a standard for the rest of the industry.

The three sides failed to reach an agreement, so the National Mediation Board stepped in on May 31, 1960. During the waning months of the Eisenhower Administration the mediation process dragged on, and President Kennedy inherited the situation when he took office. Secretary of Labor Arthur Goldberg intervened.

The strike was precipitated by a decision of the National Mediation board on February 6, 1961. This was a case that involved United Airlines' negotiations with the pilots and the flight engineers. United did not want to negotiate with each group individually, but instead argued that pilots and engineers should be considered to be a single class of employee. After all, they all were in the cockpit. The National Mediation Board agreed with the airlines and decided that the collective bargaining of both groups should be consolidated. On February 6, the National Mediation Board ordered the flight engineers to dissolve their old union and join the Airline Pilots Association as a single bargaining unit. There were many more pilots than flight engineers so the engineers believed that this arrangement would eclipse their own power in the negotiations; they went on strike against the airlines.

There were 3500 members of the flight engineer association; though not all of them walked off the job, the effects of their strike were devastating.

Eleanor Roosevelt spoke for most Americans when she wrote on February 22, 1961, "It is even more difficult for the average person to understand much about the grievances that exist, as among the pilots, the flight engineers, the airlines, the stewards and the stewardesses, and the International Association of Machinists. It is hoped that Secretary of Labor Arthur Goldberg will be able to effect a truce so that in future, the public will not be as badly inconvenienced as has been the case early in the week."

The flight engineers, who were blamed for the massive inconvenience, were losing the public relations war. Each of the airlines embarked on their own plans to lay off employees as a result of the strike. The airlines said they wanted to maintain some skeleton service, but on February 19, 1961 more than 70,000 workers were laid off by six major airlines.

President Kennedy described Arthur Goldberg, when he appointed him as Secretary of Labor, as a man who was "from the unions but not of them." He was an old pro in negotiating labor disputes and had served in various high positions in the labor movement for decades. In the early 1950's he midwifed the merger of the American Federation of Labor and the Congress of Industrial Organizations to create the AFL-CIO. When Kennedy was still a senator and was involved in the McClellan Committee investigation of corrupt union practices, Goldberg was his right hand man. So it was not a surprise when Kennedy chose him to be his Secretary of Labor.

The strike lasted for six days and we read about stranded passengers, tough labor negotiations, and how much it was costing the country in productivity. I was fascinated, but never dreamed that eventually, I would participate directly in these events.

Goldberg finally intervened with the solution that the President would appoint a special commission to study the problem. Nathan P. Feinsinger headed the commission. I knew Feinsinger from a class I attended one summer when he taught at Stanford. He was a highly respected, Brooklyn-born labor lawyer whom Roosevelt appointed as associate general counsel of the War Labor Board in 1942. He then went on to be the Director of National Disputes in 1943 and continued his service in settling strikes for every president after Roosevelt. Truman appointed him to be on the fact finding board for a massive steelworker strike in 1945—that one involved 700,000 steelworkers—and even though they were unable to avoid the strike, his report did help lead to its settlement.

Feinsinger headed the commission that was charged with the Flight Engineers resolution, but there were two other experts in labor law who also were involved. I had taken classes from one, who was a professor of labor economics from Princeton, and the second was one of my closest friends and mentors from Stanford, Keith Mann. He has gone down in my personal history as one of the professors who gave me an A+—this one in labor law—when I was at Stanford! But far more important, he was a leading expert in labor law and labor arbitration, and was considered the leader in the field of post-World War II arbitrators. When he was only twenty-seven years old, in 1951, he gave a tutorial on labor arbitration to the U.S. Senate Committee on Labor and Public Welfare.

I was sitting in my office one day when Keith called me. "Bill, we need you back here," he said and explained what was going on. I had some passing familiarity with the strike—everyone did at the time—but I did not know any details and was certainly not a labor lawyer. But having studied with all three of the lawyers who were on the panel gave me some insight into the way that their minds worked.

"We have a deadline for writing and submitting a report to the president while we try to mediate and settle the strike," he said. "We don't have very much time to write. We want you to come back to Washington and write the full report for us." I had a lot of clients at that time and many commitments, but a summons from the President (and Keith Mann) was impossible to ignore. When I went to Bob Taylor and Ed Tuttle and presented the situation, they did not hesitate. Their attitude was simple: this was a matter of public service. There was no question that when called one must serve the country, and I was given the principal responsibility for writing the report.

Away I went, convinced that I would only be away for a very short period of time. I arrived in Washington in late April and went to work. I worked very hard. It took longer and longer and longer, the weeks turned into a month because the details were incredibly complex.

Spring was beautiful in Washington that year, as it always was, but I cannot say that I noticed the cherry blossoms or the gentle sunny days. My head was buried in work and the more time that passed, the more concerned I became for all that I had abandoned in Los Angeles. Kitty and the children, of course, but I felt especially guilty about my job at Tuttle & Taylor. Bob and Ed had supported me without any question, but my own sense of duty and obligation to my clients haunted me.

The deadline for the delivery of the report was May 25, and it was fast approaching. That same day, Kennedy had planned to make one of his most important speeches to a Joint Session of Congress—so he was a bit distracted by other matters at the time. In this speech he asked Congress for an additional $7 to $9 billion over the next five years to create one of his most enduring legacies: the space program. While I was slogging away on the report, he and his speechwriters were crafting the stunning, mind-blowing words: "This nation should commit itself to achieving the goal, before the decade is out, of landing a man on the moon and returning him safely to earth."

The words that I was laboring over were hardly that memorable, but I was feeling the pressure. It had been a long time since I pulled all-nighters, but in finalizing this report I had two! Suddenly a volunteer offered to help me; his name was Willard Wirtz and he happened to be the Deputy Secretary of Labor (and would eventually become the Secretary of Labor). He was an absolutely wonderful man.

A calm, warm, solid Midwesterner from DeKalb, Illinois, he was a 1937 graduate of Harvard Law. He immediately became a professor first at the University of Iowa College of Law and then at Northwestern University. But Roosevelt summoned him to Washington to serve on the War Labor Board, and then Truman asked him to chair the National Wage Stabilization Board. He went back to Northwestern and was a prominent campaigner for Adlai Stevenson. Eventually Kennedy appointed him to be Under-Secretary of Labor.

Wirtz appeared at my office and worked with me, encouraging me, helping me during the crucial final days of the drafting the report. He certainly stayed a lot later than most high government officials would. Before he left on the last night, we could see the light at the end of the tunnel. We knew that we had a fine report and that it was going to be ready to submit to the President the next day.

The report generally recommended a three-person cockpit with the third person trained as a pilot. And although the report tried to soften the transition for the flight engineers, it did conclude that the two unions should discuss cooperation and merger, because "neither peace nor safety on the airlines will be fully assured as long as there are two unions in the cockpit."*

I am not a man who has many regrets. In fact, my temperament and personality are forward looking, optimistic, generally free from the burdens of a past. I have had a great life, how on earth could I possibly have any regrets?

Well here is one.

Wirtz said that night, "Bill, the Secretary and three members of the commission and I will be meeting with the President at ten o'clock tomorrow morning, I want you to come along."

"Now look, I know we're finishing up," I replied. "But I have made a commitment to a client to be back by the end of the day tomorrow." I had been away for such a long time, even an hour delay struck me as impossible. What was I thinking?

"What time's your plane?" Wirtz asked, calm and unflappable.

I replied that I was flying out of Baltimore around noon. Wirtz said that if I would come and join them, his driver would be waiting at the

---

* Commission's report as summarized and quoted in David J. Walsh, *On Different Planes* (Ithaca, N.Y.: Cornell University Press 1994), p. 52.

White House gates to take me to the airport and get me on the plane on time. Here I was, still a kid from Turtle Creek, being told by the *Assistant Secretary of Labor* that his *driver* would be waiting at the *White House gates* to take me to the airport after I met with the *President of the United States*.

Clearly, two all-nighters had taken their toll. I said, "Okay, but I've got to leave by 10:30."

There I was the next morning, in the White House, meeting with them, waiting for the President to have time to meet with us. I remember that Lyndon Johnson, a huge and powerful presence in the room, was talking with a group of important looking men in dark suits in a corner. I was dazzled and torn, constantly worried about missing my flight and disappointing my clients and family. "Well, time's running out on us," I said to Willard Wirtz.

"Just relax," he reassured me. "We're just about to go in." We had this exchange a few times and my thoughts became more and more muddled. Finally, I could not stand it any longer.

"Okay, it's eleven o'clock, I have to go," I said.

He looked a bit incredulous and I saw Keith Mann staring at me. No one in the room could believe what I was doing. "I have to go, I'm sorry," I said as I gathered my things. Why I insisted on leaving, I am not quite sure. It would have been easy to just call Ed and Bob, and they would certainly have understood. All the time in Washington had disoriented me. I was there much longer than I expected to be, instead of just a week, it took nearly a month. Obviously my judgment was lacking. I said goodbye to Keith, to Willard, to others in the room and left Kennedy's White House. I got in the car; Willard's driver took me to the airport. I felt grateful that I did not miss my flight.

Only when I was back in Los Angeles and told the story did I realize that in fact, while I did not miss my flight, I did miss the chance of a lifetime.

13

GOVERNOR BROWN AND THE
STATE BOARD OF EDUCATION

When I first met Pat Brown, I was fresh out of law school and he was the Attorney General of the State of California—and someone who seemed destined for greatness. He certainly was one of the most influential men in my life. Of course, I had been following his very public and very successful career during the six years that passed since our meeting during the historic Colorado River case, when I was a junior member of California's legal team. In 1958, he ran for Governor of California and won by an extraordinary margin. Up to that point in the twentieth century, he was only the second Democrat to become California's Governor.

Pat Brown embodied all the liberal values that I cherished. He called it "responsible liberalism," which can be summed up as having a firm and visionary commitment to using government to improve the lives of as many citizens as possible, while still being smart about paying for it. Whether that improvement was in expanding the quality and reach of education, or the access to potable water, or in securing a social safety net, Brown would look at a problem and devise a practical government solution. The historian Kevin Starr put it so well when he described the time when Brown was governor as "an exhilarating period in which California assembled itself as the cutting edge of the American experiment."

Yes, it was so exhilarating to be in California during those years. We witnessed a seismic shift in what government was willing and able to take on as our population simply exploded. In 1950 California's population was 10.6 million and by 1960 it was 15.7 million, with most of the growth coming from people who were migrating from other states. Pat was audacious in his plans to make California continue to be a magnet: he increased resources for parks, transportation and schools, and with bi-

97

partisan support that is impossible to imagine today, he worked for fair-housing legislation and the creation of jobs. He and I shared a passionate opposition to the death penalty, and he was inspiring in his willingness to debate these issues publicly.

He was a force of nature in California. The *New York Times* had a wonderful description of him in his obituary as "burly and ebullient."* He just vibrated with energy and enthusiasm, and when a problem needed solving, he became even more enthusiastic. In that obituary, Prof. Bruce E. Cain, associate director of the Institute of Governmental Studies at the University of California at Berkeley, was quoted saying: "He was part of an era when growth was considered a good thing, when we could afford public services that would encourage people to come to California, to add to the tax base. Everything then had a golden aura to it." Golden indeed.

If Governor Brown stood for anything, if there was any single legacy from his tenure that one could point to as being the most significant, I think that his work in education would probably be the one. He knew that the best way to fulfill the great promise of the state, to get people off public assistance, create new jobs and create innovation, was to focus on education, and he started at the top, with the college and university system. He was responsible for the California Master Plan for Higher Education, which was signed into law on April 27, 1960. This law made college possible for millions in the state, first by making it affordable, and then by coordinating all the colleges and universities into a fully integrated system of higher education from community colleges to graduate programs in universities. The timing was brilliant. The baby boom generation was growing up, and college needed to be in their future.

He also appreciated that resources needed to be directed towards primary and secondary education and that is where I ended up being involved. I was sitting in my office at Tuttle & Taylor in 1962, working on a brief, and found out that the Governor wanted to appoint me to the State Board of Education, a governing board that was responsible for interpreting and applying the state statutes governing the public school system, from kindergarten through twelfth grade. I was also unusually young for the honor—I once heard that I was the youngest person ever appointed to the board of education.

Education was a field that was both personally and professionally important to me. Not only did I have four school age children who were educated in the public school system, but my entire life was a result of the

---

* http://www.nytimes.com/1996/02/18/us/edmund-g-brown-is-dead-at-90-he-led-california-in-boom-years.html

education that I was lucky enough to have been given. I was thrilled to be given the opportunity to contribute to the field of education and told the Governor that I would be honored to serve.

As anyone who has ever attended a PTA meeting can attest, education is an extremely emotional subject and one in which everyone has an opinion. I was not sure what to expect when I went to my very first meeting, but I think that I had assumed it would be a calm, businesslike discussion of pressing educational issues and I would simply absorb as much wisdom as possible. Tom Braden—the journalist with the massive family who wrote *Eight is Enough*—was the President of the Board of Education when I served, and Dorman Commons, who was head of Natomas Co., a San Francisco-based energy company, was another board member with me.

The first meeting focused on the very contentious issue of whether to approve the reorganization of a particular school district in southeast L.A. County. There was a group that wanted to split off a portion of one district and create a new and separate district. This required State Board of Education approval. I sat and listened to it and saw the discussion becoming more and more passionate and heated. People were clearly furious and at first I couldn't figure out why they were so angry with each other.

I looked around and saw one of the staff members from the State Department of Education and asked him to come over because I had a question. I asked him very quietly, "Does this have anything to do with race?" He answered by nodding his head in the affirmative. It was all I needed. I had learned how to cross-examine by that time, and one of the most effective techniques is to feign ignorance. Since I was the newest member of the board and this was my first meeting, everyone gathered there assumed that I did not know what was going on. I asked some questions, and soon the racism and paternalism of those who were pushing for the redistricting came out in the bright light of day. The clarity made it easy for the board to reject the proposal.

I was able to see the kind of power that was concentrated in the state board. The outcome of that meeting was that I was appointed as a committee of one to draft some regulations relating to the process of approval or rejection of a proposed reorganization of a school district. While many of the requirements were boiler plate, one that I drafted was that whoever proposed reorganizing a school district needed to provide an impact assessment on how the redistricting would affect the racial profile of the district. Do any aspects of the proposal, directly or indirectly, have to do with race? This became a part of any discussion of redistricting and continues to this day.

One of our major responsibilities was to approve the textbooks for the public school system from K through 12. It was a fascinating process for me, because I had never paid too much attention to all the textbooks that my children hauled in and out of our house. My benign indifference stopped as soon as I started looking; I became very curious about textbooks, both their content and the business behind them. The way the process worked was that the Board of Education had an advisory group of teachers and superintendents who would review the books and make recommendations to us as to which ones we should purchase. Then we would meet with the textbook publishers who would pitch their books.

When I looked at the history books, for example, I realized that those for the middle school and high school level were biased in favor of the South on the issue of slavery and the Civil War. Nearly one hundred years had passed since the Civil War was fought—a curiously short period of time actually—but clearly the North was victorious in that national cataclysm. Yet our students were studying textbooks that were incredibly sympathetic to the South. In fact, the story was told from the southern point of view.

But why? This question led me to the realization that southern states had a disproportionate influence on the textbook publishers. Textbook publishing, I learned, was *very* big business. So when it was time for the history textbook publishers to meet with the board, I began to give the publishers and the whole system a bad time using my well-honed skills in cross-examination. They were incapable of providing decent answers. I do not know whether they started publishing books for California, which was certainly a large and growing market, or publishing different books for the southern states, but for whatever reason, during my time on the board, we saw the content of the history books of my state change.

I worked closely with Tom Braden and Dorman Commons, and we adopted some new regulations that required the books used in the California system to reflect a balanced approach to United States history, particularly in its treatment of the Civil War. We could not control the textbook publishers directly, but we had the power of the purse and our system was one of the largest in the country, so these publishers knew that it was in their interest to comply.

History was not the only area in which the textbooks were found wanting. This was the era of what was called "the new math." Math and science were never my passion nor my best subjects. But I looked at these textbooks because it was my responsibility as a board member in getting ready for the meeting. And I realized that the content of these books was not making a lot of sense to me. I began to wonder if we could get a volunteer on our board who *really* knew his stuff. The most dazzling mathematician I knew of—well, he was actually a Nobel Prize winning physicist but he clearly knew math—was at Caltech and his name was Richard Feynman.

I called my friend Barclay Kamb, a Caltech geologist who will figure prominently in the next chapter, and asked him, "What do you think? Do you think if I asked Feynman to come up and attend a meeting, he would a look at these books and tell us what he thinks?" Barclay said, "I don't think he's ever done anything like that before. But you know, I was talking to Feynman recently, and he was ranting and raving about how awful the school textbooks were in his field of math, science and physics. He just might do it."

So I called Feynman and he described our first encounter in his wonderful memoir, *"Surely You're Joking Mr. Feynman!"* He said that he was giving a series of freshman physics lectures at the time and after one of them, his assistant complained about his daughter's math books. At that point, Feynman wrote, "I didn't pay much attention to what he said." But the next day, I called Feynman and asked if he would serve on the state Curriculum Commission in which we would have to choose some new textbooks.

Feynman wrote that "since usually the only people to look at the books were school teachers or administrators in education, they thought it would be a good idea to have someone who uses mathematics scientifically, who knows what the end product is and what we're trying to teach it for, to help in the evaluation of the schoolbooks." Amazingly, he agreed to work with us.

The word got out to the publishers and immediately they bombarded him with letters and telephone calls offering to explain to him, a Nobel Prize winning physicist, the contents of an elementary school math text book. They were all terrified—and they should have been! Feynman thought that they all seemed crazy. He was an objective scientist and found the lobbying effort absurd. Either the content of the books would stand on their own or they would not. He called me to explain what was going on, and I suggested that he go see one of the teachers who was also on the math commission and talk to her about the books. Her name was Mrs. Whitehouse.

Feynman went to visit with her, and she started talking about everything that was going to be discussed at the meeting about the math textbooks. "They are going to talk about the counting numbers," she told him. Feynman did not know what on earth she was referring to! He realized she was talking about integers, but every term she used was a completely different one from the time honored mathematical terms he had employed for his entire and very successful life. She explained our completely arbitrary assessment of the texts, which involved getting as many copies of each book as we could and then sharing them with teachers and administrators in various districts. They would then give us their reactions but there was no rubric, no uniform standard, just a random collection of impressions about whether a book was good or not.

Feynman would have none of that. First of all, he did not know any teachers, so he decided that he wanted to evaluate the books himself and told that to Mrs. Whitehouse. A few days later, he said that someone from the book depository called him to announce that three hundred pounds of math books were about to be sent to him. He was then told that someone would be sent over to help him read them. He did not need someone to read them for him. He needed to read them himself.

And he did. And the more he read, the more furious he became. He later wrote, "The books were lousy, they were false, they were hurried.... The definitions weren't accurate. They were faking it. They were teaching something they didn't understand which was in fact useless at that time, for the child." When he came to the first meeting of the Board, he impressed us all. Other members had given some perfunctory ratings to the books, but no one went through them the way he did. He told us in detail what was good and bad in each book and actually had a reason for his ratings. In one moment that was pretty embarrassing for some of the members, they had rated a book that was actually filled with blank pages!

He was funny and tough, and at one point he said, "Here they are, talking about where energy comes from. It comes from here, comes from coal, it comes from there." He said, "There's only one source that energy comes from—the sun! That's *that!*" The committee's recommendations were presented to the full Board of Education, but we did not have enough money to pay for the books that we wanted to recommend. Finally, we met with the publishers' representatives, and this was my turn to step in.

There were two books that we were unable to decide between, so we figured that we should solicit bids from the publishers to see who would give us the best deal. We asked if we could get the books a bit earlier to prepare for the coming term. One publisher's rep said, Absolutely! We are delighted you accepted our bid, and we can get them there in time. The second publisher said, we want to bid again because we based our bid on the old deadline.

"And how much would it cost for us to get your books at an earlier date," I asked the guy from the second publisher.

He gave the number and it was less!

Then the first publisher got up and said, "Wait! If he changes his bid, I will change mine!"

But I would not let them off and became very naïve. "But how is that?" I asked. "That we can get the books earlier and cheaper?"

They both fell over each other trying to explain how, if they used a special offset method of printing, they could do it more quickly and when they did it more quickly, it would cost less. To the tune of *two million dollars!*

I was furious. What happened was that the uncertainty of the date created the possibility for a competitive bidding process. Richard Feynman had a wonderful time in telling this story. But for me, the joy of working with him also taught me some important math lessons about competitive bidding that even I could understand.

I remained on the board for several years and was able to witness the passage of Lyndon Johnson's 1965 Elementary and Secondary Education Act, which was an absolutely momentous piece of legislation that did more than any other bill to build up secondary education for poor and minority students. After it passed, there was a *lot* of federal money available to address the problems in the impoverished districts, many of which were home to a large proportion of African American children. Each state was required to designate someone to have the administrative responsibility for the implementation of the Elementary and Secondary Education Act and thus to oversee the distribution of that money to the school districts.

California has a unique situation in which we have a Board of Education that is appointed by the Governor, but a Superintendent of Schools who is elected by popular vote. Our Superintendent was a pugnacious, difficult, racist, and extremely anti-progressive man named Max Rafferty. Somehow the board was not paying attention in 1963, and he got himself elected to statewide office, after serving as the Superintendent of the local district in the very wealthy L.A. suburb of La Canada. We did not realize what we were getting into. He was unbelievable.

We may have been the board, but the Superintendent of Schools is the CEO, if you will, to the Board of Education and also managed the whole Department of Education. Our disagreements with Rafferty were endless, but when it came time to use the federal money, he acted like an impoverished relative who could not wait to get his hands on the family inheritance.

We did not let him have it because this money was to implement programs that he clearly opposed. The way we prevented him from getting it was we made a deal with Governor Brown and some of the leadership in the legislature. A law was passed giving the Board of Education the power to determine who would administer the federal funds. We had worked with someone, an African American official at the state Department of

Education named Wilson Riles. His job was to deal with issues of race in the school system, and he was the perfect appointment to be in charge of implementing the Elementary and Secondary Education Act. The board appointed me—as a committee of one—to work with him in developing President Johnson's program under the regulations of the federal statute. We worked closely together and those programs became an example for how to do this in the other states.

And during this time, in the Board of Education, I started to get to know Governor Brown better and better. Our relationship deepened. He trusted me. And soon we would have a chance to work together even more closely.

Governor Edmund G. "Pat" Brown, Sr.

14

COOPERATIVES AND REACTORS

Cooperatives are a fundamental part of the history of agriculture in California. Farm cooperatives began back in the nineteenth century, predominately in the orange industry. As with all cooperative farming, the tradeoff was clear: a loss of some autonomy in great years, and perhaps fewer profits, outweighed by the benefit of collective bargaining with packers and those who worked the farms.

One of my most significant cases involved not oranges, but avocados, a cooperative Tuttle & Taylor also represented. The case eventually found its way to the Supreme Court; its full name was *Florida Lime & Avocado Growers Inc. v. Paul, Director of the Department of Agriculture for California*. The basic issue that had to be resolved was when a state statute is different from a federal statute, which should apply?

Nearly all the avocados that appear in the produce departments in the United States are either grown in California or in South Florida. California always had very protective laws concerning their avocado crop, specifically the amount of oil contained in the avocado when it went on sale. In 1925, California passed a statute that required that all avocados that were sold there had to have eight percent of their weight from oil. Ripe avocados release a certain amount of oil and California believed that consumers should purchase avocados that were ripe. But Florida avocado growers grew a different kind of less oily avocado, so their state had no such stipulation. They distributed their avocados according to a federal law that did not address the oil content or the ripeness of the fruit.

California refused to permit Florida avocados to be sold in the state, because they did not meet with the standards with which the California avocado growers had to comply. Hard, unripe Florida avocados could be sold for less than our fruit and they would have an unfair competitive advantage. Florida, of course, argued that this was not fair at all, and that these California laws violated the Equal Protection and Interstate Commerce Clauses. But their stronger argument was that the California standards were preempted by federal law. They argued in federal District Court that the regulation that was part of the Federal Agricultural Marketing Agreement Act of 1937 had a different standard for what constituted a mature avocado, and that was the only standard with which Florida avocados need comply.

The case began in 1954, when I was still in law school.

It dragged on for years, and in 1962 it became clear that it would go to the Supreme Court, which is when I started devoting a lot of time to those avocados. I was one of the lawyers behind the scenes in crafting the arguments for the California Deputy Attorney General, who would argue the case before the Supreme Court. We were determined to prove that not only was there no conflict between California law and the federal law, but most important, that California law was not preempted by federal law. I was in the Supreme Court and felt the thrill once more when the case was argued on January 8, 1963. On May 13, 1963 the court found in favor of California. I had a lot of input into the brief, as you could imagine, and I went with California's Deputy Attorney General back to Washington when he argued the case. He did not get a single question that we had not already figured out in advance. We won.

To this day I am passionate about Haas avocados. Jane realized very early in our marriage that when it came to picking out the fruits and vegetables for our home, this would be my responsibility!

Good litigators are known to have a certain agility, the capacity to become experts in one field and then another. This variety makes litigation endlessly absorbing, as illustrated by the huge change in subject in my next case, which involved the construction of a nuclear power plant in Malibu. It was 1964, and as ludicrous as it sounds now, a 1000 megawatt nuclear reactor in Malibu was a very serious possibility. The Department of Water and Power of the City of Los Angeles had decided to build a nuclear power plant in Malibu County, just past what is now Pepperdine University. The site was just on the northern side of the highway, right up against the hills. While anyone with his or her head on straight would say you would *not* build a nuclear power plant at that location, common sense was generally not the driving force in these matters. The City of Los Angeles was planning to petition the Atomic Energy Commission for clearance to build the power plant and it appeared that they were unbeatable.

There was a problem with this plan—well, there were many problems with this plan—but the most immediate concern was the Adamson family.

The Adamsons were a hugely influential family in Malibu. Today, one can tour their historic mansion—what the brochure accurately describes as the "enchanted site"—which is located where Malibu Creek meets the Pacific Ocean. The Chumash people called this area home until the eighteenth century. The Rindge family owned 17,000 acres and twenty miles of this coastline. The Rindge family's daughter, Rhoda, and her husband, Merritt Huntley Adamson, used the site to construct a beach house, which became the historic Adamson House museum. Some of the land was donated to create Pepperdine University.

The second generation, headed by Merritt Huntley Adamson Jr., had gotten to know me and asked me to represent them in opposing the application to the Atomic Energy Commission. Tuttle & Taylor was still a very small operation at the time. I had no assistants, no paralegals to dig into the research. But I realized that what I needed was a good geologist. Only an argument predicated on science and safety could possibly carry the day, so I needed to bolster the science.

In *The Atom and the Fault*, a book about these issues, Richard Meehan wrote, "The landowners, no ragged band of bucolic peasants awaiting discovery and salvation by urban activities, hired one of the West's most brilliant litigators, attorney Bill Norris. Norris wasted no time in seeking out the soft, unprotected geological parts of the Los Angeles Department of Water and Power's position." (I can certainly attest to the first and the last parts of that sentence!)

The problem was that those who would be able to knowledgeably discuss this case had already been co-opted by the Department of Water and Power, who had them all lined up from Stanford to UCLA. The Atomic Energy Commission had gotten support from the U.S. Geological Survey, which assured the Commission that, "The probability of permanent ground displacement by faulting in the Corral Canyon in the next fifty years is negligible." To read these words fifty years later, just makes you want to scream, "And then what?"

Frustrated with my search for an expert, I turned to a number of the Caltech scientists I had gotten to know through Rudd Brown's husband who was a professor there. As usual, I seem to be blessed with the immense good fortune of having someone tremendously important appear in my life at exactly the right time. Over and over again this has been the case, and it happened once more with the providential arrival of Barclay Kamb as my star witness.

He was a brilliant young geologist who was admitted to Caltech when he was only sixteen and was educated there from his freshman year through his Ph.D. He had studied under the great, Nobel Prize winning biochemist and peace activist Linus Pauling and also married Linda Pauling, his daughter. Barclay Kamb now taught at Caltech and was one of the youngest full professors they ever appointed.

I went to talk to him and saw that he was not one of those university scientists who augmented a professor's salary by a robust side business as an expert for law firms. In fact, he had never done anything like this before in his life, because he was so deeply involved in his research and teaching. But he was also from California, and his father even lived in the area that was under dispute. So we met and talked and somehow we just clicked. He was a little bit younger than I and one of the few genuine geniuses I have ever met. Linus Pauling said he was, bar none, his best student ever—and that was well before he became his father-in-law. I finally persuaded Barclay to be at least tempted by the possibility. He said that he would go down, have a look at the property and see if he could find anything that interested him.

And he did. And away we went.

We had to face nearly six weeks of hearings before a three-man panel appointed by the Atomic Energy Commission. The chairman was an administrative law judge and ran the hearings, one member was a chemist from DuPont, and the other the dean of the Engineering School from the University of Virginia. It was a fantastic David and Goliath scenario. Our team consisted of Barkley and me, ably assisted by one of the Adamson sisters who served as our administrative assistant and general back office helper. We faced a legion of lawyers, geologists and U.S. Geological Survey staff.

What did I know about geology? It did not matter at all. I had Barclay Kamb, and we had a marvelous time. I was making him into a lawyer, and he was making me into a geologist, and somehow it worked.

One of the key issues was whether or not the site was within one quarter mile of an active fault. Our first glimpse that our team might be making an impression was when the Commission ordered the Department of Water and Power to dig a huge trench at that location. It was a major undertaking—about thirty feet long, eight feet deep and ten feet wide—which was to give the geologists an opportunity to go beneath the surface and see what the geology told them about the viability of the project. It was quite a sight to see all of these geologists crawling around in the trench, but none of them saw what Barclay saw. I would just tag along with him, and he would explain things to me.

Some of the other Malibu landowners who opposed the project were delighted by this excavation, and Frank Morgan, who had been the president of Richfield Oil, arranged a picnic on the site for members of the American Association of Petroleum Geologists. Over a hundred geologists gathered there, ostensibly for a party to drink some beers and feast on a few steaks. But Morgan had another idea, which was to get them to sign a petition opposing the power plant and saying that the location was not safe. And they did. Even though this was useful for the case, there is no reason to think that this was a strategy based on environmental and public interest concerns. These were *petroleum* engineers after all, and according to Meehan's book, "Suspicions still linger that the whole affair was a plot on the part of the oil industries to destroy nuclear power."

Barclay prepared me thoroughly for the cross-examination of the Department of Water and Power witnesses. I have worked with innumerable experts and I love to cross-examine them. It is one of my favorite indoor sports. And I have found that I am pretty good at it, knowing how to take the lead from my experts while also making some connections that perhaps they had not considered. But Barclay was the only witness I have ever had to whom I said with total and complete confidence, "Barclay, say whatever you want to say. I am not going to tell you how to answer these questions."

As a lawyer you always prepare your witnesses rigorously. You try not to put words in their mouth, but you encourage them not to talk too much. They just have to answer the question and I would always say to them, "If you fail to say something that you think you should say, then we'll have a break and you can tell me and I'll decide whether or not you need to make the point." Not Barclay. He was a virtuoso. When he testified, he was riveting, as he explained the geology in the rocks and the implications of this proposal. At one point he got a piece of paper—he was a gifted artist— and started drawing the rocks! And then he summed up his point. "The disturbed zone at Malibu passes directly beneath the proposed reactor installation," he said. "In relation to the possible range of exposure to fault hazards in southern California, the Malibu site ranks as among the more hazardous possible."

Need we say more?

When the hearings were over, after both sides wrote and submitted our long briefs, we got the decision.

We won. This was the *only* time that the Atomic Energy Commission turned down an application to build a nuclear power plant on the basis of safety. We made a little history on that. I have always been very careful about inserting my own opinions when addressing matters of the law, but I honestly could not *believe* that they were even *thinking* about it. From a safety point the notion was preposterous. And I could not imagine a nuclear power plant in that little stretch of precious land that people ought to be able to enjoy.

And thanks to Barclay, they always will.

And thanks to the Atomic Energy Commission, I made a friend for life.

Years later when I began skiing and taking my family on ski trips to Mammoth, Barclay joined us. Together we would drive up to the mountains, while Barclay would talk about the geology of the mountains, explaining their formations to my children who stared out the back seat window, transfixed by his way of bringing this part of nature to life. He was such a natural teacher, such a modest person and such a wonderful friend, my children never realized until they were grown up, that they were learning science from one of the greatest scientists on the planet.

Barclay Kamb and Bill Norris, 1995

15

CAMPAIGNS AND CONVENTIONS

They were quite a pair of opponents, Pat Brown and Richard Nixon. Could they possibly have presented a starker choice in 1962? Pat Brown, ebullient and charming, flush with the successes of four years as governor, with bipartisan victories behind him and a vision for California's future that was so consistent with the aspirations of our young and vigorous population. And Richard Nixon, whose name today has become so much a shorthand for paranoid and resentful politics that it is difficult to remember what it was like back then, before his presidency and before Watergate, when he was a frontrunner and a natural leader in the Republican party of California.

California, though changing, was still very Republican. John Kennedy defeated Nixon two years before, but by a tight margin, and in that election Nixon had won the Republican stronghold of California. He had also been our senator and, of course, had risen to the office of Vice President. But there were tensions within the Republican Party because not all Republicans were like Ed Tuttle and Bob Taylor. The John Birch Society continued to hold a tremendous amount of power. Even though he was never a member of the John Birch Society, the California State Assemblyman and Minority Leader in the State Assembly Joe Shell had their support when he ran in the Republican primary, and he was on record as having said some very positive things about the Birchers in the past.

I was beginning to get more deeply involved in state politics. My role in the State Board of Education brought me closer to the Governor's office, and I began to spend some time with Pat Brown. I liked our Governor more and more, and he became a father figure, mentor and trusted older friend to me. At the same time, my top priority and my major focus was working at Tuttle & Taylor and building up my law practice. Even though the number of billable hours at the time was a mere fraction of those today, it was still a very demanding job. In 1962 Pat Brown asked me to be one of the three southern California co-chairmen of his campaign, which was mostly a symbolic position. Pat knew that I was not going to be able to devote a great deal of either time or money to his campaign. But he liked me, trusted me, and (not to be cynical) I fit a demographic—young, professional, father of a bunch of kids—that was useful for him as the champion of California's future.

We knew that Pat would be the Democratic nominee, so before the Republican nomination was settled, we sat back and watched Nixon and Shell engage in one of the dirtiest campaigns California had ever witnessed. I confess we enjoyed the scene of Republicans tearing each other apart!

Finally, Nixon did win the Republican nomination, but he was already a bit bruised. Then it was our turn. Nixon did have a lead early on but we kept chipping away at it. Much as Hollywood is seen as a liberal bastion today, there was a strong and powerful conservative group then—as we later saw with Ronald Reagan's rise to power—so they were a particular challenge. Brown kept hammering on Nixon to declare his allegiance to being the Governor of California and not just use the office as a stepping-stone to challenge Kennedy again in 1964. "Make a commitment to California," Brown said, and Nixon assured the voters that of course he would serve his full term, but he was sounding more and more defensive all the time.

On November 6, election night, we were tense. We thought that we had done a good job, but Nixon was still favored to win. Slowly the votes rolled in and one county after another went for Pat Brown. Nixon did not concede on election night, and his press secretary held a news conference at two in the morning saying that even though Nixon was 90,000 votes behind Brown, the votes that had not yet been counted were in strong Republican districts.

Not strong enough. We had a long night in Brown headquarters. There were times that I was tempted to head home, but it was all just too exciting and important to leave. When the ballots were counted, Nixon only won 46.87 percent of the vote. Finally, at ten o'clock Wednesday morning Nixon sent Brown a telegram, "Congratulations on your re-election as Governor. I wish you the best in your great honor and opportunity which you now have to lead the first state in the nation." That was pretty standard stuff—but then came his famous concession speech in the Beverly Hilton Hotel, where he memorably said to the press, "You don't have Nixon to kick around anymore because gentlemen, this is my last press conference."

It was a fascinating experience to watch the great Brown Democratic operation handle that campaign using the speeches, the media, and the strategic moments to make certain points. In a way, it reminded me of the elements that come together when litigating a case: how at the core of a campaign strategy lies strategic deployment of evidence. During the course of it I became even more a part of Pat's team, and I would bring my kids, every once in a while, to a campaign event so that they could appreciate that history was not just something in their textbooks, but was made by real people. They got to learn about the issues and met many politicos and VIP's.

A year after the election came the catastrophe of Kennedy's assassination. My daughter Kim was only seven, but she vividly remembers being told about his assassination during lunch break at her elementary school. She felt a special bond to JFK not only because of our family politics, but when I was in D.C. working on the flight engineers' case, I missed her birthday—which was coincidentally on the same day as Pat Brown's—and sent her a postcard with a picture of Kennedy. The message was, "Hi Kim, Who's handsomer? Kennedy or your daddy? Save those hugs and kisses for me. Daddy." She still has that postcard!

My parents were visiting us at the time; we were planning to spend Thanksgiving together. My mother always had a little bit of a psychic gift. She could feel when things were going to happen, and the morning of the assassination she woke up and told Kitty that she felt something terrible was going to happen that day. They were watching television together in the pool room when the news broke. I was at work, sitting at my desk, and heard the terrible news. We were all in our separate worlds—the kids at school, Kitty at home with my parents, me at the office—and then over the next few days, we were all together. We watched when Oswald was murdered, and I remember trying to quiet the family down so we could hear what was going on. It was a sad Thanksgiving.

In 1964 Governor Brown asked me to be one of the delegates to the Democratic Party Convention that was held in Atlantic City. The drama surrounding this convention was profound. Only nine months before, Kennedy had been assassinated, and the sense of shock and grief still lingered. The violence of his death was followed by still more violence in the South, especially in Mississippi. In the spring of 1963 the South erupted, as several years of sit-ins, Freedom rides and voter registration projects led to wide spread mass protests throughout the region involving the local African American population and hundreds of volunteers from the North.

The terrorism, the church burnings, the heroism and subsequent murders of civil rights workers—including Medgar Evers, and James Chaney, Mickey Schwerner and Andrew Goodman—unfolded in living room television sets all over the country. On July 2, 1964, President Johnson signed the Civil Rights Act, a momentous piece of legislation that outlawed all discrimination on the basis of race, religion, sex, color and national origin. The Act only inflamed racist passions further in the South, and the violence continued to escalate.

The Civil Rights movement embodied all the values that were most important to me. I could never reconcile the true greatness of our country and our Constitution with the utter injustice with which we treated so many of our citizens. I saw it as a kid in Turtle Creek, as a young man in our segregated nation's capital, as a lawyer in Los Angeles and as a representative on the California State Board of Education. I had become friends with some African Americans in California Democratic politics, like Mervyn Dymally, who had been elected to the U.S. House of Representatives in 1960. We were close in age and our paths crossed on many occasions. Things were changing, slowly and for the better, but the process of change was violent and only underscored an essential, fatal flaw in our society.

The establishment in April of the Mississippi Freedom Democratic Party (MFDP) presented a fascinating opportunity and problem. The party was formed by civil rights activists—including Fannie Lou Hamer, Ella Baker and Bob Moses—in order to increase the participation of African Americans in the political life of the state. The organizers wanted to extend the ongoing work on voter registration to full involvement in the Democratic Party, which was the dominant party in state politics. As they envisaged, the defeat of four MFDP candidates in the Democratic primary for Senator and three House seats made clear that the reason for their loss was not because eligible voters rejected them, but rather because the majority of eligible African American voters were not even permitted to register to vote.

At that point, the MFDP took the next step towards changing the Democratic Party from within and focused on the all-white Mississippi delegation to the Democratic National Convention that was going to be held in Atlantic City in August. Since they knew there was no chance that they could be elected to be a part of the official Mississippi delegation, they held their own convention in early August and elected sixty-eight representatives to go to Atlantic City and attempt to be seated as the true delegates from the State of Mississippi.

I was also going to Atlantic City as part of the California delegation. This was my first convention, so I was thrilled to be going. No one had thought that it would be a very exciting event. Lyndon Johnson clearly was going to be the nominee, but there was still a great deal of party business to take care of, and the vice presidential slot was going to be interesting, though it looked as if Hubert Humphrey was the obvious choice.

There were 5,260 delegates to the convention that year but the group— or perhaps more accurately the two groups—that attracted the most attention were from Mississippi. There was the all-white official delegation, and then there were the MFDP members who wanted to replace them. Initially it looked as if there was general sympathy for the MFDP cause, but eventually it became clear that if they were seated other southern delegations would revolt and that was the last thing that the party leadership wanted. President Johnson and Hubert Humphrey were determined to avoid any controversy at this convention. Johnson was always worried that Bobby Kennedy would somehow move in and supplant him as the party leader, and racial strife at the convention would give Kennedy the perfect opportunity to become the grand peacemaker and seize the day.

It all boiled down to a question of credentials, which were going to be voted on by the delegates to the convention. So Johnson and Humphrey twisted a lot of arms, hammering out what they believed was a reasonable compromise of the credentialing issue raised by the MDFP. Pat Brown was the Chairman of the California delegation and he joined forces with the President and Senator Humphrey in working out a compromise and selling it to the delegates. Put simply, the compromise entailed giving the MDFP two non-voting at-large seats in the convention. It was ludicrous. Fannie Lou Hamer, one of the great Civil Rights leaders and a member of the MDFP said, "We didn't come all this way for no two seats." But it was not her choice. The decision would be made by the full convention in a roll-call vote, which we did in state-by-state caucuses. California had the largest number of delegates and I was one of them.

Here we had our governor, who not only supported the compromise but also actually had been involved in crafting it. The more that I learned about the compromise, the more impossible it became for me to support it. I spoke with Mervyn Dymally and other friends, and on the merits the compromise was simply unfair. For the first time, I was faced with the painful and difficult choice between my loyalty to Pat Brown and my conviction, which favored the delegates from the Mississippi Freedom Party who objected to the compromise and felt that their voting rights had been trampled on.

There was a roll call vote, and I was still debating to myself which way I was going to vote. Was I going to vote my conviction? Or would my vote reflect my loyalty to Pat Brown, whom I admired and loved? Finally, they got to the M's and I heard the name of Stanley Mosk, the Attorney General of the State of California.

"No!" he said.

"Well, if Stanley is going to vote "no," I thought, "*I'm* going to vote "no"! His vote tipped the scales for me; it bolstered the courage of my convictions. The woman who was recording the vote knew who I was, she knew my relationship to Pat Brown, and she knew that I was there because of him. When I said "No," she cleared her throat and said, "Now I will restate what the issue is." She couldn't believe it! She re-read it and said, "Now, Mr. Norris, do you want to vote?"

Out came another "no."

It was hard, but I did it, and I think I did the right thing. In the end, the motion was defeated; the members of the MFDP walked away having made a powerful point. The Mississippi delegation remained intact—at least for the time being. And the convention carried on. The next day, I saw Pat Brown at a luncheon and he came up to me and asked, "Bill, did you think that was fair? Did you think what we had worked out with the President was okay?" He was not giving me a bad time. He just wanted to give me a chance to talk and hear what I had to say.

There is an odd postscript to the story. Perhaps not connected but it certainly occurred shortly after the convention, so in some ways it was all a part of that tumultuous year of 1964 and a part of my relationship with Pat Brown. Later in 1964, Pat Brown appointed Attorney General Stanley Mosk—who preceded me in opposing the Mississippi Compromise at the convention—from Attorney General to Justice on the California Supreme Court, where he went on to have a long and really outstanding career. His seat as Attorney General was now open.

Warren Christopher called and said that he wanted me to meet with him and Fred Dutton, the great Democratic power broker in California. Chris was back at O'Melveny by this time and Fred was still the chief of staff to Pat Brown in Sacramento. I was to meet the two of them at Chris' home on Lorraine Avenue close to Hancock Park. I went, and they told me that Pat was thinking about possible appointees to finish out Stanley Mosk's term as Attorney General and they wanted to talk to me about my possible interest. I think they also wanted to check me out as to what kind of candidate I would make.

I had never run for any office at that point, and while I was becoming a bit more visible, I was unknown and I was young. Pat really had taken a liking to me and he had put me on his short list. It became clear during our discussion that they did not know whether, during the very short period when I would actually serve to finish off Mosk's term, I would be able to become sufficiently well known to run for election and win.

But even in 1964, Pat was getting worried about the competition and the opposition that he would face in the 1966 election. There were so many factors at play in his decision of who would be his next Attorney General. So he played it safe and appointed his old friend from San Francisco, and the incumbent district attorney, Tom Lynch. It was a good choice. Tom was a fine Attorney General and got elected easily in 1966, an election, we all know, that Pat Brown lost.

If I needed any more proof that my vote against him during the 1964 convention never changed our relationship, this was as good a piece of evidence as any. I think that Pat would have liked to have appointed me, partly because of my youth, but also because he could see in me some of his own ambition and interests. He too had been Attorney General when he was a relatively young man. He may have wondered what I might have done with that opportunity.

And sometimes, so do I.

Bill Norris, Tuttle & Taylor attorney, around the time of *Miranda*

16

ARGUING *MIRANDA*

One Friday night, in November 1965, after a long week at work, I came home in time for Kitty and me to have a drink together before dinner. We had a busy weekend planned with our four kids, so there was never much time for fatigue in our family, but somehow I do remember that even after a good night's sleep, I was still tired when I woke up on Saturday morning. Kids were running around; we were getting breakfast ready; maybe there were some cartoons on the television when the sound of the telephone cut through the chaos.

It was the Clerk of the Supreme Court of the United States. He was not a law clerk, but a lawyer who was the overall administrator of the activities of the Court. I immediately felt my fatigue vanish—adrenaline can do that. He told me that Chief Justice Earl Warren "wants you to represent a defendant from California in this case." Roy Allen Stewart's case had won review by the Supreme Court, but he had no lawyer to represent him. So the Court was going to appoint one for him, and that lawyer was going to be me.

How do you say no to the Chief Justice?

And that is how I became the lawyer arguing a companion case to one of the most important right to counsel cases in American jurisprudence: the 1966 *Miranda* case.

An article in the National Law Journal (April 4, 2000) put it so well: "The procedure the police now routinely used to inform criminal suspects of the right to remain silent and to have a lawyer present during interrogation could have been the *Vignera* warnings, the *Westover* warnings, or even the *Stewart* warnings. But because of a simple matter of timing it is the *Miranda* warnings that are embedded in the nation's crime-show-watching consciousness...."

119

As the article pointed out, despite the association with the name, there was not just one *Miranda* case; there were five different cases associated with that ruling. Five cases were pending before the U.S. Supreme Court, with fifty-eight lawyers from fourteen states contributing appellate briefs, and they all involved the same issue: what were the rights of criminal defendants once they were in custody? The Supreme Court had already taken a look at interrogations while suspects were in custody in *Escobedo v. Illinois*. That case ruled that a suspect was entitled to a lawyer if he asked for one—the critical factor here being the actual request for representation. But these cases carried the issue further.

I knew from my time clerking for Justice Douglas that when a group of cases involving generally the same issue appeared on the docket, the typical procedure was to take one case and hold the others. But the court was clearly aware of what a momentous decision this would be, so in a highly unusual procedure they grouped the five cases together to be argued consecutively. Of the five cases, four were from the states, one was a federal case that came out of the District of Columbia, and they each addressed different aspects of what happened during an interrogation in custody. Each of the defendants had been isolated while being questioned—we can also say interrogated—by a police officer or a detective or a prosecuting attorney. In all the cases this interrogation resulted in the admission of guilt—signed statements that were presented in trial, or a tape recording of the confession—and in all the cases the defendant had no attorney present and had not been informed of his rights.

Ernesto Miranda was the appellant in the first case on the docket. On March 18, 1963, he was arrested in his home in Phoenix and taken to the police station, where some witnesses identified him as the man who had raped a local woman. He initially said he was innocent, but then the police interrogated him for two hours, and Miranda broke down and signed a confession, which was later presented in court as evidence of his guilt. Written on top of his confession was a statement that said that this confession was made with full knowledge of his legal rights and given freely. Both statements were not true. He was sentenced to 20 to 30 years in prison for each count of rape and kidnapping, and when he appealed the case, the Arizona Supreme Court said that his constitutional rights had not been violated when his confession was obtained and upheld his conviction. As we all know, the case then went to the U.S. Supreme Court.

The other cases were variations on this theme, one from New York, another from Kansas City. In the case that was assigned to me, *California v. Stewart*, the Los Angeles police arrested Roy Allen Stewart while they were investigating a series of robberies—purse snatchings involving blows to the head—that took place between December 21, 1962 and January 30,

1963. In one of them, the assault became a homicide; the purse snatching was so violent that the victim died. Checks from the deceased were cashed. Stewart was arrested at his home on January 31, after police determined that he was responsible for endorsing and cashing checks that had been stolen during the purse snatchings. And they did not stop at Stewart: everyone in the house was arrested, including his wife and three people who were visiting the couple.

Over the next five days, police interrogated Stewart nine times. He held out for four days saying he was innocent, but finally on the fifth they broke him. He admitted that he robbed the woman who died, but did not mean to kill her. This was all recorded, and that recording was then used during his trial as evidence. After Stewart confessed, the police released the four other people arrested with him, because there was no evidence to connect any of them with the crime.

Stewart was convicted of robbery and first-degree murder and sentenced to death, but eventually the California Supreme Court reversed the decision. They said that Stewart should have been advised that he had a right to remain silent and a right to counsel. The state of California then petitioned for certiorari to the United States Supreme Court.

At the time I was appointed, I did not know where his state court lawyer was, but that was not a major concern. I immediately called Bob and Ed—who were completely supportive of my taking on this pro-bono assignment—and when I went into the office Monday morning I mobilized the troops and got them working. We needed to check every possible relevant citation that might exist and go through the previous record of the case with a fine tooth comb.

Tuttle & Taylor had grown a bit by then, though we were still quite small compared to the giant firms like O'Melveny with their hundred lawyers. I had been pretty aggressively recruiting young lawyers, and there were now about thirteen of us at the firm. I had three young associates working—Joe Mandel, Eli Chernow and Nancy Howard, all of whom went on to great and prestigious careers. They were young then, just starting out, and while nearly every attorney wanted to be a part of that case, I chose them and chose wisely.

Tuttle & Taylor had moved from our old offices on 5th and Hill Streets to a more prestigious location on 6th and Grand in an old building that still stands. Ed and Bob provided all the support that they possibly could for this case, and my secretary, Gloria Lujan, began typing one brief after another. I did not have much time. The arguments were scheduled to be argued in three months, from February 28 to March 2, but my brief, my written argument to the Court, had to be submitted considerably earlier, and I was starting from scratch.

So many profound issues were involved in these cases: the rights of the police to perform their important work as they always had and questions about the balance between their professional obligations and the rights of those accused of crimes. What about the length of detention? Should that be a factor in weighing the rights of the accused? Then there were the basic rights to counsel and the privilege against self-incrimination. And what about the timing of the confession, did that make a difference?

The legal giant Solicitor General Thurgood Marshall, who had famously argued the *Brown v. Board of Education* case and in fact argued more cases in the Supreme Court than any of their justices—he argued thirty-two—was going to argue the federal case that was known as *Westover*. This involved the FBI and zeroed in on two key issues: does the system, as it now exists, discriminate against those without much money? After all, obtaining a counsel for those with means was usually a matter of course. Not so for people who were poor or underprivileged. Then there was the other basic conundrum: how practical was this whole idea of warning the accused of his rights?

As our deadline for submitting briefs drew closer we worked nearly round the clock. I can still see my young associates in the library, going through the cases while Gloria typed up each iteration of our brief from scratch: it had to be perfect. (Of all the people who celebrated the arrival of word processors, I have to believe that legal secretaries were among those who celebrated the most!). We submitted our brief that would then be copied and distributed to the nine Justices before our oral arguments.

I flew out to Washington at the end of February for the oral arguments. I remembered my time as a clerk for Justice Douglas and knew that he would be one of the Justices listening to my arguments, while his current clerk was certainly doing the same hard work that I had ten years before. There was a special thrill to walk into that grand building again, so familiar after all the time I spent there, but my role as a lawyer arguing a case in the Court was a new one for me, and I felt the great responsibility to my client, to the Court and yes, to the Constitution.

The five cases were on the calendar of the Court, one to be argued after another, starting with the lowest number, which was *Miranda*. The arguments began on Monday, February 28. I knew that we would not appear on the first day, so I could sit in the courtroom, absorbing all the arguments. In one of the cases, the famous attorney F. Lee Bailey argued on behalf of the convicted murderer Sam Sheppard. He was pretty good, but there were some flaws in his logic and we broke for lunch in the middle of Bailey's presentation. The judges went to their chambers, and the rest of the lawyers and I went to a private lunchroom. I walked right up to Bailey and gave him some suggestions about how he should handle his time remaining. He looked astonished, but that did not deter me. When I saw a way that argument could be improved, I didn't hold back.

On Tuesday, March 1, it was my moment to engage with the Justices for the first time since I was a clerk, in the case of *Stewart v. California.* Gordon Ringer was California's Assistant Attorney General, and it was his job to persuade the Justices that the Sixth Amendment right to counsel was sufficient protection for defendants. He did not touch on the central issue of the case, which involved not the Sixth Amendment but the Fifth Amendment's privilege against self-incrimination.

And then it was my turn to stand at the lectern. I looked at the assembled Justices and began slowly, perhaps, but increasing in my conviction and intensity as I went on. I pointed out that "in some circumstances where there is a spontaneous confession to the police.... California Supreme Court is just saying fine that those confessions or admissions are admissible as evidence."

Bang! Justice Fortas interrupts me. "Mr. Norris, that's exactly where I'm having a little difficulty in understanding your position and it may be that I am responsible for interrupting you so often," he said. "But as I get it from this point what you have said, you do not believe that the State's obliged to furnish counsel immediately upon the arrest." I agreed with that. Then Justice Fortas dug in, "If the person in custody volunteers and then that's admissible even if he doesn't have counsel?"

I knew just where he was going with this and I was prepared. "I would qualify my response along that line," I replied. "I think the police must engage in this process of interrogation," but went on to qualify how they would go about doing that. Fortas just kept coming back at me and we were completely engaged in the back and forth argument that for me is one of the best parts of being a litigator. I had to be fast on my feet and I was engaging with the best legal minds on the planet. Bang! Bang! Bang! I loved it. *That's* a real argument.

Later, when I became a judge, I appreciated the fact that the argument was not for the lawyers, it was for the judges. The lawyers had their shot in the brief, and that was where the cases invariably turned. When it came time for the argument, the lawyers have to do their best to understand what is troubling the judges, and respond as best they can. I was up there for nearly two hours explaining my position on the case. Justice Black pressed the point and said, "You are not arguing, I am sure, that every time a man is arrested he's got to have a lawyer appointed at that moment—that we should establish such a rule?"

I thought that was not the argument at all, and I said so. But I did point out that "the only effective way to protect the right to remain silent, the right not to testify against yourself, is to make sure that he has a lawyer. It is counsel that is the vehicle for protection of all of these other rights," I concluded. I pointed out that the ACLU in its amicus brief argued that this was a Fifth Amendment case "on the ground that there may be some other way of protecting the right to remain silent. But when all is said and done, they agreed that the only one they could really think of was the right to counsel."

There was only one judge who did not ask me a question. Yes. Justice Douglas.

What stands out to me today was that everyone seemed to be arguing about what the law *should* be. They were not really arguing in a way that cast their particular client in the most favorable light. Well, I had a couple of things that *I* wanted to say about Roy Allan Stewart and why he should not be executed. I did not realize at the time that I was departing from the way that others approached the case. I had written my brief, of course, and addressed all these issues. And finally, I concluded, "What he confessed to was a single act, but he did not understand what a legal consequence is. Thank you, Mr. Chief Justice."

I returned to the counsel table and after Gordon Ringer tried to rebut my argument and we were done, it was time for Thurgood Marshall, the Solicitor General of the United States, to rise and argue the federal case. He stopped where I was sitting and took my hand and when he shook it he said, "Good job!" This was the high point of my career as a lawyer! I just floated out of the courtroom!

On June 13, 1966, the Supreme Court made its decision: "High Court Puts New Curb on the Powers of the Police to Interrogate Suspects," the *New York Times* headline read. "Dissenters Bitter." The decisions were all five to four, with one exception, the *Stewart* case, where the decision was six to three in favor of my client. I have no idea why my old golfing buddy, Justice Tom Clark, provided the sixth vote in *Stewart* and voted with the minority for every other. But he did.

The victory was enormously gratifying for me and important for Tuttle & Taylor. We were gaining a real reputation as a small firm with a lot of horsepower. When I went off to recruit other young lawyers, even those prize lawyers who had clerked in the Supreme Court, they knew that we were a force to be reckoned with. But then there is also that sense of history: In a case that has protected the rights of countless defendants, that truly changed the course of our history, I had a small part. It is one of the many reasons that I love being a lawyer.

17

BOBBY

The greatest tragedy of the 1960's was the Vietnam War. Its effects resonated for decades in the horrific loss of life, the terrible divisions it created in American society and the ruinous effects on the Johnson presidency. Its overwhelming presence overshadowed some of the truly great social change that was a part of Johnson's Great Society program. During that time, there were no politicians that were spared having to cope with the Vietnam War, and the Democrats were especially on the defensive. Even if politicians were not crafting our foreign policy, the association with the Democratic Party was enough to make them very vulnerable.

At some point, I became totally disenchanted with the Vietnam War. I was never very enthusiastic about it, but eventually I just wanted to get out there and protest with the young folks of this country. In 1968, I realized that I could not possibly support Lyndon Johnson for another term as president. Obviously, I would have voted for Lyndon Johnson against any Republican—but if there was any chance to have another Democratic candidate, say Eugene McCarthy, he would have had my support.

McCarthy beat Johnson in New Hampshire, but I think that many of those who liked McCarthy, as I did, also felt, as I did, that he did not have what it took to be an effective president. My antipathy towards Johnson was so strong because I could not stand how his leadership was directly responsible for our horrible position in the Vietnam War.

There were many people who had looked at Bobby Kennedy as the best alternative to Johnson. One of my very close friends from the Supreme Court clerkship days was John Nolan. He remained in Washington to practice law, and I used to say that John was part of the Kennedy "mafia" in the D.C. area—he was so very close to all of them. In fact, he had been Bobby Kennedy's personal assistant at the Justice Department when

Kennedy was the U.S. Attorney General. John was a real witness to history when Bobby sent him into the South to get James Meredith admitted to the University of Mississippi.

John and I spoke regularly, and increasingly our conversations turned to the impossible presidency of LBJ and the importance of an alternative. I would say to John that Bobby Kennedy, who was then Senator from New York, had to run. But John would be non-committal. My persistence was not restricted to recruiting young lawyers, and I would badger John and ask him if Kennedy were any closer to making a decision to run. I was just trying to put a little pressure on him; I did not expect him to tell me.

One afternoon I sat in my office and received a telephone call from Fritz Burns, who was one of the insiders with the famous speaker of the California State Assembly Jesse M. "Big Daddy" Unruh. I knew Jesse. He was one of the great and colorful characters in California state politics. He was elected to the California State Assembly when he was 32 years old in 1954. In 1959, he wrote the Unruh Civil Rights Act, which would be a model for the Federal Civil Rights Act of 1964. He was Speaker of the State Assembly from 1961 till 1969, and was at the height of his power as a kingmaker during 1968. He was such a colorful character. He once said that *refusing* to touch lobbyists' money would just leave him on the outside of the action and the deal cutting. Who would want to be an ineffective purist? In his obituary, the *New York Times* quotes him, "So, stilling our doubts and scruples, we began to play the dangerous game of taking money from would-be corrupters--to elect men who would fight corruption." Wikipedia quotes him on lobbyists, "If you can't eat their food, drink their booze, screw their women and then vote against them, you have no business being up here." We could use that kind of gutsiness today!

Unruh was very close to the Kennedys, and I was intrigued when Burns asked me if I wanted to meet him late that afternoon. We met for a drink and Fritz got right to the point. "Bill, you know they're meeting back there in D.C. as we speak," he said. "The Senator is not prepared yet to make any kind of public statement about what he is going to do, or not do, in terms of becoming a candidate. They need a little more time."

He then went on to explain that if Bobby Kennedy took the time he needed to make his decision, he would not qualify for the crucial primary in California because the papers had to be filed within the week. He then entrusted me with the responsibility to get the papers, with all the necessary signatures, filed on time with the Secretary of State. I was cautioned that if the news got out prematurely there would be deniability back in Washington.

I did not know what to make of it. I certainly had some experience in politics, but this was on an entirely different level. I knew how close Fritz Burns was to Unruh and Unruh to Kennedy, so I figured the request was for real. There were only about half a dozen names that were required, so my job was not impossible, should I decide to do it. But I needed to think before I committed. The next morning, I called John Nolan, my friend in D.C., and told him what Fritz had told me. "John," I said, "I don't quite know what to do." John was masterful. He did not tell me to do it, he did not tell me not to do it, but he couched what he said in such a way that left me, his old buddy, with no doubt that I should do it. So I did.

In no time at all I received a call from Warren Christopher. Christopher at that time was Deputy Attorney General under Ramsey Clark. Johnson had not announced that he would not run again, so he was still the incumbent and would in all likelihood be the nominee. We had a very good conversation, and no one could make a more persuasive presentation than Chris did. He talked about how damaging a split in the party would be between these two giant figures. He knew me so well all he needed to say was, "Well, you know, Bill, if you go down that road, we're going to have Richard Nixon as president." That was a pretty powerful and astonishingly prescient argument.

But I leveled with my old friend. "Chris, given the choice between Bobby Kennedy and Lyndon Johnson, I have to take my chances with Bobby Kennedy," I said. "I've lost so much confidence in the president, no matter how much good he did with civil rights and the elementary and secondary education program, I can't do it. I'm going to do what they've asked me to do, and I'm going to support Bobby Kennedy."

Of course, Chris was prescient, but for the wrong reason.

Bobby's hesitation gave Eugene McCarthy a substantial head start. Eugene McCarthy was looking like a viable Johnson alternative and had been running against Johnson since December. On March 12, he had received 42% in the New Hampshire primary, to Johnson's 49%; it was not great for Bobby Kennedy's image to join the fight against Johnson only after blows had been landed by someone else. Surprisingly, in New Hampshire, McCarthy's strong showing came from votes from both pro-Vietnam hawks, who were upset with Johnson's failure to win the war, and doves, who were upset with Johnson's escalation of the war.

Even so, after McCarthy's victory in New Hampshire, Bobby announced his candidacy on March 16. We had to put together a campaign in California at warp speed. If anyone could do it, Jesse Unruh could, and I became his right hand man. This was a much better use of my time than joining the kids demonstrating in the streets! Jesse Unruh was statewide chairman, and while I do not remember what my title was, Jesse and I were in charge of putting that campaign together. Working at one of the hotels down by the L.A. airport, we assembled the Kennedy delegation for the upcoming convention in Chicago.

I had two strong connections to the Kennedy campaign: Jesse in the west and John Nolan in the east. Early on, John came out to California with a cigar box full of cash from the Kennedys to pay for our start-up expenses. John joked that they would just go into a vault and get a shovel. That was the Kennedy way. We kept the box in our home, which gave Kitty migraines.

One reason I was so supportive of Bobby was that he had finally become very outspoken in his criticism of LBJ's Vietnam policies. The widespread view was that he was holding off from challenging Johnson because he expected to lose—so he would speak on campuses and see signs asking if he was "Hawk, Dove or Chicken?" Those who most wanted Bobby in the race were unhappy with his straddling both sides. He appeared to be giving greater weight to the political game than to the war itself. He would attack Johnson's Vietnam policy and then say he would campaign for Johnson's re-election.

On the other hand, Bobby had two big strengths in this anti-Johnson showdown. The country looked more and more like it had gone off the rails, and the symptoms—race riots, campus protests and the war—were blatantly beyond Johnson's ability to control. They were trends that had become obvious only under Johnson, so it was easy for Kennedy to represent a return to the remembered sanity of life during the last Kennedy administration.

Kennedy's second major strength was that the President and the country were almost no longer on speaking terms—LBJ was largely barricaded in the White House. It was very good for Kennedy that he was *the* candidate who could really communicate with the people. (As it turned out, on March 31, 1968, Johnson announced in his stunning "I shall not seek, and I will not accept" television address that he would not run for re-election.) When Martin Luther King was killed on April 4, Bobby was campaigning in Indiana. At a night rally in Indianapolis, he gave a mostly black audience the news in a speech he delivered extemporaneously. Indianapolis was one of the only American cities not to suffer badly from riots that night. Kennedy, in his ability to really connect with ordinary citizens, provided a stark contrast with McCarthy's professorial and analytical campaign style.

Hubert Humphrey, meanwhile, was not participating in the primaries themselves—he was trying to get the nomination by lining up states' delegates directly, winning the commitments of delegate-controlling politicos. In several primaries, governors running favorite-son candidacies unofficially represented Humphrey on the ballot, but this tactic did not always work—in the Indiana race, Kennedy beat out that state's governor. The primaries were the opportunity for either Kennedy or McCarthy to pull decisively ahead as the change candidate before a confrontation with Humphrey in August's Democratic National Convention in Chicago.

In Kennedy and McCarthy's competition, California was central—the biggest of the four states where the two directly campaigned against each other. The other three were Indiana, which RFK had won, Oregon, where McCarthy beat out Kennedy one week before the California primary, and South Dakota, which would vote on June 5th, the same day as California. Each senator acknowledged that California could give his campaign crucial momentum so the stakes were high for their only one-on-one debate, which was broadcast on ABC on June 1.

McCarthy did his most visible campaigning on California's campuses; Kennedy gave a great deal of attention to the state's inner cities, which was one of Jesse's smartest strategies. The campaign, even with all the hard work, was absolutely exhilarating. We all felt as if we were embarking on such an important break with the past and making a commitment to a new future. On the evening of June 5, we were all at the Ambassador Hotel, eagerly waiting the returns. I was there, and my secretary Gloria came with a group of her friends. We were euphoric. Kennedy came out on top, with 46% of the vote to McCarthy's 42%.

Kennedy gave his victory speech at midnight, four hours after the polls had closed. There was an enormous crowd in the Embassy Room Ballroom of the hotel, where the supporters pumped their fists and chanted, "We want Kennedy! We want Kennedy!" while Robert and Ethel stood smiling and waving at the podium at the front of the room. I was just offstage with Bobby's sister Jean Kennedy Smith. We chatted, applauded, and were thrilled as we listened to Bobby's speech.

He gave a shout out to Don Drysdale, who had pitched his sixth straight shutout that evening. The first person he thanked was Jesse Unruh, and he and I exchanged a quick glance. Kennedy made a point in his speech of referring not only to the primary outcomes in California and South Dakota (which had also voted for him that night), but also in New Hampshire. "The country wants to move in a different direction," he said. "We want to deal with our own problems in our own country, and we want peace in Vietnam."

It was such a chaotic scene of euphoria. This victory put the presidential nomination within reach in ways that even the optimists among us—and I was certainly one of those—had never imagined. I watched Bobby and Ethel as they made their way with the rest of the entourage from the ballroom into the kitchen, headed for a press conference. Jean and I had drifted close to the kitchen when we heard the shots and saw the flash of the gun. Suddenly it was pandemonium. I have never been in a situation like that before or since, and you never know how you are going to react. Unruh was in the kitchen and witnessed the assassination. Knowing so well what could happen, he leapt on top of a table, according to columnist Jimmy Breslin, and screamed at the police: "I want him alive! I hold you responsible for him being alive! I want him alive!"

A lot of people were running around, calling for ambulances. I said to myself, "Uh-oh, Steve Smith is back there with him. I'd better stay very close to Jean." I just gave myself that role to play at that point. Rumors had immediately filled the hall, and the rumors were wild. One rumor had it that Steve Smith was the one who had been shot. Of course, we now know that twenty-four-year-old Palestinian Sirhan Sirhan shot and killed Bobby Kennedy. But in the midst of that chaos, we were all just trying to figure out what to do next.

Steve Smith appeared and came towards Jean and me. He told us that Bobby had been shot and it looked bad. Paul Schrade of the UAW was also wounded, but less seriously. Steve asked me if I would go up on the stage, take the microphone and tell the people there that Kennedy had been shot and that he was going to the hospital. They should all leave the auditorium, leave the hotel, go home and hope and pray for the best. "Steve, that should come from a member of the Kennedy family," I said. "If you want me to go with you, I'll go with you, Jean will go with us, but you have to be the one to talk to these folks."

"Yes," he said. "I think you're right." So Steve, Jean and I went up on the stage and Steve took the microphone. I was unconscious of all the TV cameras, all the reporters. It never occurred to me that I would be hearing the next day from friends and family all over the country who saw me on TV as they watched the assassination scene replayed over and over.

We were shattered with grief. And there is no doubt in my mind that Bobby Kennedy would had become the nominee and would have been elected president, and the course of American history after that year would have been much different. But we had to move forward. I was a member of the California delegation, and we were going to the convention in Chicago in two months without a candidate. By the time of the Democratic National Convention, Johnson had removed himself from the process, and his Vice-President Hubert Humphrey had become a sure thing to be the nominee. He got to town with roughly one hundred more delegates committed to him than were needed to secure the nomination.

But the California delegates were a big block, and we had no candidate. We arrived the weekend before the convention began on Monday, August 26. Jesse asked me to be the delegation representative on the rules committee dealing with the nomination process at the convention. I was working on this committee that had two delegates from each state while Jesse was meeting with some of the real heavyweights in the Democratic leadership nationally including the famous mayor of Chicago, Richard Daley.

When Jesse emerged, he had some interesting news. "Bill, there's some talk in that meeting about Ted Kennedy, rather than Humphrey," he said. But he wanted to have some eyes and ears among the actual delegates to see how they would react. He pointed out that I had met a number of the delegates and asked me to work the convention hall to see if there was any support for a Ted Kennedy nomination. Jesse knew how to play to my strengths, and over the next few hours I did exactly what he told me to. I did not need to talk to that many people: I trusted my gut on this and always had the feeling that if Ted Kennedy had been the nominee, he would have won. I reported back. "As far as I can tell, Jesse, they would be relieved, they would like to have Ted Kennedy," I said.

The convention was televised chaos and police brutality. On August 28 came what was called the "police riot," when police and activists verbally provoked each other, threw things and clobbered one another on the streets outside the International Amphitheatre. This also was the day that the party's nominee was made official. When Sen. Abraham Ribicoff nominated George McGovern, he referred to the Chicago police department's behavior as "Gestapo tactics."

During the nominating process, fifteen state delegations unsuccessfully tried to replace Humphrey's delegates with anti-war delegates. When the Convention considered the party's Vietnam plank, Phil Burton, who was one of our representatives from California, spoke for the peace advocates in language that we all had discussed in private. It was no use. Ted Kennedy was not a possibility, nor were any of the other candidates. And the Johnson/Humphrey language won out in the party's Vietnam plank. When the final vote for the party's position on Vietnam was tallied, we staged our own very peaceful protest. The California delegation began to sing with the New York delegation, "We Shall Overcome." It was a powerful, painful moment.

After the vote, I went to my hotel room and prepared to leave the convention. I watched the rioting on television as I packed my bag. I was heading east with my two oldest kids, Don and Barbara, to look at colleges. I would miss being present at the last day of the convention, but I knew that my work was done.

On August 29, the final day of the convention, a film tribute to Bobby Kennedy was shown. Don, Barbara and I, in our hotel room in New York, turned on the television set to watch the proceedings. We sat silently as the tribute to RFK unfolded on the screen. All the youth and idealism, the vision and the special Kennedy charisma, was captured as if he were still alive. I remembered my first convention in Atlantic City. Was it really only four years before when a similar tribute was paid to his brother and the applause lasted for twenty minutes? Everything was different in Chicago. Times had changed. The violence was unprecedented. The country was in the midst of a year of turmoil that we had never before witnessed, with two assassinations of great young leaders, and violent demonstrations in the streets where young police attacked young demonstrators and vice versa.

I am an optimistic man. I always look ahead and not behind. And as I looked at the thousands of Democrats gathered in the Amphitheater, and at my two teenagers on the cusp of embarking on their lives as college students—the same generation as those who were demonstrating in the streets—and imagined the millions of people of all parties also watching this on television, I truly believed that despite all the violence and the bitter conflicts, we were joined not only in grief, but always as Americans.

18

HIRE THE BEST TALENT, THEN TURN THEM LOOSE!

If there were only one ingredient that separates a good law firm from a great law firm, it would be its lawyers. I am not simply referring to finding the superstars from Stanford, Harvard and Yale—naturally these young lawyers tend to be pretty smart and driven—but there are superstars in other schools as well, and superstardom alone is not enough. Their education and capacity for hard work is a given; they would not be where they are without those characteristics. But what distinguishes the great lawyers who can create a great firm is a level of creativity and ease in working with clients, with fellow attorneys, and with ideas.

This may sound obvious but some would argue (and because they are lawyers you can imagine how they would argue) that the size and breadth of the firm is far more important. When there are 150 attorneys, a firm can bring vast and varied resources to a client. There is some obvious merit in that case, but as evidence to the contrary, I need only point to Tuttle & Taylor.

When I joined the firm, I was the only litigator, and I was also the "recruiter-in-chief." As such, I was able to bring in a number of exceptionally talented lawyers to a firm that, by design, never became very large. My favorite hunting grounds were Stanford Law and the Supreme Court—targets that did not set me apart from most firms—but over the years I found great lawyers from many different schools, and some of the truly great lawyers came from schools that may not be ranked among the most elite. But I found lawyers there who had those special qualities.

My recruiting trips to Stanford, I later found out, had become something of lore among the third year students. I never realized that but gradually it became clear that somehow my appearance stood out from the collection of attorneys from the largest firms. My strategy was simple: I would talk to the professors, then look at the Law Review editors, and work through a number of the top students, seeing if they were for us, and if they were, taking the time to relentlessly persuade them to give our small firm a try.

The Supreme Court clerks were tougher nuts to crack, but I was determined to bring a few into our firm, and one year in particular proved to be a banner year for that effort. Recruiting Ray Fisher can be seen as a pretty good example of my strategy and my great success. I had already visited Stanford in 1965, but Ray was out interviewing with the giant firms of Covington, Wilmer Cutler, and Arnold & Porter, so he missed what he later referred to as Bill Norris' "legendary recruiting trip to Stanford." A few weeks later I received a call in my office. "Hello, Mr. Norris, my name is Ray Fisher and I am president of the *Stanford Law Review*," he said. This was a good place to start for me and I became more interested. "If there is any chance that you might be still be interviewing for your firm, I would like to be considered."

Ray once described his own nervousness in making the call and how I "casually allowed as to how [I] *might* make room in [my] schedule" to interview him. I knew that this was exactly the kind of young lawyer I would be interested in pursuing. And pursue him I did! I interviewed him in Los Angeles and we hit it off. I brought him and Nancy, his wife, home for dinner with Kitty in Pasadena. They had two young children, so that too set him apart.

Then he got a clerkship on the U.S. Court of Appeals for the District of Columbia Circuit with Judge J. Skelly Wright. Wright, nominated by President Kennedy, had been in office since March 1962 and had already made his mark as one of the judicial greats—visionary, a powerful sense of social justice, a great writer. I tracked Ray down in Washington and made it clear that a job would be waiting for him when he finished this D.C. clerkship. I was willing to be patient and the clerkship, obviously, only made Ray a more appealing candidate. He clerked for Wright for a year and then was offered a clerkship with Justice William Brennan on the U.S. Supreme Court.

"Even better!" I thought. I was tenacious and determined to get this man for Tuttle & Taylor. But Ray was not sure. He was tempted to stay in Washington and join the prestigious Covington firm, but there was considerable attraction to moving his family back to Southern California, which was home for both him and Nancy. Then there was the size issue. Covington was a large firm at the time, with 150 lawyers, while Tuttle & Taylor had twelve lawyers. I helped him realize that he could succeed in ways with us that may take him many more years at Covington.

In 1968, Ray joined our firm and so did two other former clerks from the Supreme Court. Our firm jumped from twelve to fifteen lawyers (and the following year I would hire four more, bringing us up to nineteen). Another notable recruit, in 1965, was Jerry Brown, a recent Yale Law grad and California Supreme Court clerk. He was brilliant, to be sure, but had quirky work habits, like preferring to be in the office at three in the morning and absent at three in the afternoon. But never mind, before you knew it, he was elected to the Los Angeles Community College Board of Trustees and away he went. I wonder what ever happened to that guy.

So we were on a roll, recruiting the best and the brightest. Ray later told me that I was the main reason that he joined Tuttle & Taylor, but another appealing aspect was that we were politically active and that "it was the attitude of the firm that this was an honorable thing to do in addition to being a lawyer." We were also much more sensible in those days about the almighty billable hour. Today firms require 2600 billable hours for their lawyers; when we hired Ray, the average was about 1600. (His starting salary was also $11,000 a year!) One could do some great things with those extra thousand hours a year, and we did. As Ray once said, reflecting on Tuttle & Taylor, "In short, non-billable hours were valued almost as much as billables, sometimes more so."

But most important, we were lawyers and litigators, and Ray worked with me on two very important cases during his early years there. Our challenge was to demonstrate to clients that we were competitive, because we were what would now be known as a "boutique firm": high level, concentrated, attentive involvement in each case, unlike other large firms in which the work would be handled by easily a half dozen lawyers. This kind of engagement would be far more likely to both win cases and be cost efficient in doing it.

Meanwhile, our litigation practice was making a name for itself. In 1972, I got a call from Keith Mann, one of my mentors at Stanford Law School. He was my connection with President Kennedy's commission on the airline dispute several years before, and continued to be a very close friend. On this occasion Keith called me and told me that Stanford had a case on its hands that involved a very popular, tenured English professor—he specialized in Melville and cultural history—named H. Bruce Franklin whose politics were on the far extreme of the Left. He was thirty-seven years old and was one of the founders in the late sixties of a Maoist organization called the Revolutionary Union but split from them because they were too moderate!

Clearly, Franklin was extremely anti-war and anti-government, but so was much of the rest of the country. This was 1972 and a time when anti-war protests exploded on the campuses against Nixon and Kissinger's escalation of the Vietnam War into Laos and Cambodia. When Henry Cabot Lodge, the Ambassador to Vietnam, came to speak at Stanford, Franklin incited a group of students in the audience to shout him down so he could not give his speech. Dick Lyman, the President of Stanford, was outraged by the way that Franklin encouraged students to undermine the free speech rights of Lodge and brought charges against him before the faculty Senate. He sought a reprimand, which the professor chose to frame as the persecution of an anti-war professor.

Any appeal from faculty discipline of this sort had to go to the Board of Trustees, which was ordinarily represented by a major, establishment San Francisco law firm. Lyman's decision on hiring outside counsel was very strategic. He sought me out because of my reputation as a liberal and a strong advocate of the First Amendment. Of course, Keith must have influenced his thinking. By this time, I had also served on the California State College Board of Trustees. After Pat Brown's defeat by Ronald Reagan in 1966, he took advantage of his lame duck status to make a few appointments, and I was one of them. As this was also a time of great student unrest, I had some experience in working with these issues.

The bombing of Laos triggered violent student demonstrations on many campuses including Stanford. Of course, Franklin was involved: he gave a passionate speech in the Student Union that essentially accused Stanford of being complicit with Nixon and the military complex through its research. Ground zero for that research was the Computer Center. That night, there was violence. Some shots were fired at members of the conservative student organization, the Free Campus Movement. There were also other acts of vandalism. Franklin spoke to students again, and that triggered the actual occupation of the Computer Center. The incident escalated, with more violence and property damage.

Consequently, the stakes were much more serious, and Lyman decided to fire Franklin. Lyman thought Franklin manipulated students to engage in suppression of speech; more importantly, Franklin used his position as a professor to encourage illegal behavior by students, leading to gunfire on campus, property damage and risk of greater damage to the Computer Center. The subsequent hearing over Franklin's dismissal threatened to become a proxy battle over war policy.

When Keith called me and told me about it, I said, "Well, you know, that's all kind of interesting. I'm generally considered to be liberal, but if these facts are as you have given them to me, I may have to reconsider my liberal credentials!" He asked me if I would come up and advise the president, Richard Lyman, on how to proceed. Lyman described how Franklin led a group of students in taking over the building, how it was impossible to enter the building because they had barricaded the doors and there were some people inside the building who were both frightened and intimidated. When he finished, I said to him, "Dick, if I had been in your position, I'd have fired him too."

A tenure review committee composed of about eight professors outside of the English department was charged with reviewing the case and holding a quasi-legal hearing. Under Stanford's rules and regulations relating to the faculty, Franklin was entitled to due process. The chairman was very good. They were all very good. But the University needed someone to speak for its point of view. I conferred with Keith again after my meeting with Lyman, and he explained that while Stanford normally had very large law firms representing it, the University wanted someone who was independent of those firms to speak to this issue. "They would like to have someone who's not all that well-known up there, but has a reputation for being very liberal on First Amendment issues, and in particular the issues of faculty," he said.

I agreed to take this on and brought fellow Stanford Law grad Ray Fisher with me. There was another younger lawyer named Chuck Rosenberg who was right out of Harvard, and really good, very liberal, and very interested in litigation. When I interviewed him I had asked him if there was anything that he found particularly interesting. He immediately responded that in Harvard, he was very interested in the question of First Amendment issues relating to faculty. Perfect.

We shaped our constitutional legal strategy in ways a more conservatively ideological firm likely would not have done. We had to concede that Stanford was subject to the First Amendment constraints on public universities. Given all of Stanford's government funding, it would likely have lost the argument that it was a private institution subject to a lesser standard. We had to meet the then governing constitutional standard for what was required to punish a speaker for incitement to riot and assemble the evidence that Franklin clearly crossed the line.

A medium sized lecture hall that was usually used for Physics had been converted into a kind of courtroom. Franklin defended himself with some help from a law student, but there were rumors that the flamboyant but impressive lawyer William Kunstler was going to defend him. He did not, but Alan Dershowitz, who had already made a name for himself as a constitutional lawyer, was briefly involved.

Franklin did not help his case by his supreme arrogance. He tried to avoid accountability for his leadership actions by blaming the students and denied his own critical involvement because he was "too important to the Movement." He said that he could not have unlawfully incited the students because he knew what the constitutional line was. He almost explicitly said that he was so important to the anti-war movement that the movement would not want him to cross the line, whereas the students were expendable.

The case we made against Franklin was straightforward. Stanford had an absolutely explicit policy known as the "Disruption" policy and this is what it said:

> Because the rights of free speech and peaceable assembly are fundamental to the democratic process, Stanford firmly supports the rights of all members of the University community to express their views or to protest against actions and opinions with which they disagree.

The policy then goes on to point out that the University is a community and everyone, faculty, students and administration, share a "concurrent obligation to maintain on the campus an atmosphere conducive to scholarly pursuits, to preserve the dignity and seriousness of University ceremonies and public exercises, and to respect the rights of all individuals." When those activities are disrupted or it is impossible to carry out "a University function or approved activity," or if free movement of anyone around campus is somehow made impossible, then the university law is broken.

I made the opening statement we had crafted as a team, and then went out and handled the press. But I had received a call from one of my other clients whose case was going to trial, so I could not stay for the entire proceeding. I left Ray and Chuck to continue. The hearing was conducted as if it were a real jury trial, with evidence heard on both sides, the cross-examination of witnesses and summations of the case. The process lasted for six weeks. Franklin tried to characterize his actions as pure speech that was not directed to inciting imminent lawless action, but he failed to do so convincingly. He also failed to make a good argument that the disruption policy denied his First Amendment rights rather than protecting the First Amendment rights of all members of the university community. The panel finally left to consider its verdict, and when they returned they said Franklin was guilty of violating the University's Disruption Policy, and the punishment was revocation of his tenure and termination "with prejudice."

I was not there for the closing arguments or the verdict. When Ray and Chuck came back to Tuttle & Taylor, I asked, "How did it go, guys?" And they both said, "I think we got the son of a bitch!" Franklin thought he knew where the First Amendment line was and insisted that he had not crossed it. But he did, because there were issues about the community in the disruption policy that were fundamental.

Ray and I also worked together on one of our very large cases, which became known as *Pacific Coast Agricultural Export Association v. Sunkist Growers, Inc.* It was a huge antitrust case that consumed an enormous amount of our time. We represented T&T's long-time and loyal client Sunkist Citrus Growers, which produced about 75 percent of the oranges that were grown in Arizona and California. Once the fruit was harvested, it was processed through a large network of 105 packinghouses that were further divided into groups of twenty sales exchanges. The packinghouses processed the fruit and then stamped each orange with their name as well as that of Sunkist. Each packinghouse had a limit on the number of brand oranges that it could sell in a given time period. Purchasers in the United States—the big grocery stores and other wholesale buyers for, say, hotels and restaurant chains—had some choice as to the sources from whom they bought their fruit.

In contrast, when Hong Kong imported oranges from the United States, it was not entitled to request specific brands, although they were able to say that they wanted their oranges to come from, for example, the Central Valley or Southern California. A number of different exporting companies generated and maintained the sales to the Hong Kong importers, but the largest was Pacific Coast Agricultural Export Association, a loose confederation of several exporters.

In 1966, Sunkist broke off their agreements with Pacific Coast and decided, instead, to have complete control over those exports. They began to sell directly to Hong Kong through a new, exclusive agent known as Reliance. This arrangement was a huge success for Sunkist; by 1970 Reliance captured almost 70 percent of the Hong Kong market for American oranges. Obviously, this did not make the Pacific Coast Agricultural Export Association happy, and in July 1968 it sued on behalf of seven of its members alleging that Sunkist had violated federal antitrust laws. In August of 1969, two other export companies who had the same complaint joined them.

The basic argument was that Sunkist stole their clients by giving Reliance a list of their Hong Kong customers, and that Sunkist harmed their business by refusing to sell them oranges to resell in Hong Kong. Sunkist's 70 percent market share, they argued, constituted a monopoly and had to be broken up. It was an incredibly complicated case, and Ray and I traveled often to Hong Kong during the years that we worked on it. Finally, the trial date was set in 1972. Ray had become a very experienced young lawyer by that time, and we were a good team.

In 1970, Kitty and I had very amicably separated. We were great friends, and continue to be, but as with so many couples that marry when they are very young, our lives had drifted apart to the point where both of us realized it was time to move on. What this meant was I was now living alone.

When it came time for the trial, Ray and I decamped to San Francisco for nearly three months in preparation. It was an unusual length of time for a trial. Ray's wife Nancy would come up and visit, and even make us some home cooked meals. This was when Ray and I became quite close, living together and working such long hours, not only in San Francisco, but also during the many months of travel for discovery.

The trial was a big battle and in the end, the jury found against Sunkist. We lost on the antitrust claims. Then came the damages trial, and I let Ray handle it. The trial lasted for two weeks and Ray did a fine job. The appellants asked for $3 million in damages. The jury made Sunkist responsible for only $1 million in damages. Of course, Sunkist appealed, and in 1976 the case went up to the Ninth Circuit, but to no avail.

As far as I was concerned, limiting the damages to $1 million was a victory for our client, and Sunkist agreed. But it was also very much a turning point with Ray. After this case, he was no longer my second chair but became the lead attorney in many significant cases for the firm. In fact, Ray eventually became Associate Attorney General under Janet Reno, served on the L.A. Police Commission, and also became a Ninth Circuit judge—although after I had left the bench, so sadly we did not have the opportunity to sit together as fellow judges.

Tuttle & Taylor was now one of the best firms in Los Angeles. Young attorneys were eager to work for us, and my "legendary recruiting trips" to Stanford only became busier. There were many fantastic lawyers who worked at our small firm over the years. But the story of Ray Fisher tells so much about the firm, the generation of lawyers who grew up then, the great variety of cases that are involved in a litigation practice, and about how hard work can create a long friendship.

This is also about generations. The Sunkist case marked the turning point for Ray; he was now in the first chair in litigation. But we were constantly bringing in new young lawyers who would ably assist in the second chair. My strategy was to always hire the best talent and then let them loose! Give them the work and see what they could do with it. Because I had good instincts for the people I recruited, one young lawyer after another had those moments of terror and, eventually, those moments of supreme confidence. I never stopped recruiting.

19

RACE POLITICS AND THE TRIUMPH OF TOM BRADLEY

When the Princeton class of 1951 celebrated its 50th reunion, I was asked to write a piece that I entitled "The Judiciary in the Last Half Century" for our alumni publication. I began by reminding my fellow classmates that when we began Princeton in 1947, Jackie Robinson had been jeered by fans and players alike when he broke the color barrier in Major League Baseball and that when we graduated four years later there was not a single black face in our graduating class. When I was asked to write about the judiciary, "I thought immediately about the courageous and historic role federal judges have played in changing the hearts and minds of Americans on the issue of race." I then offered my own reflections on the long history of civil rights and the judiciary.

I wrote:

> I believe the performance of the federal judges on the core issue
> of racial justice in the last half century confirms the wisdom of
> fellow alum James Madison in fighting to establish in the Con-
> stitution an independent judiciary as a separate and equal
> branch of government. It also confirms the wisdom—and arro-
> gance, Jefferson charged—of Chief Justice John Marshall in
> reading Article III of the Constitution as conferring upon him-
> self and his fellow federal judges the supreme authority to de-
> cide when the Congress, the President and the individual states
> violate the Constitution.

The piece was a great opportunity for me to write about an issue that had been a major concern for my entire life—the issue of race. Lucille Bagley was the only African American girl in Turtle Creek High School. Oliver L. Brown was a father in Topeka Kansas who only wanted his children educated properly; he became the Brown of *Brown v. Board of Education*. Thurgood Marshall was one of the greatest heroes of the twentieth century, who braved threats to his life as the head of the NAACP legal defense fund and later was the first Supreme Court Justice to break the color barrier.

As much as I love the United States of America—and I do love this country—its capacity for crude injustice for those who were "different" never failed to cause me pain. How could citizens such as these men and women be marginalized in any way? Even when I was a boy I was outraged by the patronizing, not aggressive, but utterly racist treatment of Lucille Bagley. How was it possible that our magnificent Constitution could apply only to white heterosexual men?

As I repeatedly saw how the racism of our country played out, how it was inextricably woven into our lives—our neighborhoods, our schools, our television programs, our representatives—I have become convinced that our legacy of slavery continues to hang over every aspect of our society. I knew that racism was wrong with the same conviction, as fixed as the color of my eyes, that I knew I had to try and change things, address the wrongs of the past, and transform the future. Certainly profound Supreme Court decisions such as *Brown* or momentous government policies such as Johnson's 1965 Civil Rights Act drove social change. But so did the actions of men and women day after day.

And of course, so did the ballot box. I saw this first hand in two California elections—Wilson Riles and Tom Bradley—that changed the course of history.

My service on the State Board of Education taught me about the many layers of entrenched racism in our educational system: the de facto segregation of our schools, the uneven distribution of resources, the low expectations we had for so many of our young people of color. While no individual could ever be held singly responsible for the status quo, one of its greatest champions was Max Rafferty, the California State Superintendent of Public Instruction who had been in the job since 1962. When the *New York Times* reported his first election, the headline said, "School Post Goes to Conservative: Dr. Rafferty Defeats Liberal in California Contest."

If there was something that I was for, Rafferty opposed it: busing, sex education, creative teaching, and breaking down the color barrier in our schools. His reaction to the progressive movement in education during the late sixties when I was on the State Board of Education was only to dig in deeper and become even more inflexible and conservative. He had a national reputation as a reactionary, or as the man upholding traditional values, like memorizing and drilling, which were being attacked by dangerous liberals. His books, *Suffer Little Children* and *What Are They Doing to Your Children,* were bestsellers, and their titles reveal their intended audience. He was a major impediment to necessary reform in the California school system, and I remember returning home from some meetings practically hyperventilating in fury. He was up for re-election in 1970, and given the turmoil of the times, we could see that his supporters would be motivated to get out and vote. But maybe there was a chance to get him out of office.

How could he possibly be defeated? My vision was that the perfect candidate would be an African American educator, someone who understood the full range of the needs of the children and also appreciated what had to be changed. On the other hand, the idea that an African American candidate might have a chance had been severely compromised by what had happened to Tom Bradley. We had all just witnessed the terrible, unexpected upset of Tom Bradley in his first race for mayor in 1969. Bradley was an African American man I passionately supported in his bid to be mayor. He had been an L.A. police officer, joined the California Democratic Council, and was elected to a City Council seat in 1963. He was a brilliant and brave politician, who suffered levels of explicit and implicit racism in every chapter of his career. More radical African Americans disparaged his moderation, while whites associated him with the extremists in the streets who were rioting in Watts.

In '69, when Bradley challenged the two-term incumbent Sam Yorty, he got portrayed as a radical and a tool of black militants—this, just four years after the Watts riots, and at the height of the Black Panthers' notoriety. Yorty was completely out of step with the city and with the times. I remember that Bobby Kennedy wrapped up his speech at the Ambassador Hotel on that fateful day of June in 1968, by saying that Mayor Yorty was demanding he and his people get out of town. I believed that Yorty was extremely vulnerable and worked hard on Bradley's campaign.

Bradley had spent most of the campaign with a commanding lead in the polls, and we began to feel confident that he would eventually be our mayor. But in the last week of the campaign, Sam Yorty unleashed the ugliest, most racist campaign imaginable. He had lots of money and spent it lavishly on prime-time TV spots. The weekend before the election on Tuesday those of us who were on the committee were monitoring the polls very closely, and we saw them shifting dramatically. The shift was directly connected to those racist spots in which Yorty preyed on the fear of white folks throughout the city. He zeroed in on the police force, in which Bradley had served, but Yorty said that if Tom Bradley were to be elected the police officers would resign their positions! It was that blatant and that dishonest. Yorty mobilized not only his base, but preyed on the fears of many Angelinos by associating Bradley with the violent, Afro and Dashiki wearing, pistol packing Black Radicals who were on the news every night. The unfairness was breathtaking.

So was Yorty's success. He defeated Bradley by a hair's breadth. And I was stunned by how easily manipulated otherwise intelligent voters could be in the face of blatant, unfair, race baiting.

Those of us working for change and angered about what happened to Tom Bradley had to wait four years to take our revenge against Yorty. But just a year later, Max Rafferty, the Superintendent of Schools and my nemesis on the State Board of Education, was up for re-election. I was eager to see him defeated. But this was a statewide office, so the political dynamics that had to be managed were different. Dorman Commons had been appointed to the State Board of Education by Pat Brown in 1961 and was an oil company executive. Dorman and I developed a very solid personal and working relationship. When we realized that Rafferty was up for re-election I said, "We've got to find someone to run against Max." Dorman could not have agreed more.

We started scratching our heads, and Dorman said, "Okay, let's try to find a nice moderate, non-threatening Republican, who was maybe the superintendent of a suburban school district. No liberals, just a nice moderate, and let's have him run against Max." We discussed this idea and even reached out to a few of these so-called "dream" candidates and realized that we were not happy with any of them. In fact, we were discouraged.

We then became more audacious and decided not to think about someone who was cautious in the extreme, but instead imagine someone whom we would have appointed ourselves, if we could bypass an election altogether. We looked at each other and had one of those wonderful moments of perfect, non-verbal communication. We knew that we were thinking of exactly the same person and that everyone would think we were crazy. Our dream candidate was the African American Deputy Superintendent of Schools named Wilson Riles—an educator, and man of substance and depth. We knew he would be perfect. We also knew that convincing the voters of his perfection was not going to be easy.

Dorman and I presented our idea to Wilson, who was described in the newspapers as a "tall, earnest black man," and he was absolutely incredulous. He just shook his head in disbelief, reminding us that Tom Bradley's defeat in his mayoral bid was only a year ago—as if we needed any reminding of that debacle—and the racism evident in that campaign clearly had not dissipated. Besides, he rightly pointed out, he had no money and absolutely zero name recognition.

But he did not say no, and that was all that Dorman and I needed to move forward. The next step was to start fundraising and see if there was any way we could get a little money to start the campaign. We went to see Max Palevsky, who was one of the biggest contributors to Democratic politics in the state, and one of the biggest in the country. He founded a company called Scientific Data Systems, SDS, a computer manufacturing firm. Eventually SDS merged with Xerox, and the financial press described it as the first billion-dollar merger. Max, who described himself as "a poor Jewish kid from Chicago" when he began, by this time owned ten percent of the Xerox stock. And he was thoughtful, strategic and visionary in the way he used his considerable wealth.

We went to talk to Max and had lunch in his office, and when we told him our plan, he too was incredulous, and he too referred to Tom Bradley's recent defeat. "If we can't get Tom elected in Los Angeles," Max said. "How on earth are we going to get another African American elected for a statewide office?" He was insisting that our focus should not be in the lower level superintendent race, we should aim high and focus on the Senate. But that was not our intention, and we stuck to our commitment to getting Wilson Riles some money for his campaign. We told Max that if we did not walk out of his office with $25,000 seed money, there was not going to be a campaign.

Finally, Max pulled his desk drawer open, took out a checkbook, and wrote us a check for $25,000. "I'm giving this to you guys only because it's you," he said. "Now go spend it." Spend it we did, and soon we began to see some results. Nobody knew who Wilson Riles was before we started. The campaign was bruising and complicated, and I worked hard to help in any way that I could.

But what was most astonishing was that on Election Day, despite all the prognostication that Riles would be defeated, the voters made the right choice! It was called "one of the most stunning upsets in California's political history" by the *New York Times* on November 5. The headline was "Rafferty Is Defeated by a Negro as California Education Chief; A Black Unseats Rafferty in California School Race." Note that the *Times* still gave Rafferty the dignity of his name, and Wilson was only "a Negro" and "a Black." But he was also a great Superintendent, winning a second and then a third term. He was not only the first African American to be elected to statewide office in California; he was also the first African American in the United States to be elected as Superintendent of Schools.

Then it was time for another mayoral election. Bradley decided he was going to run again, and again he faced Yorty. I remember that Tom and I discussed whether or not he should subject himself to this kind of punishing experience again, but he was committed to trying—and to succeeding this time. This time, when he faced off with Yorty, Bradley was a better-known candidate, no longer a city councilman whose name was recognized by only seven percent of Angelinos as he had been at the start of the last campaign. If Yorty made a less direct issue of race the second time around, this time he accused Bradley of corruption, saying that he lacked integrity and accepted money from gamblers in Las Vegas. Yorty seemed to be getting desperate when he said that Bradley "seems to think that blacks should vote for him because he's black." He was trying the same old tactics, but this time they did not work.

One reason was because this time, we nailed Sam Yorty. All of his accusations about Bradley's imagined financial corruption were distractions away from Yorty's real financial shenanigans. We came up with some information having to do with money and insurance policies. We had the story but we needed someone to go public with it. Ultimately, we got a Republican member of the City Council and tax lawyer by the name of Joel Wachs. Joel was a terrific guy. He took the Yorty story and ran with it. He held a press conference and said, "Here's our case against him."

Los Angeles' mayoral races are non-partisan run-off elections, so if no one gets 50 percent of the vote the first time around, the two highest-placing contestants move from an open primary to a general election run-off. Bradley and two others were Yorty's opponents in '73. In the April 3 primary Bradley came in first, with 35 percent, and Yorty second, with 29 percent. Yorty had long been falling out of step with L.A.'s politics—he had moved right as the city had gone left, holding out (despite being a Democrat) on endorsing Humphrey in 1968.

We also knew how to run Tom's campaign this time—it was a bare bones, don't-mess-up campaign. He was 55 and had been in public service for a long time—had served on the city council for ten years, after twenty-one years in the police department—and his campaign strategy was to appear a steady hand at the tiller. The day after Bradley announced his candidacy on December 5, 1972, he stressed "governmental economy and stemming crime" and he talked about passing balanced budgets. "The people of Los Angeles are entitled to a safe city," he said. Asked whether L.A. was ready for a black mayor, he said, "I think that this city is ready for a mayor who has the ability, who will deal with the issues in this city. And I believe that ... they're going to respond by electing me."

Tom dialed back all the passion that he had, and it worked to his advantage. On April 14, 1973, nine days after the primary, the *Los Angeles Times* reported, "the racial issue has been made less of publicly than it was in the same period four years ago," and then stated that Bradley was "making little news with mostly bland speeches.... The Bradley camp thinks the voters are fed up with vehement campaign charges and that it would be counterproductive." The same piece commented, "in many Jewish precincts, some voters complained that Bradley was bland to the point of dullness."

The general election was going to be on May 29, 1973, and in early May the *Los Angeles Times* published a poll showing Bradley leading Yorty, 43 to 28 percent. But twenty percent of the voters said they were undecided, and many of these suggested they would wind up going for Yorty, so we were not taking anything for granted. In man-on-the-street interviews in ethnically varied neighborhoods, some whites openly talked about their reluctance to vote for a black mayor, though others said they were ready to give Bradley a chance. A Mexican American woman was quoted talking about the disillusionment she was experiencing with Watergate and expressed the view that voting in any election was pointless. "Strong enthusiasm for Bradley was rare," the paper reported.

Our campaign may have been dull, but it was very effective.

On May 29, 1973, Bradley beat Yorty, 56 to 44 percent. We were ecstatic! Los Angeles had an African American mayor for the first time in its history and was one of the few American cities that did. In fact, it was the only city in America with a majority white population that had a black mayor. On election night at the Los Angeles Hilton, we were jubilant. Tom went up to the podium and was at last able to speak with the passion that he had contained during the campaign. He said he received the highest honor that this city could give, and he called this night, "the fulfillment of the impossible dream." He pointed out that the election proved something fundamental and crucial about our political system and held "great significance for young people in this country, because it reaffirms their belief in the political process." Political transformations, he said, "must be done from the inside." And that began Tom Bradley's twenty years and five terms as one of the greatest mayors Los Angeles ever had.

His success was not assured during that first term, and he knew that he needed help. Our work was not over on election night. In fact, it was just beginning. Max Palevsky never wanted anything for himself in an election. He did not care about getting his name out front, but he did want Tom to make me his chief of staff. I did not want to be his chief of staff, and Tom already had a fabulous chief of staff named Maury Wiener, who was just the right guy for that job.

I was ready to step back, but Tom had other plans for me. He insisted that I become his first President of the Police Commission. "Bill, I think you could go in there and handle Ed Davis, and embrace him, so you could build some bridges for me," Tom said. I did not really want to do it, but how could anyone say no to Tom Bradley?

In fact, he did have a serious problem with Ed Davis. Davis had been the LAPD's Police Chief for four years when Bradley was elected mayor, but the two had known each other since 1940 when Bradley also served in the then segregated police department. The day after the election, the neutrality with which Davis spoke was as close to hostile as it could come. He refused to give his own views about Bradley's win and offered the most boilerplate comments about working with the new mayor and that Angelinos had spoken. He did, however, say that Bradley would have a hard time matching outgoing mayor Sam Yorty's degree of support within the LAPD. Yorty had again used the line that Bradley was anti-police throughout the mayoral contest. Davis did not comment on that accusation directly, but stressed that Bradley had been in the LAPD at a time when it was segregated, and said ominously "that the situation may have had some effect on Bradley's current attitude." It was a gratuitous shot across the bow directed at his new boss, the mayor of Los Angeles.

The consequences of Bradley's win were immediate: three of the Police Commission's five members resigned at once. Looked at one way, this was pretty standard when a new mayor takes office, but given all that Yorty had done to poison the well, it was a bad beginning.

The LAPD also had bad relationships with multiple minority groups at the time. A year before, the *Times* had reported: "Most Los Angeles County law enforcement agencies Friday declined to testify before an Assembly committee probing relationships between the police and minority groups. Only Beverly Hills and South Pasadena Police Departments broke the otherwise solid police boycott against the hearing...."

The women's movement had also affected the police department; internally, policewomen were pressing to be given equal promotion opportunities. Four months before Bradley's election, the *Times* reported that "The LAPD, which has not hired a policewoman in three-and-a-half years, was instructed Thursday [by the City Council] to assign women officers on a trial basis to traditionally-male law-enforcement activities." Davis responded that the imposition of standardized criteria for the hiring of police officers would lead to their being fewer policewomen, his logic being that height and weight standards would disqualify some women who were currently on the roll. Yet another festering challenge that faced the new mayor.

Probably the group with which the LAPD tussled most publicly and frequently when Bradley took office was the homosexual community. Davis, whose flagship project in these years was Team Venice—intended to cut crime by half in five years through neighborhood-specific police units—found himself frequently insisting that gays not be allowed onto the police force and defending the LAPD's targeting of gay bars.

Tom clearly had a police problem, and I was honored that he trusted me to be the one to solve it. The Police Commission is to the city of Los Angeles what the State Board of Education is to California's public school system. They review and sometimes create the regulations, they appoint the chief, they review the budget, they set policy, and they run investigations of the institution. It polices the police and is the locus of a lot of power.

All of a sudden, I was the president of a commission overseeing a very conservative police department with a very intelligent, very flamboyant, and very hostile chief, Ed Davis. He was the man who set the climate of command, and I focused on creating a good relationship with him because Tom Bradley had asked me. Slowly we began to get along. He even went so far as to attend an ACLU event with me! He gave me my own police department badge—which I accepted and still have—and attempted to give me a gun, which I emphatically did not accept!

"Ed, you're kidding!" I said. "I might hurt somebody, including myself!"

One day the chief and some of the other ranking officers took me up to the police academy for breakfast and to review the troops. I always enjoyed bringing my kids to as many events as possible, and this time Kim was lucky enough to be chosen. I am not sure she felt especially blessed, but I was certainly happy to have her with me. It was a great morning, and I was mingling with all of them and asked no one in particular, "Why do they all look alike? Why do they all have the same hair cut?" I think I took them by surprise by asking the kind of naïve question that no one would ask because the answer was thought to be so obvious. But once the question is actually asked out loud, it seemed no one had a decent answer.

There were some rumblings, and then someone said, "Discipline!" Which was not a sensible answer at all. And I said, "Well, you know, the Israeli Army, they had all these guys out there, and boy, they were good! Didn't seem to bother them that they didn't have the same hair cut!" That certainly took them by surprise! But I also pointed out that there were practically no African American officers in that department. Clearly that was what we would call, bureaucratically, "an area in need of improvement."

When he was there, Tom Bradley had actually been one of the few black officers in the ranks. I wanted to see if we could develop an outreach program to get more African Americans in that department. And I think I had some success. Bradley had appointed as my vice-chairman Sam Williams, who was a prominent African American lawyer. We were both committed to changing the racial composition of the department and imposing some incentives for recruitment of a more diverse police force.

Many direct and indirect benefits come from this, a point that should have been obvious then. Police should not be considered to be aliens but representatives of the community who were charged with maintaining safety. How on earth could that happen if there was an atmosphere of hostility and mistrust?

By this time, I had been on several public boards, and I knew what to look for. One of our responsibilities was to review the budget that the LAPD submitted to the City Council for approval. As I looked at that budget, I saw one entry with a great deal of money attached to it, but not a very clear category. I could not figure out what it was. So I started asking questions, just as I had done on my very first day at the meeting of the State Board of Education when I suspected a racial motive was driving a decision. This time, the issue had nothing to do with race—at least not directly—but with politics. The budget line item supported what appeared to be a somewhat mysterious group in the police department that was carrying out secret investigations.

It was practically like Richard Nixon's enemies list! For example, I discovered that they had been keeping tabs on Women4!—a very liberal West Side women's political action committee, and there was much more. I could not believe it. Davis knew that he had a few things to explain. "Okay," he said. "Come down to the station, I'll show you around, and we'll go through the files."

I had opened up a whole can of worms that went back to Davis' predecessor, a man named Bill Parker who had served in the police department for thirty-nine years, sixteen of them as chief. He inherited a very corrupt police department when he took over in 1950, and had actually tried to modernize it and clean it up. But in the process, he also instituted his own version of corruption by targeting minorities and anyone who did not meet his approval. Many considered him responsible for police brutality and the hostility that existed between the community and its officers. He wanted a lean and mean police force and was the guy who created the expression, "thin blue line."

What he also did was to direct the organized crime and intelligence division of the force to investigate not only gangsters but citizens he did not like. These included politicians and actors, community activists and liberal public figures. When he retired in 1966 the surveillance did not stop, and Sam Yorty probably benefitted from it. A politicized police department is one of the most dangerous institutions on earth, and I was determined that under my watch this would stop.

I was becoming a pretty seasoned veteran in two areas that are basic to the present and the future of our society: education and law enforcement. I recall a celebratory moment when these came together at an event at the

Los Angeles Music Center's Dorothy Chandler Pavilion. Both Mayor Tom Bradley and Superintendent Wilson Riles were there. Somehow these two big men decided to pick me up and carry me down the grand staircase between them. I cherish that memory to this day.

I had figured out how to make best use of what power I had to serve the community, and to serve my new, historic mayor. I loved working behind the scenes, and slowly I was seeing the great state of California, and the spectacular city of Los Angeles, changing for the better. To have been a part of that seismic change was a deeply gratifying companion to my legal work. I loved politics, but being a candidate for anything—even dogcatcher—was the furthest thing from my mind.

Candidates Bill Norris and Edmund G. "Jerry" Brown, Jr., 1974

20

"YOUNGER FOE": MY RACE FOR ATTORNEY GENERAL

One evening in January of 1974, Hal Kwalwasser, one of my young associates at Tuttle & Taylor, and I had been hard at work on a case in our downtown offices and took a little time out for dinner. We were just beginning our main course when he posed a question that radically changed my life. "Bill, why don't you run for Attorney General?" he asked, with the kind of casualness that seemed out of sync with asking me to become the most powerful lawyer in the State of California.

I almost burst out laughing. "What are you talking about?" I said. I had never considered running as a candidate for any office myself. When I came to L.A. after my clerkship with Justice Douglas, I was focused on earning a living to support my family. And besides my financial circumstances, I had no public recognition outside of the Democratic Establishment. "I'm not going to run for Attorney General!" was my reply.

Hal was unperturbed. He obviously had been thinking about this, and as any good lawyer he had planned his arguments for careful deployment. "Well, no other *serious* Democrat who is known is running for that office," he replied mildly.

Hal had qualified his statement by the word "serious" because another Democrat had entered the field: Vincent Bugliosi. He was a controversial and flamboyant lawyer, who had served in the L.A. District Attorney's office and prosecuted Charles Manson for his hideous crime. He had left the DA's office in 1972, and had just published a blockbuster book about the Manson case called *Helter Skelter*. Bugliosi seemed to be ubiquitous, in the papers, on television, on the radio, and took every opportunity he could to mention his work on the Manson trial. He brought up the case at *every* press conference and speaking engagement to sell both books and himself. One always had the impression his run for office was less about public service and more about sustaining his fame.

"No Democrat with his or her head on straight wants any part of him," Hal said. Then he began to gain steam. "Besides, you would have a really good ballot designation, 'President, Los Angeles Police Commission.' It will persuade the voters that you know something about crime."

I started to laugh, "Aw, c'mon Hal," I said. But the seed was definitely planted.

As I said to Hal, I knew the Democratic establishment in California very well—the relationship was a long and positive one. I had leadership roles in a number of campaigns with them from Rudd Brown's runs for Congress to Tom Bradley's successful and historic campaign for mayor. Hal's advice had ignited a flame of ambition for elected office in me, and I knew to whom I should turn for some smart advice.

The first person I talked to was Nelson Rising, a former O'Melveny lawyer who had brilliantly managed Bradley's mayoral campaign as well as John Tunney's bid for the Senate. He eventually went on to become the chairman and CEO of a huge real estate company called Catellus, which held all the property of the Southern Pacific Railroad. He was heavily involved in Democratic politics. He too was encouraging and suggested that we go visit Max Palevsky.

I had become friends with Max during Bobby Kennedy's campaign, and a few years later, he financed a significant chunk of Wilson Riles and Tom Bradley's campaigns. Max and I had a something important in common; we both grew up poor—he as a young Jew in Chicago—and the only reason we managed to get educated was because of the GI Bill. He studied math and philosophy as an undergraduate at the University of Chicago, and entered the doctoral program in philosophy at UCLA. He attended a lecture at Caltech by John von Neumann, the father of computers, and left academia to work on what became the first computer developed by Bendix in 1956. He went on to all of the business success I described before, and by now another of his little projects had begun to pan out, a little semiconductor startup he helped fund named Intel. He also still kept his hand in philosophy, and he was a great collector of art. In other words, he was a phenomenal brain, but as most geniuses he was not always the easiest person with whom to get along. He liked me though, and we got along together.

Nelson was enthusiastic about my Attorney General run, and together we went to have lunch with Max. The three of us met at a restaurant near Max's office, which was in a modern bank building in Westwood. Nelson and I told Max our idea and asked him what he thought. "Billy, if you are crazy enough to do this, of course you have my full support," he said. "My one concern is that I don't think that you are crazy enough to run for office!"

I guess I was just crazy enough. I resigned the presidency of the Los Angeles Police Commission and got to work.

Max was very clear about how he would fund campaigns. If he believed in you—as he did in me and in Tom Bradley—he would give as much as he could without being too far out of line. He would go to a certain point and then require his candidate to raise more money before he would give more. He would not want to be responsible for half the campaign chest, and that was fine with me. I knew that I needed to have a much broader base of support than just one genius.

I started to put together my campaign staff. I needed people I could trust and people who knew what they were doing. Fortunately, I was blessed with an abundance of both. My law partner and thoroughbred Republican Ed Tuttle wanted to chair my lawyer's committee! He was such a good friend and such a wonderful partner; I was extraordinarily touched by his confidence in me. Vic Fazio was my campaign manager. He was young and energetic and had built a great base of support in Sacramento where he was on the Planning Commission. Eventually he was elected to the U.S. Congress and served for nine terms, even as the Democratic Caucus chair. He was born for politics and had a fertile strategic mind.

My finance chair was Ira Yellin, the son of an Orthodox Rabbi, a Harvard Law graduate and a Marine (incredible combination—the man really had everything). He later became a visionary real estate developer who restored Grand Central Market downtown, and developed the Bradbury building, the Million Dollar Theater, and the Metropolitan Water District headquarters, but as a young lawyer, he already understood finance and had contacts throughout the city.

Eli Chernow was the brains heading up my issues team. We first met when he was a math major at Caltech in Pasadena and was working on the Henry Waxman for Congress campaign. I just saw something in him and persuaded him to go to Harvard Law, where he eventually became the editor of the Law Review. Of course when he graduated, I immediately recruited him for Tuttle & Taylor! I always had an eye for talent, and Eli was exceptionally talented. He ultimately became an L.A. Superior Court judge and highly sought after mediator and arbitrator.

One of Eli Chernow's main assistants was a bright young man who was still in college. I could not have trusted him more. His instincts were keen and his knowledge of me and my work was deep. His name was Don Norris and, yes, he is my son. Don was a natural in campaigns. We became especially close during those campaign days.

Phil Angelides also worked on my campaign as my driver. He was still in college but had already gone through his own, unsuccessful, campaign for City Council in Sacramento. Phil was a Coro Fellow—winning the very prestigious fellowship that was established in San Francisco in 1942 to train young people in leadership skills to become civic and political leaders. Phil later became a Treasurer for the State of California and a prominent developer.

I received a call at this time from my dear friend and college roommate Don Stokes. Don had just been appointed dean of Princeton's Woodrow Wilson School of Politics and Public Affairs, our old haunt, and was eager to tell me the news. When I told him I was going to run for Attorney General, he said, "Bill, you just trumped my ace!" But Don built an enduring legacy at Princeton, remaining as dean for eighteen years, developing the undergraduate program in public affairs, building a strong graduate and professional program, and doubling the size of the Woodrow Wilson School's faculty.

By the beginning of February, I was an official candidate. The *Los Angeles Times* ran a story on February 9, 1974 with the headline "LA Lawyer to Run for Attorney General; Norris Attacks Bugliosi; Hits Younger on Watergate." Hal was right when he noted that my Police Commission work would be significant. There it was, right in the lead! The story began:

> William A. Norris, an attorney and former president of the Los Angeles Police Commission, announced his candidacy Friday for the Democratic nomination for Attorney General. Norris, 47, said that a main Democratic foe, the former Los Angeles Dep Dist Atty Vincent Bugliosi has been waging a campaign that is an "insult to the people of California." And he said that the Republican incumbent, Evelle J. Younger, who is running for re-election, has not taken action or expressed moral indignation over Watergate....

Those few sentences pretty clearly sum up not just the main issues but also a sense of the times. The Watergate scandal, the "second rate burglary" that destroyed Nixon's presidency, was a continuing story throughout 1973 and 1974. The televised Watergate hearings began in May 1973, and the country was riveted by the story of corruption that unfolded before us. Vice President Spiro Agnew resigned in October of 1973 and revelations about the nefarious activities of the Nixon Administration constantly appeared in the news. Nixon was not going to resign until August, but the story colored all the politics of that off-year election year of 1974 and gave us the feeling that Democrats were once more going to surge back into power.

Governor Reagan had decided not to run for re-election—clearly he had greater ambitions—so the field for governor was wide open, and the young man who emerged as the Democratic candidate was Jerry Brown. We had recruited Jerry to Tuttle & Taylor in 1968 fresh out of Yale Law School, but he had not remained with us for long. In the late sixties, Brown moved from one political position to the next. He was appointed to the Los Angeles County Delinquency and Crime Commission (a political favor to his dad), was elected to a seat on the Los Angeles Community College Board of Trustees (a public election), and then in 1970, during a bitter campaign in which Reagan defeated my old pal Jesse Unruh, Jerry Brown became California's Secretary of State.

This was a very low profile and uninfluential office before Brown got into it, but he used it to compel members of the State Assembly to reveal the sources of their campaign donations. He also got the public's attention by pointing out how politicians were merely paying lip service to existing standards of campaign finance disclosure. He churned out press releases and held press conferences on this issue. Jerry was only 36, and he was running hard to become the governor. His campaign had the aura of inevitability about it. So my plan was to get through the primary—where we had to defeat Bugliosi in order to secure the Democratic nomination— and then grab Jerry Brown's coattails to sail into victory. I confess it was a bit strange to be grabbing the coattails of my former employee at Tuttle & Taylor!

The first step was to win the nomination. I loved being a candidate. My major opponent, Vince Bugliosi, was someone who I disagreed with on the issues and considered to be fundamentally untrustworthy—out to promote himself and lacking in judgment, if not personally erratic. For this reason, many prominent people in the Democratic Party wanted me to make sure he did not become the party's candidate. This made getting out there and campaigning every day very easy.

The California Democratic Council, the impressive affiliation of party groups throughout the state I learned about when working with Rudd Brown in 1958, snapped into action to support Jerry, of course, but also on my behalf. They all knew Bugliosi and appreciated not only that he should not be trusted, but also that he almost succeeded in beating an incumbent for L.A. District Attorney. That was scary for a lot of folks, and they were mobilized to make sure he did not get another shot at an elected office.

The first time that Vince Bugliosi and I met face to face was at the CDC endorsing convention. We both were keen for their endorsement. When the CDC vote was taken by the members, it appeared that I was the clear winner, but my euphoria was short lived. My son Don came up to me and brought me back down to earth. "They made a mistake," he said. "You have to have a super-majority of a certain number of votes. You got a simple majority, not a super-majority." That did not mean that Bugliosi won, only that I did not win by a sufficient margin.

By this time the CDC was proudly announcing that I had won and was their candidate. Don asked me, "What do we do?" And it was clear to me that we had only one option: "You go tell them of the mistake. Just go tell them. They have to withdraw the endorsement." He said okay, and he went up and explained the super-majority issue and in the end, it only worked in my favor. The press loved the fact that the winner had so much integrity, he refused the victory if it did not conform strictly to the rules. In the end, the voters gave me their endorsement and I secured the nomination to be the Democratic candidate for Attorney General. Then I dove into the campaign against Evelle Younger.

Younger had been the L.A. County District Attorney from 1964-1971 and was the incumbent Attorney General, so he was very well known as a solid, moderate Republican.

During the primary season I had gotten a lot of newspaper attention, the *Sacramento Bee*, the *San Francisco Chronicle*, even a backhanded compliment from the staunchly, resolutely Republican *Los Angeles Times*. On May 30, 1974, before the primary, the *Times* ran an editorial that had seven paragraphs in support of Younger, inevitably concluding, "The Attorney General is the people's lawyer. Younger has been an excellent one and we endorse him for re-election in November." Then came a scant, obligatory three paragraphs at the tail end on the Democrats in which they did allow that compared to Bugliosi, I "clearly [had] the better background and temperament for the office."

I was optimistic that the *Los Angeles Times*—the leading newspaper in my city, where I had made a name for myself as a lawyer and community activist—would cover my campaign with fairness and energy. But that pre-primary editorial was the last time that they actually were willing to mention my name! Throughout the general election, I was referred to as "Younger Foe"—relishing the pun, I am sure, where Younger could be both the proper noun referring to the incumbent, but also a little jab at my relative youth and implied inexperience. Forget about giving me any name recognition!

There was another reason for this, aside from the historic *Times'* alignment with the Republican Party—which of course, would have been enough. Otis Chandler, the publisher of the *Times*, had an exceedingly close and troubling relationship with Younger. Stories were beginning to come out in other news outlets about business deals involving an oil drilling company known as GeoTek, which was owned by a close friend of Otis Chandler's named Jack Burke. Burke and Chandler were deeply connected—Burke even was the godfather of Cathleen Chandler, Otis's oldest daughter. And when he had become a successful oilman, early on, he asked Otis if he wanted to invest in oil deals and if he knew of other potential investors.

One of them was Evelle Younger.

This became exceedingly complicated because the deals were not as pristine as people had imagined. Over eight years, from 1964 to 1971, Burke raised more than $30 million for investments in joint ventures to explore and drill for oil. For all these joint ventures, Geotek was the general partner and the investors were the limited partners. Geotek hired other companies run by Jack Burke to do the actual exploring and drilling, the investors just put up the cash. The relationship of all these companies to Jack Burke was never fully disclosed to investors, and there were allegations that Burke milked the joint ventures of an estimated $2.6 million.

When Burke was putting the joint ventures together, he let Chandler invest $200,000, gave him a seat on the Geotek board of directors, and also used him to recruit other investors. Somehow, Chandler did not tell the other investors that he was receiving almost half a million dollars in a combination of finder's fees and promotional shares of GeoTek stock through a secret deal structured so that there was no downside risk. Burke was eventually accused of fraud, and Chandler got dragged into the mess. Evelle Younger remained above the fray, even though he was an investor in this questionable arraignment. Moreover, as first DA and then Attorney General, he presumably could have had some involvement in prosecuting Burke, but declined to do so.[*]

The SEC began investigating in early 1970, but the story first broke in the *Wall Street Journal* in 1972. The *Los Angeles Times* had some difficulty covering the case and said as little as possible. Otis Chandler was one of the defendants—later cleared in 1975 at a cost of about $1 million in legal fees. The GeoTek story was in the background during the campaign. But the Chandler and Younger connection to the scandal never surfaced in the press, because Younger would not debate me and the *Times* was silent on the issue.

---

[*] See *SEC v. Geotek*, 426 F. Supp. 715 (N.D. Cal. 1976) (for structure of investment scheme) and Dennis McDougal, *Privileged Son: Otis Chandler and the Rise and Fall of the L.A. Times Dynasty* (New York: Perseus Publishing 2001), pp. 285, 299-301 (for Chandler's role in the scandal, and Younger's investment).

Other than the *Times*, the press was very positive about my campaign, and I began to garner strong support all over the state. My team compiled a list of supporters and they were, from A to Z, the most prominent and influential Democrats in the state. Tom Lynch, who had been Attorney General under Pat Brown from 1964 to 1971, was the honorary chairman and on the list there were literally hundreds of bold-faced names, a combination of "This is Your Life" and "This is California!" Actors, like Warren Beatty, my old friend the Caltech professor Barclay Kamb and his wife, politicians Henry Waxman and Willie Brown, I look at the list today and marvel at what a distinguished group of people had confidence in me.

Tom Lynch, along with Michael Traynor and several others, also helped form a *Lawyers Committee to Elect Bill Norris Attorney General* —a remarkable group that included a long list of stellar attorneys from San Francisco. Some, like Frank Farella, were friends of mine from Stanford days. Boalt Hall Professor Bob Cole was a co-clerk with me on the Supreme Court. Coincidentally, the list included John Levin and Michael Kahn whose law firm I would join many years later when I retired from the bench.

The year promised to be a strong one for Democrats. Nixon had resigned on August 9, 1974, so the mid-term elections took place three months after that and two months after Ford had pardoned Nixon. Pundits thought they were seeing a long-term Democratic realignment. My challenge was that Younger was just not that controversial a candidate—not a great Attorney General, but not horrible either. He was lukewarm, amiable and competent, someone who flew just under the radar and wanted to get his job done quietly.

It was hard to engage him vigorously on the issues, especially since he refused to face off with me in a debate. At one point in August, I focused on California utility rates and promised that I would fight for consumers instead of cave in to the Public Utilities Commission's recent award of a $200 million rate increase to the Pacific Telephone Company—this was a time of a monopoly in the telephone business. The award was egregious, especially when the staff recommended that phone rates be reduced by $114 million! It seemed a perfect example of the way that Younger backed off of the watchdog role of Attorney General that was so important.

Running for public statewide office provided me with a crash course in campaign finance. I had never before appreciated how unbelievably expensive it was to make things happen. Because Younger refused to debate me and the *Times* could only refer to me as "Younger Foe," I had a real challenge in gaining widespread name recognition. This made it tougher to raise money, so I needed to get on television. David Garth, who was the famous political guru back in New York and seen as the inventor of the political commercial, was a friend of Nelson Rising and had been involved in the Tom Bradley campaigns. Garth came up with one spot that was designed to tell the voters who I really was, from my modest beginnings in Turtle Creek, my military service, my education, my law career and all my public service—in about 30 seconds! Apparently I did pretty well in the spot, but when I heard it for the first time and saw it on television—it was over so fast, and cost a fortune!

Another element of the campaign that was exceptionally expensive but critical was polling, and when we took a field poll in late September, we seemed to be doing well, but not that well. We were not going to raise the white flag, but the lackluster numbers did have an effect on my fundraising ability. So once more, I needed to turn to Max Palevsky. He was having some serious health problems that required heart surgery. He had always been clear that his support had its limits, but at that point we needed to buy some TV spots and we needed Max's support. He was going into surgery again, and when we reached him he was literally lying on the gurney on his way into the OR. His wife Lynda, who was a big supporter, followed him down the hospital corridor with a pen and a form he had to sign for the funds to be transferred from his bank account to ours. And Max, on the gurney, signed it. Max was very demanding. He had very high standards. He would say what he wanted to say. And he was never one to equivocate, never one who wanted his name to be everywhere. He had nothing to gain by helping me get elected Attorney General—but he was loyal.

There were so many powerful moments in that campaign. Tom Bradley sent mailings into South Los Angeles and the black community just came alive for me. At one point, Teddy Kennedy visited California, and John Nolan made sure that we were in touch. I travelled with Kennedy and he always let me get off the plane first, so I could enjoy some of the attention from his presence. On another occasion, I went up to San Francisco to campaign in the charismatic Assemblyman Willie Brown's territory. Willie Brown always insisted on introducing me, but he was such a fantastic speaker, such a spellbinder, that I could only begin my remarks after his introduction by saying, "And now I have to follow *him*?"

My contacts and my friends back at the State Board of Education, and the Wilson Riles campaign, came out in strong support of me. I loved traveling all over the state and talking to folks, seeing parts of California I had never before visited. And even though I was forever "Younger Foe" in the *Los Angeles Times*—later some *Los Angeles Times* reporters even apologized to me for my treatment in that paper—I had fantastic support in other papers throughout the state. The *California Journal* said, "The word seemed to spread by word of mouth that Norris was one of the best

Democratic candidates for anything this year. Norris ran like gangbusters, even in the 'cow countries' where he had previously been unknown." And of course, we could count on the great coattails of Jerry Brown.

My last interview during the campaign was with Bob Abernathy on NBC—another Princeton grad—and he spoke to me about the GeoTek scandal. It was the only time that I felt that this issue was being at all examined in the context of the election. But we knew it was too late.

After the interview was over, he apologized. "Bill, in Los Angeles, the TV stations, the radio stations, can't deal with an issue like this," he said." It requires too much depth, and we don't have the resources to dig into it. The only place that can do that kind of investigation is the *Los Angeles Times* and they won't touch it." At least I felt a certain solace in the knowledge that the deck was stacked.

By the end of October, my numbers had improved but all of a sudden, what we had assumed would be an easy victory for Jerry was turning into a real nail biter. Brown ran a good-government campaign, but his lead on his opponent, the state controller Houston Flournoy, shrank as the campaign was winding down. A very good guy, Flournoy was a former political science professor at Pomona College and a state Assemblyman, and he almost pulled off a win. We faltered going down the home stretch as Jerry's coattails all but disappeared. In the end, Brown won—I am happy to say—but his margin of victory was only 2.9 percent, and I lost.

So I did not become the Attorney General of the great State of California. My brother George came out for what was supposed to be our victory party. He loved the banner that we had put on the wall that said, "Go Turtle Creek!"

Of course I was disappointed that we did not win. Of course I wished that all that time, effort and money contributed by all those supporters would have resulted in a successful campaign. But when I gave my concession speech, I knew that this was the genius of American democracy. One person. One vote. One winner. One loser. But always, new opportunities around the corner.

"My Pop"

Mayor Tom Bradley and Bill Norris

21

MCDONNELL DOUGLAS AND PROP 13

Naturally I was disappointed not to have become California's Attorney General, but my disappointment was soon replaced by a kind of relief that I would be able to devote my attention once more to my law practice, politics, and civic engagement. I was back in my natural habitat! I had been on leave from the firm to run my campaign when the aircraft manufacturer McDonnell Douglas was involved in what the *Los Angeles Times* referred to as "the worst disaster in aviation history." On March 3, 1974, one of its planes—this one a Turkish airliner—crashed nine minutes after taking off from Orly airport.

I was campaigning at that point, but like everyone else, I was riveted by the early reports of the crash on television. A cargo door had blown off after takeoff, causing the pressurized air from the cabin to explode into the atmosphere and crush the cabin floor and steering equipment. The plane plummeted into a forest just outside of Paris and killed 346 people— nearly two times the previous aviation fatality record for a single flight.

I knew that Tuttle & Taylor would have a huge piece of litigation on our hands, and the firm immediately jumped into action. I had built a solid team, and they began the preliminary work for McDonnell Douglas in the months after the crash, but the company was chomping at the bit for my involvement. The *New York Times* lambasted McDonnell Douglas Company, the contractor, General Dynamics, the subcontractor, Turkish Airlines, and the Federal Aviation Agency (FAA), the United States government body that inspects the safety of all planes produced domestically, for their "fatal irresponsibility."[*]

I immediately took over the case after the election and began to focus on what would be one of the longest and most complex cases of my entire career. It consumed an enormous amount of my time over the next six years. The scope was unprecedented—1,100 wrongful death suits worth more than $125 million in total claims, which would be over $610 million today.

This was not a class action; there were many individual claims originally filed all over the country. The courts of appeals, in all of the circuits, had a system whereby if disparate cases in different circuits or districts had common facts, they consolidate. This is a classic situation: one aircraft, one airplane crash, so a committee met and conferred and determined which district would serve as the central district where every case would be tried. All the cases were consolidated in Los Angeles.

An investigation of the wreckage found that the jet—a DC-10 model—was not equipped with a support plate, which had caused the cargo door to malfunction. Plaintiffs blamed the manufacturer for willfully putting a poorly designed aircraft on the market. After painstakingly going through all the records, we argued that the door was properly equipped and inspected before the plane was delivered to Turkish Airlines in 1972, two years before the crash. We pointed out that the malfunction must have been due to alterations to the door made by the airlines during those years. Still others pointed the finger at the FAA for failing to properly inspect the plane before it was sold to an international company, going so far as to call the agency a "machine ... that is woefully outdated."[†]

There was a traditional airplane crash law firm in town, which was taking the depositions but the part of the case that was my responsibility was not the facts of the wrongful death lawsuits but rather the overall strategy and the questions of law. I recognized very early on that it would be much too costly for McDonald Douglas to go to trial with all the plaintiffs. I realized that if some of the evidence ever got before a jury, it would be very adverse to the interests of my client. So I took the initiative and decided to try to settle the case.

There were two other defendants in the case, General Dynamics, which was responsible for the fuselage, and of course the carrier, Turkish Airlines. I went back to New York with one of my Tuttle & Taylor

---

[*] "Fatal Irresponsibility," *New York Times* (1923-Current file); Mar. 23, 1974; ProQuest Historical Newspapers: The New York Times with Index p. 30.

[†] Richard Witkin, "The Nation: On Trial—DC-10 and F.A.A.," *New York Times* (1923-Current file); June 3, 1979; ProQuest Historical Newspapers: The New York Times with Index p. E5.

attorneys and negotiated with the other two defendants and all the insurance carriers, including Lloyds of London. We made a favorable agreement among the three defendants in which they would not contest liability with each plaintiff and would go forward and try the cases (or settle) as to the amount of damages. The condition of this deal was that the plaintiffs would not seek punitive damages for the defendants' alleged malicious misconduct. I figured most of the plaintiffs' lawyers would want to get their fees fast and move on. By September 1976, lawyers had worked behind the scenes to settle the claims of nearly 200 passengers through agreements worth an estimated $35 million, or about $200,000 per passenger. This would be more than a million dollars today.

Though we settled more than half of the claims out of court, the remaining claims went to trial in Los Angeles—a major hub of the McDonnell Douglas Company, the third largest commercial aircraft manufacturer in the world and the largest defense contractor in the United States. Judge Pierson M. Hall, a Senior District Judge considered a preeminent authority on aviation law, presided over these claims. Judge Hall had previously presided over nine air-disaster cases with a no-nonsense approach that often led to mutually agreeable settlements.

Most of the trials were just straightforward examinations of the amount of damages suffered by the individual plaintiffs. But there were some plaintiffs who refused to waive punitive damages and tried to really cash in. From 1975 to 1980, I argued a number of cases on behalf of the McDonnell Douglas Company and questioned the legal basis for seeking punitive damages in these wrongful death suits. The issue whether they would be entitled to punitive damages in a wrongful death case went up to the Ninth Circuit Court of Appeals.

I briefed that case with my colleagues at Tuttle & Taylor. By that time, President Carter nominated me to be a Ninth Circuit judge. Eventually, I would be arguing the McDonnell Douglas case before the very judges that would soon become my colleagues, but that is a story for a later chapter!

As hard as I was working on my clients' cases, I did not live in a complete McDonnell Douglas bubble. Politics demanded some of my attention, because 1976 was also a presidential election year. There was a sense of real optimism among Democrats that we would win this race. Gerald Ford was a very decent, but not particularly inspiring, president, and I had real confidence in Jimmy Carter as a candidate. I had already checked him out with some of my friends around the country who knew him very well, and I was quite impressed.

I was involved in his campaign in California, particularly leading up to the convention in Madison Square Garden in New York. When Jimmy Carter made his sweep through California to secure delegates for the convention, I put together a small group of extremely powerful Democrats, including my old friend Max Palevsky. These were heavy-hitters, especially in terms of their historic financial support for Democrats. After they met, they had a press conference with Carter. That did a lot to help the California campaign of this peanut farmer governor from Georgia.

Some of us who were supporters of Jimmy Carter, and planning to go to the convention, were still unsure about who the best vice presidential candidate might be. We got together and sent Jimmy Carter a telegram. When we met and there was some discussion about this, he had said, "Why not the best?" In our telegram we wrote, "Why not the best, why not Fritz Mondale?"

The most thrilling moment of the convention was when Barbara Jordan, a Texan and the first Southern African American woman to be elected to the U.S. House of Representatives, delivered a keynote address. She immediately pointed out how unusual it was for a person of her gender and her race to be addressing this convention. But she refused to belabor this, or level any attacks on the Republicans. She said in ringing tones, "We are a people in a quandary about the present. We are a people in search of our future. We are a people in search of a national community. We are a people trying not only to solve the problems of the present: unemployment, inflation ... but we are attempting on a larger scale to fulfill the promise of America. We are attempting to fulfill our national purpose; to create and sustain a society in which all of us are equal."

I watched her, remembering the bruising campaigns of Riles and Bradley, and felt a sense of hope and optimism about this country that seemed so fitting during the bi-centennial year. We all worked hard in California to get Jimmy Carter elected President, nonetheless Gerald Ford and Bob Dole carried the state with 49.5 percent of the vote to Jimmy Carter's 47.6 percent. But Carter became our President, and whatever else you might think of his tenure, I must say he made some very good judicial appointments!

Even though not a presidential election year, 1978 was a very significant year for several elections. Yvonne Burke is a very prominent and elegant woman who was the first African American woman to represent Los Angeles in Congress. Many years later she served in a very powerful role as one of the five members of the L.A. County Board of Supervisors. In 1978 she did not run for Congress again, but ran for Attorney General—the same position that I had tried for and lost four years before. In the Democratic primary she ran against Burt Pines, who was a very decent City Attorney. I was extremely conflicted about whom to support—Burt had been a good friend and a great political colleague of mine—but in the end I had to support Yvonne. The possibility of electing an African American woman to be our Attorney General was impossible not to support, so I made the difficult call to Burt and told him that I was going to work for Yvonne. She won the primary, but lost the election to State Senator George Deukmejian—who would later become our governor.

In June of 1978 the biggest event of Jerry Brown's first term as governor created a tsunami in California—the passage of Proposition 13, dubbed the "People's Initiative to Limit Property Taxation." The driver behind the proposition was Howard Jarvis, a lobbyist who had lost races for U.S. Senate and mayor of Los Angeles. Jarvis was an anti-tax true believer. He and Paul Gann had it written up, gathered the required signatures, and raised the money to get it on the primary ballot. They campaigned hard for its passage and found a very receptive audience in the electorate.

Prop 13 appealed to many more voters than just the ideologues. Property values (and the corresponding tax assessments) in California were rising precipitously—by up to 120 percent, according to the *Los Angeles Times*—in the four years that Brown had been in office. Property taxes in the state were a reflection of both the tax rate and the assessed value of properties. Since tax rates went as high as ten percent, and the assessed values were increasing every year, people's taxes were spiraling, and fear of losing one's home was widespread. Jarvis, campaigning for Prop 13, claimed that there were older Californians who were reduced to eating cat food in order to pay their taxes.

A related issue was the California Supreme Court's 1971 decision in *Serrano v. Priest* that wealthy and poor public school districts had to receive equal funding. Redistribution of tax funds had been used to get money to poorer districts in the years since Serrano, much to the resentment of taxpayers in higher brackets who did not want their higher taxes going to support schools in other districts. Prop 13 dealt with this perceived injustice and the spiraling level of taxes by setting the state property tax rate at one percent of the worth of a home as assessed in 1975-76, as long as the home had the same owner since that assessment.

All the changes created by Prop 13 were to be written into the California State Constitution as an amendment and would be changeable only by another public initiative; it could not be altered by the state legislature. Governor Brown and state legislators freaked out about the usurpation of their power and the prospect of severely lowered public funds. Jurisdictions would lose about 57 percent of existing tax revenue, eliminating $7 billion of the $11.4 billion in property tax revenue collected each year. Brown told voters, "[There's] no sugar daddy in Sacramento who will bail you out if Proposition 13 passes."

The legislature wrote up the rival Proposition 8 and placed it on the same primary ballot as 13. Prop 8 would have likewise cut property taxes dramatically, but it wouldn't have made the changes structural or placed possible future changes out of the hands of legislators. Much to my shock and dismay, my horror really, Prop 13 passed with 65% of the vote and Prop 8 failed with 47%; moreover, 70% of eligible voters turned out for the June primary election, as compared with the 45% of eligible voters who had participated in '74's general election. This was clearly the start of what was to be called the "Taxpayers Revolt."

Brown switched his course and endorsed 13 as soon as it had passed, arguing that his job was to reflect the expressed will of Californians.

Shortly after the passage of Prop 13, I was asked to represent the twenty-two school districts throughout the state in their challenge to Prop 13. Its effects on education were devastating as school districts throughout the state saw their budgets not just slashed but eviscerated. Why did they come to me? I figured that they knew me through my work on the State Board of Education, and I could not say no to them. I thought it was a terrible thing for the State of California and made no secret of my opinion.

Once again my colleagues at Tuttle & Taylor stepped up with their commitment to pro bono representation and worked with me to file a direct action in the California Supreme Court. The court had discretion as to whether to hear it or send it back to the trial court. They of course took it. I thought we had a pretty good case, and our brief was exceptionally good. I was aided in the writing of the brief by my colleagues Stan Fickle and Nancy Howard. Stan Fickle, a graduate of the University of Indiana Law School, had clerked for a federal District Court Judge who was a friend of Bill Brennan. His judge had urged the Justice to hire Stan as a law clerk. We reached out and recruited Stan Fickle for Tuttle & Taylor, and even though he had never even been to California he accepted. He had a wife, a couple of kids, and had served in the Peace Corps. At first blush he was not very impressive. He mumbled, had a little beard, shuffled around, and was a constitutional lawyer of the first order!

The case had a name as large as its importance: *Amador Valley Joint Union High School District et al. v. State Board of Equalization*. We argued to the California Supreme Court that Proposition 13 represented such a drastic and far-reaching change in the nature and operation of our governmental structure that it had to be considered a "revision" of the state Constitution, not just a mere "amendment." It did not merely change the way property taxes were imposed, it made changes to the way the state legislature could make decisions regarding all other types of taxes, and it greatly limited the powers of local governments to change or initiate taxes.

A revision of this magnitude could not be made to the Constitution by process of the initiative, but only by a constitutional convention.

I was very proud of the brief and said as much when I was at a meeting in Mayor Tom Bradley's home in Hancock Park. One of Tom's advisers who was there was Paul Ziffren. Paul was a major political force in California, national Democratic committeeman, quite a few years older than I. He had three sons, all lawyers. Paul asked me how the case was going, and I said, "Well, I've got the brief here, but I haven't argued it yet." Paul wanted to read it and took a copy of the brief. And then the next time we met, he said, "Bill, it's one of the best briefs I've ever read. But do you really think that this Supreme Court is going to strike down Proposition 13, when they all have to face the people at the ballot box for re-election? Take the needle out of your arm!"

Paul was right of course.

I was scheduled to give the opening argument on September 22, 1978. But I had gotten terribly sick to my stomach the night before. I just did not know what I was doing, but I knew that I had to get up to San Francisco to make the argument. The adrenaline started flowing and I made the opening arguments. Then the Attorney General, Evelle Younger, argued on behalf of Prop 13 very briefly (which was more than I got him to argue against me during our campaign four years earlier). Then the deputy attorney general took over from there. When it was my turn to make the final argument, I addressed the Supreme Court Chief Justice, Rose Byrd.

"I would like permission to have my colleague Stan Fickle argue the final argument, your Honor," I said.

I gave him no notice! Absolutely none.

Stan, incredulous, looked up at me. "Go ahead, Stan," I said. "You can do it." I knew that I had to get out of there. I was feeling wretched. And Stan took over brilliantly, as I knew he would. I walked outside the courtroom and was immediately surrounded by all these cameras and microphones. I was getting all these questions, and I did not know what I was saying. All I knew later was that a lot of folks heard me and saw me on television from all over the country. Unfortunately, our challenge was not successful. The Supreme Court said that it was their solemn duty "to zealously guard" the initiative power, it being "one of the most precious rights of our democratic process." Paul Ziffren's prediction was spot on. In the years to come, I was proven right about the terrible consequences of Proposition 13. And I took up the fight again many years later.

All this was business as usual. I had a lot of balls in the air, and 1979 was going to toss a wildly colorful and quite unexpected ball my way that was to become one of the most exciting, demanding, and fulfilling legacies of my life.

In front of MOCA: Eli Broad, Founding Chairman; Mayor Tom Bradley;
Bill Norris, Founding President; and Richard Koshalek, Director

22

MOCA AND ME

During my campaign for Attorney General, some dear friends introduced me to a woman named Merry Wiester. She was a contemporary art consultant and occupied a world that was very interesting for me but miles away from one with which I was familiar. Wandering through a museum or an art gallery had never been a part of my life, and I often looked back and asked myself why, when I went to a university with the most outstanding art history department in the country, did I not take a single art history course taught at Princeton? But kids from Turtle Creek don't tend towards art history classes. And yet, Merry must have thought there was some hope for me when she came to my apartment on Bunker Hill and saw a lithograph by Sam Francis hanging on the wall. I had bought that piece all on my own from Gemini G.E.L. Art Gallery and love it to this day. Merry and I got married after the campaign was over, and I embarked on my education in contemporary art from my passionate and knowledgeable wife.

When the Pasadena Museum of Modern Art ran out of operating funds in 1974, it made a deal with Norton Simon, the Hunt Food entrepreneur whose business holdings were vast. He was a serious art collector of old masters and impressionists. In the sixties he spent $4 million dollars on a huge collection of Old Masters from a private gallery in New York and was looking for a place to house his impressive collection. When the Pasadena Museum became desperate, he stepped in, renamed it the Norton Simon Museum and moved most of the contemporary art into the basement. The consequences were significant. All of a sudden, there was no modern or contemporary art museum in all of Los Angeles!

The need for a permanent home for the contemporary arts in Los Angeles had long been a common refrain among artists and art patrons.

173

Despite boasting the second largest population of working artists in the United States (second only to New York City) and some of the top art schools, these conversations rarely amounted to more than a collective catharsis. The financial collapse of the Pasadena Museum made the situation more acute. Many of the city's talented artists, collectors, and dealers had little opportunity or institutional support to thrive. They were instead left to look to other cities with a more established and centralized art infrastructure.

I would certainly not have paid as much attention to all of this had Merry not been as involved in the art scene as she was. The loss of the Pasadena Museum had been a topic of conversation for years, but it became more urgent in 1979. Merry and I had moved into our new home in Hancock Park, and one morning she said, "Bill, all the art enthusiasts in the city have no idea what to do other than stand around, wring their hands and say, 'Ain't it awful?' Somebody should try to do something about that, and that somebody should be you." I looked up at her and wondered what she possibly could be getting at. I was working hard on my law practice. The McDonnell Douglas case and Prop 13 were hugely demanding, as she well knew. Besides, she was the art expert. I knew law and politics.

She was suggesting nothing less than the establishment of a new museum of contemporary art in Los Angeles, and she appreciated that this was not just about art, this was going to be about politics and knowing what levers to pull to get things done. She thought I was the only one in town who understood all the political lines from downtown to the West Side, and parts beyond and in between. Her suggestion seemed like a kind of impulsive, off the cuff notion and very easy to dismiss. I replied, "Look, I'd just as soon not do that." Then I realized that I did not really have a choice as far as Merry was concerned. "You've got to," she said.

I knew that this was going to involve one careful step at a time, and that it certainly would take more than just the two of us. In January, 1979, I pulled together four or five others, including Fran Savitch, who was a top aide to Mayor Bradley and real estate developer Rob McLeod, and we began touring some old buildings on Spring Street downtown that might be feasible sites for our museum. We had no money, we had no art, we had no board, we had no non-profit corporation, but we did have an idea. And we had chutzpah. We met and talked and toured potential sites, and as interesting as that all was, I knew that this was getting us nowhere. We needed to make things more formal, and we needed some political help.

I took Fran with me and went to talk to my old friend Tom Bradley. I explained to him what we were doing. Our efforts felt to me like starting a political campaign with an unknown candidate. "I need some legitimacy,

Tom," I said. "I need people who can give me some backing and some heft in the art world and the community."

Tom warmed up to the idea, but first he had to tease me a little. He said, "Bill, what do you expect from me? You know that since Proposition 13 passed six months ago, we don't have any money for this sort of thing. After all, you represented the school districts that challenged the constitutionality of Prop 13—and you lost!"

He was right. We both knew that I tried to get that misguided proposition tossed out in the *Amador* case, but was unsuccessful.

"What do you want me to do, Bill?" Tom asked.

I told him that I wanted him to appoint an advisory committee that would have his imprimatur as the Mayor's Advisory Committee on a Museum of Modern Art. Once we had that, I could get out there and do a better job of getting people's attention. He said okay as long as I was the Chair. I guess he wanted someone he trusted to ensure that his reputation would be protected. He asked that I include Marcia Simon Weisman on the Committee. He had recently attended a political fundraising event at the Beverly Hills Hotel and was seated with Joel Wachs, a councilman and patron of the arts, and Marcia Simon Weisman, an avid art collector and tireless fundraiser. They began talking about the dearth of contemporary art space in L.A., and soon it was the focus of their conversation that night. Tom would not have expected me to be such a champion of the project, but when I walked in to talk with him that day, he realized that we might be able to pull something together.

Tom's creative juices started flowing. With an eye toward transforming downtown Los Angeles into a world class city center, he agreed to explore opportunities to develop a contemporary art museum in the heart of L.A.—a move that would eventually become a key catalyst for a revival of the area that continues to this day. That was how the Mayor's Museum Advisory Committee was created and charged with exploring the feasibility of making this new museum a reality.

I was the chair and suggested we ask Marcia Weisman to serve as the committee's vice chair. The group consisted of six additional members, including: Fran Savitch, Bradley's top aide and troubleshooter; Maureen Kindell, president of the Los Angeles Board of Public Works; Gary Familian, a businessman, fundraiser, and patron of the arts; Betye Monell Burton, a former trustee of the Pasadena Museum of Art; Ira Yellin, a prominent civic leader and longtime advocate for the revitalization of downtown Los Angeles; and Rob McLeod, a downtown commercial real estate expert.

At the outset, we operated out of a small corner of Mayor Bradley's office, but soon moved to my office at Tuttle & Taylor. As usual, the firm's commitment to pro bono community work could not have been more complete. They offered us whatever we needed in terms of support, which was essential since we were broke. We were tasked with overseeing every aspect of the museum's creation, ranging from identifying a site to break ground and hiring an architect, to defining the artistic vision of the institution and amassing a reputable permanent art collection, and perhaps most importantly, fundraising for both a building and for operating expenses. Bradley's one stipulation was that no public money could be solicited for the museum's operating costs. To move forward, private donors would need to come up with the money.

I had no clue how much money we would need to raise, but I always had a good sense for matching people and projects, and I knew Robert Rowan, who lived in Pasadena and was a very successful real estate developer. He was one of the most committed collectors of contemporary art in the whole area, and he had been chairman of the Pasadena Museum.

I visited him and said, "Bob, I want you to be on the board, I need you." He agreed to be on the board, but pointed out that he was "not going to make the same mistake twice." The mistake he said he had made, or his board had made, was to use their money to build the building for the Pasadena Museum, which left them nothing for operating expenses. I appreciated this issue and suggested that we begin to raise money for an endowment that would throw off sufficient funds for operating expenses. "What's the minimum that we need for that endowment?" I asked. His reply? "Ten million dollars."

I filed this number away for future use.

In June, a journalist named Barbara Isenberg, who covered cultural affairs for the *Los Angeles Times* and had picked up some information about the Mayor's Advisory Committee, wrote a story about the committee and the hope for a new museum. In the story, she quoted Tom Bradley, who said, "A group of people had been talking, touring and looking at potential museum sites for a contemporary art museum and had approached me about my interest. I encouraged them and arranged for them to meet at my office. They understand that they have to raise the money privately and believe it can be done." Isenberg also interviewed me and I described the committee, telling her, "We represent an almost self-appointed group of people who share an interest in 20th-century art and who believe that the lack of a modern art museum in Los Angeles is a glaring void in our cultural life." Barbara followed up this piece with another article the next day about the interest of the city's art collectors in a new museum.

So we were out in the open. Five days later, I received a letter from Don Cosgrove, the head of the Community Redevelopment Agency of the City of Los Angeles. In his June 15 letter, Cosgrove wrote: "The Agency strongly supports your statement, quoted in the L.A. Times, on behalf of committee members that 'the lack of a modern art museum in Los Angeles is a glaring void in our cultural life.' We enthusiastically endorse your goal of establishing a modern art museum in Los Angeles and would like to offer our services to your committee in identifying suitable sites or facilities in the downtown area as well as other appropriate assistance."

I had no idea what that meant, but I would find out six weeks later. In the meantime, another letter arrived at my desk as a result of the Isenberg articles in the *Times*. This one was from Sherri Geldin, a Phi Beta Kappa graduate and summa from UCLA and an MBA with a specialization in Arts Management, also from UCLA. It was one of the best-written letters I had ever read, and relying on my nose for great talent, I offered her a job as our first staff member and an office at Tuttle & Taylor. She worked tirelessly on every aspect of getting the museum started, built and operating, and served as the Associate Director. Later she would move to Ohio and the Wexner Center of the Arts and become one of the most respected museum directors in the country.

Six weeks later, I brought several committee members to meet with Cosgrove at the CRA's offices. Cosgrove laid out a breathtaking proposal. "What do you think of Bunker Hill as a potential site for a museum?" he asked us. I was flabbergasted. Not two weeks earlier, Merry and I had been driving along Grand Avenue, when I pointed to the top of Bunker Hill, not far from the Music Center. "If I could pick a site for the art museum, I'd pick this one," I said. As Cosgrove pulled out plans for a proposed cultural institution in that exact location, I could not help but wonder: was this for real?

In many ways, these were the two most important turning points in the history of the founding of MOCA, and they were interrelated: the article by Barbara Isenberg and the letter from Don Cosgrove of the Community Redevelopment Agency. "This project is going to be so big that we thought maybe there would be money to build some sort of a cultural center there, like an art museum," Cosgrove said. "Are you interested?" I just said to myself, "I can't believe this! I think we have a museum!"

The CRA's proposal would not only develop a derelict swath of downtown but also provided the land to construct a wholly new structure to house a museum. Great so far, but who would pay for the building? As part of the CRA's provisions as a public agency, 1.5 percent of all funds spent on development projects were to be allocated to public arts. Usually, this funded a commanding sculpture in a courtyard or something. Why not take advantage of the large sums of money for redeveloping Bunker Hill and allocate the 1.5% toward a public art space instead?

The proposed museum would be a major feature of the CRA's effort to revitalize the neighborhood of Bunker Hill, an 11.2 acre sprawling slice of Los Angeles's neglected downtown. The facilities would occupy 100,000 square feet of the new development at a cost of $16 million. When the CRA sent out the request for proposals to real estate developers for this ambitious undertaking, they included a letter from me to the CRA, explaining our dream and what we hoped to accomplish.

Then came another meeting with Tom Bradley in which he told me that the CRA was going to give us the land in the form of a long-term lease and the developer was going to give us the money for the building. Then Tom had one more question, "Bill, where's your operating money coming from?" My meeting with Rowan prepared me with the answer.

"We will be required to have a 501(c)(3) structure for the whole thing, and we will have to raise $10 million as an operating endowment over a period of two years, a symbol of community support for the endeavor, "I said. "Or we won't be included in this development project." He said, "That sounds okay." I pulled those numbers out of the air, but did it confidently since it was the number Bob Rowan had given me.

The momentum continued from there. My first target was Eli Broad. Eli was the only man who built not one but two Fortune 500 companies in two totally different industries: one was in home building and the other in insurance. He was a great philanthropist and was very involved in education—so I got to know him in that world. But he also was a dedicated patron of the arts and a passionate collector of contemporary art. Marcia Weisman invited the Broads, the Norrises and artists Tony Berlant, Ed Moses and Bob Graham to her beach house in Trancas. Eli and I took a long walk on the beach as I described the vision for this new museum, the arrangement with CRA, and our need for an endowment. He got it immediately.

At the end of our chat, he said, "You've got your first million." I shook his hand, I said, "Eli, with the first million dollars, you're the founding chairman." He said, "Bill, you got the deal with the city, you're the founding president!" It was not very democratic, but away we went. One of his stipulations was that we would not go public with Eli's incredible generosity until we got a commitment from a second million-dollar donor.

We soon hired Andrea Van de Kamp, a professional fundraiser, to help secure large donations, and she and Merry dove into the fundraising. Together with Van de Kamp, I turned to my old friend Max Palevsky, this time for his artistic and not his political patronage. Eli and I created an architecture committee and appointed Palevsky as chairman. Maybe we would not have had to. Max was such a good friend and a visionary, he could immediately see the importance of this project. He particularly loved architecture and pledged the next million.

The campaign's third million came through yet another committee, this one comprised of local artists. Chaired by the sculptor DeWain Valentine, the Artists Advisory Council had been meeting on a weekly basis for months. When they first got together, I told them that they were forbidden to talk about art, they had to talk about money. That formula proved effective, and together with installation artist Robert Irwin, Valentine produced Robert O. Anderson, chairman of the Arco Corporation. Following an hour-long meeting with the oil tycoon at Broad's Westside mansion, Eli and I had secured our third million. Who knew artists could be such phenomenal fundraisers?

In November, 1979, Tuttle & Taylor filed the original MOCA Articles of Incorporation, naming Marcia and me, along with Jeff Grausam, a T&T partner, as the incorporators. Jeff, along with other T&T lawyers worked on the real estate and corporate aspects of the deal on a pro bono basis for many months, and I could not have been more grateful. Later, the first trustees were named—Eli Broad, Bill Norris, and Marcia Weisman.

One of the obstacles we faced in gaining support for a separate museum dedicated to contemporary art was the fact that the Los Angeles County Museum of Art (LACMA) was an important cultural fixture in town that enjoyed great support from the corporate and wealthy donor communities. Many of them did not understand why we needed another museum. Gary Familian had taken me to a meeting with the CEO of Carter Hawley Hale department stores who basically told me I was on a fool's errand. Happily, I was fortified by a discussion I had with my friend Dick Sherwood, a prominent O'Melveny lawyer who was also a board member of LACMA.

Dick was the first Jewish partner at O'Melveny and had clerked for Felix Frankfurter the year before I clerked for Douglas. We became close friends when we were both in L.A. practicing law. I had gone to talk to Dick, and let him know what I was doing. "Billy," he said. Somehow he and my mother were the only two people in my life who called me Billy. "You're right on target, you've got something important going. Hang in there. I'll do what I can." Dick encouraged me to go for it, saying there was plenty of room in our big city for two art museums to flourish. His wife, Dee, even volunteered to work on our project.

One afternoon I was in my office at Tuttle & Taylor, and Missy Chandler called me at my office. She was in the midst of the divorce from her husband, Otis Chandler of the *Los Angeles Times* dynasty. She had been reading about what was happening with the birth of MOCA and our negotiations with the City, and she wanted to try to help. I appreciated the sweet irony of having been treated so poorly by the *Times* during my AG campaign, and now being invited for lunch at the California Club by Mrs. Chandler.

I had never met her, but she was marvelous. We had a wonderful conversation about art, about Los Angeles and also about the tension that had developed between the plans for MOCA and the existing donors entrenched in the Los Angeles County Museum of Art. We both appreciated LACMA, and how it was a grand institution with an encyclopedic collection. It was located on Wilshire Blvd and began as the Los Angeles Museum of History Sciences and Art in 1910. It then split off in 1961 to concentrate on art. Its collection spanned ancient times to the Impressionists, with some modern pieces. We were far from being competitors, but the LACMA people were clearly nervous.

During lunch Mrs. Chandler offered to promote the museum with the downtown establishment by hosting a holiday dinner party at her home. She invited the major business leaders like Thornton Bradshaw (ARCO), Franklin Murphy (UCLA Chancellor and head of Times Mirror), Bill Thomas (McGuire Thomas Partners) and Bob Rowan along with their spouses. I remember the walls were covered with Otis' trophy heads from his many game hunting expeditions.

Missy asked Bradshaw, who had been a Harvard professor, to moderate a friendly debate between Murphy and me on the question of why a separate museum was needed downtown when we already had LACMA in mid-Wilshire. I explained the CRA deal, which came from the City of L.A. versus the support for LACMA, which came from the County. Murphy ended up acknowledging that there was a difference and that the structure was not in conflict because the city and the county exploited different sources of funding. In fact, he believed that Los Angeles was big enough for both institutions and that pluralism and friendly competition were positive forces. This went a long way to clear the path to gaining supporters for a museum to be situated in the heart of downtown.

By the summer of 1980, the CRA had selected a developer, Bunker Hill Associates, to execute the billion-dollar project, called California Plaza. At my urging, the developer pledged the endowment campaign's fourth million. So we were 40 percent towards our endowment goal with a few lead gifts. As word of the new museum spread, hundreds of people lined up to contribute to its operating endowment fund. This came as a result of the work of the Major Gifts Committee, co-chaired by Merry Norris and Gary Familian that included Betye Burton, Barbara and Ralph Kent Cooke, Aviva Covitz, Irwin Deutch, Jane Glassman, Lenore Greenberg, Stanley Grinstein, Hannah Kully, Michael McCarty, Mimi Meltzer, Bill

Palmer, Cathie Partridge, Lee Ramer, Robert Rowan, Sandy Talcott, DeWain Valentine, Marcia Weisman, and Malinda Wyatt.

In just fifteen months, Merry and her team secured nearly $6.3 million from 600 donors (largely in $10,000 chunks) which together with the $4 million in lead gifts and the high-end fundraising done by Andrea and Eli, significantly exceeded the required amount set by Mayor Bradley to get the enterprise off the ground. Many of these initial contributors were first time supporters of the arts, energized with civic pride and optimistic about the endless possibilities of this new space. I was up in Stanford on one of my recruiting trips and described the whole project to my old friend Keith Mann, He said, "Aw, c'mon Bill, how many people have an opportunity to establish a new art museum—without any money and without any art?"

We had addressed the first problem but he was right about the issue of art! Once more, we had a great stroke of luck. Merry came home one day from a little luncheon charity event at a private home in Beverly Hills and could not get over the amazing contemporary art collection that was there. It took place in the home of Lennie and Bernie Greenberg. We arranged to have dinner with them to see if we could get some support for the museum and, in fact, we did.

But then Lennie talked cautiously about her art collection. Her father, Taft Schreiber, had died in 1976 and was a very important talent agent in Los Angeles—he was Ronald Reagan's agent and a member of his kitchen cabinet when he was Governor. He was also a phenomenal art collector who had a huge collection with some tremendously valuable works by bold-faced names in modern painting: Joan Miro, Mondrian, and Jackson Pollock. His protégé in collecting contemporary art was Eli Broad, so there was a connection already.

After that evening I called Eli to tell him that I had the impression that Lennie might be interested in becoming a trustee of the museum. We had already enjoyed some success in fundraising and Eli wanted to raise the bar for our trustees. The $100,000 that she and her husband donated was not enough for him. (If I had tried to get on the board at that point, I would not have had a chance.) Eli asked me about the dinner and I said, "Well, there was this one piece of work that she talked about, and she kind of suggested that perhaps she might be interested in making a donation and joining the board."

I was describing the Jackson Pollock to Eli over the phone, and I could not even remember the name of the piece of art. The painting that Lennie had been talking about was Jackson Pollock's work "Number 1, 1949"— one of his most important works that eventually became the pivotal piece of the MOCA collection. Eli started to laugh and interrupted me, "Bill, you don't know what you're talking about, do you?" I said, "Eli, you're absolutely right." He said, "Do you know that that is the only Pollock of that particular genre in private hands today in the world?" Of course I didn't know that! "Can we put her on the board now?" I asked. He agreed, and she went on to donate the Jackson Pollock as well as seventeen other paintings that became the heart of MOCA's collection, including: Mondrian's "Composition of Red, Blue, Yellow and White: Nom III" (1939), Mark Rothko's "Yellow and Orange" (1949), two versions of Alberto Giacometti's 1960 sculpture "Tall Figure." and his "Interior Studio with Man Pointing and Three Apples."

In November 1981, I signed the definitive agreement providing the museum with construction funds, building site, a $1 million BHA payment to the endowment, and a share of California Plaza revenues, including rental income. MOCA was born—the result of a public-private partnership that became a model for future cultural and civic projects.

Over time, Eli, as Chairman, built up the board with members who were major collectors, renowned artists and business leaders. These included Leon Banks, Robert Irwin, Max Palevsky, Robert Rowan, Sam Francis, Betye Burton, Gary Familian, Dominique de Menil, Count Giuseppe Panza, Martin Lipton, Peter Ludwig, Seiji Tsutsumi, Lenore Greenberg, Jim Greene, Bill Kieschnick, Leo Wyler, and Fred Nicholas.

Fred brought some unique skills to the party. He is a lawyer, real estate developer, and art collector who was the founder of Public Counsel, the largest public interest law firm in the country. A dear friend and highly regarded executive, Fred was the perfect person to oversee the construction of the museum building on Bunker Hill. Max Palevsky's architecture committee had selected Irata Isozaki to design the building but there were many disagreements and issues among Max, Eli and the board that almost scuttled the process. Happily, Fred was up to the task. He also has a very wry wit and would often comment that my main contribution to the establishment of MOCA was that I managed to keep our two billionaire board members from killing each other.

Though financial solvency proved to be a nonissue during these early years, defining the museum's identity early on turned out to be a formidable challenge. We were doing pretty well with our fundraising, but we had not reached our goal yet, so we decided it would be helpful if we had a director in place. We had a meeting in Eli's boardroom which included a number of artists. Eli strongly recommended we hire a large search firm to find our director. He pointed out that this was crucial because it would immediately give us credibility in New York and that would be very important in recruiting the right candidate.

I did not know anything about the art world. I looked around that room, and said to myself, "Wait a minute, there can't be more than five people in the world we would consider for this job. Why do we need anyone to tell us that?" So I came up with this plan.

"Look, I don't know anything about who might be our director," I said. "But everyone else in this room must know who the top contenders will be. So let's play a game. Everyone should write a list, a list of the five top choices, ranked from the first choice to the last, and we'll see who emerges as our top contenders for director." Everyone thought that this was a fine idea, and while Eli bristled a bit, he relented. Two names emerged, both of them either first or second choice on everyone's list. One was Martin Friedman, the director of the wonderful Walker Museum in Minneapolis, and the other was Pontus Hultén, director of the magnificent Pompidou Center in Paris.

All of a sudden this became an international project! We sent someone to talk to the director of the Walker, who was interested but since he had just committed himself to launching a major capital campaign, he turned us down. We then sent Sam Francis over to Paris to talk to his old friend Pontus Hultén—Pontus eventually wrote a book about him. Sam brought him back on the airplane! It took a bit more negotiating. This move amounted to a resounding coup in the art world. In August 1980, our committee secured Pontus Hultén—the world-renowned museum professional who had helped found the Centre Georges Pompidou—as director of the new museum and Richard Koshalek as its chief curator.

This was one more example of the mysterious, magical synergy of how the pieces that became MOCA fell into place. The question of amassing a respected collection was next on our minds. I remember talking with Pontus about the fact that we were building a museum but did not yet have a collection. He reassured me, saying "You've got something going here. Don't worry. The art will come." Slowly but surely, a number of high-profile art patrons began to pledge their private collections to the museum, including Weisman, television executive Barry Lowen, and Robert Rowan, the former chairman of the Pasadena Museum of Modern Art's board of trustees. The museum also purchased 80 pieces from the highly-regarded collection of Count Giuseppe Panza di Blumo.

Plans for a temporary exhibition space known as the Temporary Contemporary were well underway by 1981, also overseen by Fred Nicholas. Located in a former warehouse originally renovated by Frank Gehry, the space—which is now known as the Geffen Contemporary—would house the museum collection until the new site was completed.

MOCA officially opened its jewel of a building on Bunker Hill on December 10, 1986. I was already on the Ninth Circuit and disengaged from fundraising activities. Today, the museum boasts over 6,800 works from renowned artists like Willem de Kooning, Jackson Pollock, Robert Rauschenberg, Mark Rothko, Cindy Sherman, Ed Ruscha, and others.

The whole experience remains one my proudest achievements. Most of my previous work—whether in the law or in politics—seemed like a natural trajectory for an ambitious kid from Turtle Creek, PA. But creating MOCA was beyond anything that I could possibly have imagined, especially coming from where I did.

Sure, the work in pulling it all together played to some of my other strengths: I like to deal with people, I like to talk to people, I like to try to make agreements with people and try to get something done by working together. And that took me beyond my skills as a lawyer, and even beyond what I had been used to in the political world. For the first time in my life, I had the thrill of creating something physical that was enduring. Not a legal decision or a political success. This was a bricks and mortar institution that would give our whole community art and culture for generations. As Keith Mann said, "How many people have an opportunity to establish a new art museum—without any money and without any art?"

Add to that, how many who were kids from Turtle Creek who barely knew a Jackson Pollock from a Renoir?

But now, after all that work, when I drive by the fantastic building of MOCA, even after all these years, I get a thrill. And I can answer Keith Mann and honestly say, "I did."

PART IV

SERVING ON THE NINTH CIRCUIT

"The right to dissent is the only thing that makes life tolerable for a judge of an appellate court . . . the affairs of government could not be conducted by democratic standards without it."

William O. Douglas

Celebration for investiture of William A. Norris, U.S. Circuit Judge, in D.C.

Bill Norris, youngest daughter Alison, Bill's mother Florence
Norris, and niece Karen Bretz

23

BECOMING A JUDGE

Once during one of Pat Brown's birthday parties at Chasen's restaurant on Beverley Blvd, he turned to me and said, "Bill, wouldn't you like to be a judge?" And I looked at him with just a little incredulity. "No, Governor, I don't want to be a judge!" I replied.

"Well, why not?" he said.

"Well, *you* don't want to be a judge, do you?" I asked. "Lyndon Johnson wanted to appoint you to the Ninth Circuit as I recall."

"Oh, no, of course I don't want to be a judge," he replied with a grin.

"Well, I'm just like you," I said, and we both began laughing. That was the end of the conversation.

Neither of us was dismissing the importance of our judiciary, nor were we implying that there was anything wrong with this important position. But Pat and I both understood that for the politically and civically engaged creatures that we were, the whole notion of giving up all that engagement to enter the pristine, monastic state of judicial, conflict of interest free purity was not appealing. How could you give up politics, volunteer work, being fully engaged in the world when you love it so much?

So call me a reluctant judge.

I was deep in the work of MOCA, in the litigation representing McDonnell Douglas, in the regular intensity of my life recruiting new talent and making Tuttle & Taylor the great law firm that it became. Jimmy Carter had a very mixed first term, but we were still committed to getting him re-elected. Then I got a telephone call from Sam Williams. He was an old friend, a very accomplished attorney in Los Angeles, and was the vice-president of the Police Commission when I was the president. There had been a little speculation when Carter first took office that I was on the short list for Attorney General, and I had spoken a bit with Carter at that time so he certainly knew who I was. But even with the strong support of Tom Bradley and others, the nomination never went anywhere. This was not a big disappointment. I was content to keep doing the work that I was doing.

But the President has a huge array of potential appointees in the justice system: obviously the Supreme Court, but also a myriad of federal judicial appointments. Griffin Bell, who was Carter's Attorney General, had put together a committee at this time for screening and recommending prospects for potential judges in the Ninth Circuit. The Ninth Circuit is an incredibly important court. Established in 1891 as part of the federal court system, the Ninth Circuit Court of Appeals—headquartered in San Francisco—has a vast jurisdiction, hearing cases from nine western states and two Pacific islands. In the late nineteenth century, the court serviced a mere three percent of the population of the United States. Today, that number has ballooned to nearly twenty percent—almost double that of the next largest Circuit Court. With this shift in population demographics over the past century, Congress has expanded the number of active judges serving the Ninth Circuit to twenty-nine, by far the largest of the thirteen federal circuit courts.

Beyond its enormous size, the Ninth Circuit became famous for being disproportionately liberal in its rulings—a perspective that is not entirely fair. Some argue that a higher-than-average Supreme Court reversal record is evidence of the Ninth Circuit's liberal bias; others say it is simply proportional because the Supreme Court hears a greater number of cases from the Ninth Circuit in a given year. One of my former Ninth Circuit clerks, Steve McConnell, once wrote that all those Supreme Court reversals can, "at times ... feel like a badge of honor." He continued, "In reality, the reputation 'enjoyed' by the Ninth Circuit is much ado about nothing. Most decisions are unanimous even when the panel is shared by people perceived to be ideological opposites." Nonetheless, 58 percent of all sitting judges were appointed to the Ninth Circuit by Democratic presidents.

The sheer size and supposed liberal bent of the Ninth Circuit eventually led critics to mock the court as the "Ninth Circus," the "Notorious Ninth," and the "Nutty Ninth," but this was not the case when I joined. Lawmakers and politicians periodically debate whether or not the court should be divided once and for all in order to make caseloads more manageable, but those discussions never tend to go very far. Though the Ninth Circuit may be an easy target for opponents, it has handed down a number of highly influential and historic rulings.

In 1980, in response to the expanding caseload in the Ninth Circuit, Congress had increased the number of Ninth Circuit judges by eleven, and

Sam had become the chair of a committee responsible for assembling candidates for the vacant seats. The size of the Ninth Circuit made this a formidable task, so this committee was responsible only for Southern California and Arizona. When Sam called, he said that he just wanted me to come over to his office and help him "evaluate some of these prospects." I agreed. I liked Sam and this seemed a friendly, collegial thing to do.

Of course that was a ruse.

He wanted to talk to me about letting him put me on the list of potential candidates. We sat in his office and he showed me the list— nearly every name was familiar except for a few candidates from Arizona, and slowly he began to bring up the absence of my name. It reminded me of the conversation I had with Pat Brown!

"Oh, c'mon, Sam!" I said. "*You're* not on that list. *You* don't want to be a judge any more than I want to! You know that you turned down an appointment to the California Supreme Court by Jerry Brown. Why do you think *I* want to be a judge on the Ninth Circuit or any other court?" He laughed, and he talked to me and urged me to just submit an application. Nothing more. No guarantees. But a simple application would not do any harm. Then the commission would include it in their submission of the list of names to the Department of Justice for consideration. Even with the expanded number of judgeships, the list had more names than there were vacancies.

So I submitted the application and my name ended up on their list. When the Department of Justice and the White House announced the names from that list of people who would be nominated for the Ninth Circuit, my name was not there and I breathed a sigh of relief. One of the names that did appear was that of my old friend Steve Reinhardt. He and I followed very similar paths: he went to Yale Law School and clerked for a District Judge in the D.C. District. When he returned to L.A. he started at O'Melveny and then moved to a smaller firm.

He was very liberal and also involved in Democratic politics, especially on Tom Bradley's and Jerry Brown's campaigns. In the late seventies he was on the Police Commission and had also been a member of the U.S. Commission on Civil Rights. Steve and Sam were *very* close—the three of us had all fought a number of political wars together. We were three of the five individuals who ran the first couple of campaigns for Mayor Tom Bradley.

All federal judges who are nominated for Courts of Appeals have to be confirmed by the Senate after a hearing in which the Judiciary Committee interviews the nominee. There was, however, some opposition to Steve's nomination, and it looked like the Administration was having an issue getting him confirmed. I had heard these rumors but was surprised when I received a call from President Carter's press secretary Jody Powell. He told me that the President wanted to nominate me for the Ninth Circuit. I knew exactly what was going on and I said, "It's my understanding that there is no vacancy, if you take into account the nominees."

And he mumbled and stumbled and said, "Well, we're having a little trouble with Steve Reinhardt."

"Are you asking me to substitute for Steve Reinhardt?" I asked. And after some stammering, he acknowledged that this was exactly what he was proposing. I would have none of it. I told him that I was a fan of President Carter and worked hard to get him elected, but "it would be a disservice to him to withdraw the nomination of Steve Reinhardt." I got very firm with him and pointed out that Steve was very well known and very popular in California and any rumors about his fitness for the office should be completely ignored. "There's no reason why the President should withdraw that nomination," I concluded.

Shortly thereafter Attorney General Griffin Bell also called me and said that he and the President were reviewing my record, and they were so impressed they decided they wanted me to be on the Ninth Circuit. He also said that he had heard that I was reluctant to take the position. I told him emphatically, "You're right, I am *not* going to do that. And I advise you and the President to go forward with Steve Reinhardt's nomination."

Bell assured me that the offer was not to be a substitute for Reinhardt's slot, and told me that Walter Ely, who was one of the older judges of the Ninth Circuit, had decided to take senior status. The Attorney General then said that when Ely went senior, "the President wants to nominate you."

I thanked the Attorney General and tried to imagine what this would mean. I was still immersed in the McDonnell Douglas case, and we were supposed to argue in front of the Ninth Circuit in a matter of months. I imagined that to be a judge would require relinquishing all that made life so meaningful to me. I was just starting to make some good money as a lawyer and would have to take a serious cut in pay to become a judge.

I went into a state of agony and I fretted over this for about six months. Merry definitely did not want me to become a judge, and that too was a consideration. I liked what I was doing as a lawyer and being involved in my usual variety of gratifying activities. I was right in the middle of the formation and founding of MOCA. Tuttle & Taylor had become a prominent and sought-after law firm. Mostly the whole idea of entering the judicial monastery and losing my ability to speak out on important issues or support candidates that could use my help went against every fiber of my being.

One of my partners, who was both a very good friend and someone who had clerked on the Supreme Court at the same time that I was there, was Julian Burke. He began at O'Melveny because T&T was too small to take him on at that time. He went to O'Melveny as a transactional lawyer, gained valuable skills and clients, and then eventually came to us. I confided my confusion to Julian, who I recall always wanted to be a judge, and he cut through my quandary immediately. "Oh, c'mon, Bill!" he said. "You know, you might like it! After all, they can't fire you, but you can quit." In an odd way, there was something about his argument that made perfect sense to me. I decided to accept. The Carter Administration officially nominated me on February 27, 1980.

So I found myself arguing the McDonnell Douglas case to the Ninth Circuit when I had already been nominated! For the Ninth Circuit! The presiding judge of the three-judge panel was Tony Kennedy, and he wrote the opinion that eloquently expressed all the reasons that we won the case.

My confirmation hearing was set for June 18, 1980. Merry and I headed out to Washington for the hearings. The last time we were in Washington together was in 1979 when we went to visit Justice Douglas, who was not doing well at all. We stopped at his home on the way from the airport to town, because I had arranged with his wife Kathy to see him. He was in bad shape and lying in his bedroom. That was the last time I saw Bill Douglas before he died in January 1980. I went to Washington then for his funeral.

My hearing was scheduled for June, and Washington had not yet turned into the sweltering city of the later summer. It was warm and beautiful, and once more there was that feeling of unreality as I sat in the Senate hearing room preparing for my confirmation. I was still the kid from Turtle Creek, and being in this position had never entered my wildest dreams. California Senator Cranston was going to introduce me to the Judiciary Committee and make a speech on my behalf. I knew Alan Cranston quite well and had worked with him over the years. But the weekend before my hearing, his son was tragically killed in an automobile accident, so sadly he was not there.

Someone on his staff had arranged for the other California senator, Senator Hayakawa, who was a Republican, to deliver Cranston's remarks. There was some sweet irony to this for me. S. I. Hayakawa was the Acting President of San Francisco State in 1968 during the student unrest. During one very noisy and chaotic protest, he tried unsuccessfully to outshout the protesters and make himself heard. He went so far as to climb on the protesters' van and pull the wires out of their loud speakers so that he could make his announcement that he planned to reopen the school. He became very popular with the conservative voters for confronting the radicals, and he ran for senator and won in 1977 against John Tunney.

When I was on the Board of Trustees for the state colleges, Reagan and the board were unhappy with the then president at San Francisco State for not controlling the students, and they put Hayakawa in to replace him. I voted no, but nonetheless they prevailed. And here he was, twelve years later, saying wonderful things about me for my confirmation hearing!

This was not a controversial nor a very crowded hearing. The chair of the committee Orrin Hatch presided. The hearing room was relatively empty, but sitting in one of the front rows was a wonderful man named Sterling Colton. He was the general counsel of the Marriott Corporation, an old friend, a former classmate of mine from Stanford Law, and, like Senator Hatch, a Mormon from Utah. He just somehow heard about the hearing and that I would be there, and he came!

Just before the hearing started, Sterling disappeared. I did not know where he went, but then he reappeared after the hearing was over. Senator Hatch was so nice to me. It turns out he was from Pittsburgh and attended the University of Pittsburgh Law School, which was practically in the Turtle Creek neighborhood, so we had a nice discussion. Then I noticed that Sterling Colton had returned to the hearing room. I said, "Sterling, I noticed that you disappeared." And he got slight grin on his face and said, "I just wanted to go back and have a chat with my good friend, Orrin. I told him, Bill's a friend of mine, and don't you *dare* lay a hand on him!"

Only after I was confirmed did I learn about some other back stories that led to this new chapter in my life. Early in the year, Jimmy Carter came to California and wanted to get his 1980 re-election campaign organized. My old friend Jesse Unruh was then the head of the Democratic Party and extremely powerful. The President asked Jesse whether he would take the lead in organizing his re-election campaign.

And Jesse Unruh replied, "Mr. President, I can't go out and ask Democratic leaders to support you early, when those who went for you early that last time out here were passed over for important appointments, like Bill Norris." Jimmy Carter went back to Griffin Bell in the Department of Justice and demanded to see my credentials. That was when he became aware that I was on the initial list that came from Sam Williams' committee, but not on the final list. Apparently Carter was *very* upset. That ride with Jesse was the catalyst for the call from Bell and my eventual appointment to be a judge for the Ninth Circuit Court of Appeals.

I knew that I would need some law clerks, and it was already very late in the game to start recruiting. I had called an old friend of mine who clerked at the Supreme Court when I was there. Bob Hamilton had been the brave young clerk who had successfully challenged Justice Frankfurter on a point of law when we were all clerks, so it was not surprising that he put his erudition into teaching law and became a professor at the University of Texas Law School. He told me that I had to hire a young man named Neal Manne, and I would regret it if I didn't. Neal was not planning to clerk for anyone but had imagined going straight to a law firm. The fact that we were in L.A. was a great incentive for him, so he decided to join me even though I was a brand new judge and a completely unknown quantity. Another clerk I snagged was Danny Waldman, a Harvard and Columbia Law grad and a former number one and captain of the Harvard tennis team. I always liked athletes; I found that their drive and discipline translated into a terrific work ethic. Danny had the benefit of being brilliant as well. The third clerk was John Stick, the top graduate of UCLA Law School, who even then seemed destined to become an academic in the Law. Indeed, he became the first of a long line of highly respected law professors to come out of my chambers.

Shortly after the hearing, I was officially sworn in. Nearly every important person in my life attended that ceremony, as did my law clerks. My children were there, Merry and her kids, Tom Bradley and some of my political buddies, as well as my dear friends and law partners Ed Tuttle and Bob Taylor. Even my mother made the trip and showed an unusual blush of pride. I wonder what she must have thought of her "Billy" as she looked around at all the powerful people there. Chief Circuit Judge James Browning administered the oath, and Tom Bradley said a few words.

I started work that summer. On my first day of work at 312 North Spring Street, there was no office ready for me yet, much less a suite, so I went into the one office that was available. I sat behind the desk, looked at my "in box," and saw some papers there. Before I knew it, I had before me a motion of some sort that I could rule on. It was some procedural thing, and today a motion's panel would handle it, but then there was no motions panel. The staff attorneys would look around for an available judge and I was that judge. I read the motion, thought about and said, "Okay." That decided it. I did not talk to anybody, nobody helped me out. And my life as Judge Norris had officially begun.

I kept looking at the mail in the in box and learned that the summer Ninth Circuit Judicial Conference was coming up in Monterey that month. I was supposed to attend. The Judicial Conference is a huge event, often with 600 judges and lawyers who work in the West. There are educational sessions, opportunities for business meetings that are in support of the court administration, and in general a very important event for the whole community. The description of the conference included a list of judges who would be there, and I came across the name of Bill Canby. He was another Carter appointee and started a few months before I did. I looked at his résumé, and what they had to say about him, and I said to myself, "I sure hope I like him as much in person as I do on paper." I became, at that point, a fan of Bill Canby.

So off to Monterey I went. I had not been a Ninth Circuit judge for more than a couple of weeks and had no idea what I was doing, except when they gave me a little case I took care of it. After having been in the midst of so many things, in control of my life and my work, to be the new kid on the block with so many new things to learn was quite a shock to the system of a 53-year-old man! I met Walter Ely, and he was very pleased to know that I was occupying his seat. He introduced me around, and there I saw Harry Hupp, the District Court Judge from San Gabriel.

Harry was a year behind me at Stanford Law School, and he was on the Law Review. As soon as we met he became my guide to all the other judges. He loved to take me around and introduce me as "his former boss." He would say that I was a tough grader of his papers for the Law Review at Stanford. "And I thought I would not have to deal with him again," Harry would say. "And here he is!"

Steve Reinhardt was confirmed in September of that year, so he was not yet on the court. When I met Bill Canby, I liked him even more in person than I did on paper. And I met his wonderful wife, Jane. As I looked at her, I found myself trying to remember who she so strongly resembled. Who is it, who is it? Of course she reminded me of Walter Mondale's wife, Joan—because she was her sister! Bill and I worked closely together on many panels over the coming years. He was one of my most treasured colleagues and a fellow baseball fanatic.

Slowly I got acclimated. My precocious young law clerks arrived. There were no customs or routines in how things were done. My chambers were beginning to come alive with intellectual activity, arguments, and fun. I looked around and realized that even though I was sure I never wanted to be a judge, maybe, just maybe, I was wrong. Maybe this was the opportunity of a lifetime.

24

NOT ALWAYS THE LIBERAL VOTE

I arrived at my spacious chambers in the Federal Courthouse on Spring Street in downtown Los Angeles and was struck by the power I was about to assume. Article III of the Constitution confers life-time tenure on federal judges in order to insure the independence of the judiciary. My office was large and was surrounded by smaller offices for a secretary and each of my three law clerks. By September, Danny Waldman, Neal Manne and John Stick had reported for duty, and I had three hardworking clerks and a challenging caseload. My eye for spotting talent did not fail me, and I was especially blessed in my selection of my very first class of clerks.

Every new judge has a learning curve and I was no exception. As someone who had argued a number of cases in front of the Ninth Circuit, I thought that I had a pretty good sense of what went on, but no one can really understand the process until you are there on a day-to-day basis. But now I could see the inner workings of this important court. Case management attorneys would inventory all the cases, classify them, and determine both the precise legal issue the case involved and its levels of complexity. That all determined the relative amount of time each case was estimated to require.

This inventory process enables the court to balance judges' workloads, but also organize cases so that appeals involving similar legal issues can be heard at a single sitting. The year was divided into weekly, sometimes monthly calendars that organized each of the three-judge panels. We were all expected to sit on thirty-two days of oral argument calendars; one oral screening panel; one motions panel; and one certificate of appealability panel. It made for quite a busy schedule since all of this required meticulous preparation. Most important, no judge had any individual control over our caseloads: we handled whatever was served up to us.

When I had been assigned my share of the cases and divided them up among my law clerks, they were responsible for initially reading and studying the briefs, and writing a bench memo for each case, as they saw it, with *their* recommendations. I would let them go for it, set them free to explore, struggle, research, and go through the essential processes to create a persuasive bench memo. I would rarely talk to the clerks about the case during this time, unless there was an issue of particular importance, or unless I saw that the clerk was having some trouble wrestling down the case. Only after the memo was circulated to the other judges did the clerk and I have a discussion about it.

I would read the briefs for the entire calendar. Sometimes, it would be clear to me that the decision of the district judge from the lower court was either clearly right or just dead wrong, and then I did not see much sense in either me or my clerk spending a lot of time on it. But that was rare; typically, the cases that reached the Ninth Circuit were complex and required great analysis and thought. Finally, when it was time to sit, we judges "robed" and entered the courtroom for oral argument. I would always have at least one of my clerks come to the oral argument—unlike Justice Douglas who never permitted this.

After the argument was over, the three panel judges would talk about the case in conference, and I would go back to my chambers with my share of opinions to draft. I would, in almost every case, have the law clerk that prepared the bench memo then prepare the draft of an opinion—but not before we thoroughly discussed the case and how the opinion should be structured. We would discuss the oral argument and the points raised by my colleagues, and then I would turn them loose, once more, to draft an opinion. But that first draft was only the beginning!

As my clerks will all attest, I took writing *very* seriously, and they would be required to write not one or two drafts, but often ten or twelve until I was satisfied and could tell them the words they longed to hear: "It sings!" I was told by clerks years after they had worked for me that one of the most enduring personal legacies of their time with me was the increased rigor of their writing. That level of effort, while time consuming, also was noticed by the other judges. I remember my first writing assignment for an en *banc* panel. The Ninth Circuit is so large that, unlike the other circuits, an en *banc* panel does not consist of all the judges, but rather a newly selected group of eleven. Chief Judge James Browning—a level-headed, even-handed, joy to have as a Chief Judge—had given me the writing assignment. I spent a lot of time on it, and Jim called and asked me how it was going. I imagine he was wondering when he would see the opinion. I reassured him and told him that he would receive my draft "in the fullness of time." When he finally received it he gave me his version of "it sings"; he told me that "it was worth the wait!"

My first crop of law clerks was a joy to work with. Each was accomplished and worked very hard with me and sometimes with one another. Neal claimed that since the others were brilliant, his job was to be funny; he made sure that even in the midst of the hard work, we would have a good time.

He was wrong about one thing, though. He too was brilliant.

I always wanted to be sure that my clerks felt a part of my life, that we became a kind of a family. I wanted them to call me "Bill," not just because I like the informality, but also because I wanted to break down any hierarchical relationship that might interfere with their capacity to argue with me as intensely and aggressively as they could. It became a bit of a Rorschach test: some clerks simply could not manage to get over their training or their natural sense of deference and could refer to me only as "Judge." I still pushed them to confront me intellectually, and they did.

We had a lot of fun and we worked very hard.

My first case as a judge was a memorable one and was argued on September 17, 1980: *United States v. Thordarson,* a criminal case involving the Teamsters' Union, which had engaged in the destruction of company trucks in order to coerce the Redman Moving and Storage Company into recognizing the Teamsters as their employees' union. They alleged that this was not a criminal act, because it had been a part of their collective bargaining efforts, and it was therefore a labor dispute that should be adjudicated by the National Labor Relations Board and not by the courts. I assigned Danny Waldman to work with me on this case. I would be sitting on a panel with two other Carter appointees, Judge Harry Pregerson and Judge Warren Ferguson.

While common sense might suggest that it is wrong to blow up trucks under any circumstances, sometimes common sense does not factor in the often bloody history of the labor movement in the United States. Sometimes when unions engaged in legitimate union activity were provoked in some way by management, violence might erupt. Pushing and shoving in a picket line enclosing a plant could give rise to claims that the union was guilty of extorting higher wages through threats of violence. Rather than have such incidents give rise to cases against individuals in federal criminal court, they are decided in the normal course of the NLRB's oversight of collective bargaining as possible violations by the union of federal labor law.

Thordarson raised the new issue whether the use of explosives was to be considered only as a labor tactic by the NLRB but not as a crime in federal court. I did not think so, but the other two judges on the panel seemed, in their questioning, to be persuaded by the Teamsters' arguments. I sat quietly for most of the argument, and when it was my turn to question, I posed a hypothetical: "Suppose the situation were reversed and the company kidnapped a child of the union leader to strengthen their bargaining position, would that still come under the NLRB and not the criminal court?" The Teamster's lawyer, to his credit, stuck to his guns and said, "That's right, your Honor." I overheard Judge Ferguson whisper, "That can't be the law." Danny and I served up the analysis concluding that indeed it was not the law. In the end I got Warren to vote with me for the Government, though Harry Pregerson dissented.

To this day, I am proud of my work on that very first case. To me it was a question of doing what is right and finding the legal path to getting that done. I was not and never would be a "knee jerk liberal"—an automatic vote for what was considered to be the liberal side. Danny Waldman told me later that his father, the labor lawyer, was not pleased with him at all because of that case, but that Danny always thought that it was the right result.

Interestingly, the *Thordarson* case—my first as a judge—would be complemented at the end of my judicial career by my last case, *Jacobsen v. Hughes Aircraft*, but we will get to that in due course.

Two other cases appeared on my docket during my first year that were the stuff of newspaper headlines involving the Hell's Angels in one and the grisly Jonestown Massacre in the other. I never pay much attention to popular culture, so the media circus surrounding our Courthouse came as something of a surprise. The cases were revealing in the way in which social cataclysms often are distilled into fundamental constitutional issues. In one, involving the sinister motor cycle gang, we ended up protecting their rights against unlawful search and seizure.

In the other case, Larry Layton was the right-hand man of cult leader Jim Jones, and Layton was involved in the murder of Congressman Leo Ryan after Ryan went to Guyana to investigate the cult. All cult members killed themselves except for a few, and Layton was one of the few. He was extradited to the U.S. and charged with murdering Congressman Ryan. Layton said that not only did he not kill Ryan, even though he may have wounded a few others, but that the case should be dismissed because the federal statute making it a crime to kill a Congressman did not have extraterritorial effect. This wound through the courts until, finally, I was picked to be on the emergency appeal panel that involved the use of evidence. But what was most noteworthy about this for my clerks and me was the incredible media circus that accompanied the case with all of the rumors of threats that circulated. The sense of anxiety around the courthouse was palpable during those days.

While I had entered the judicial monastery, that did not mean that I cut off contact entirely with my previous life. Every once in a while, Tom Bradley and I would have a conversation about how things were going for him. Initially the prospect of weaning myself from regular, public, and quite natural engagement in political life was a bit difficult, but eventually the boundaries became second nature to me. MOCA was still very much on my mind, and I would include my clerks whenever there was an event there.

After one MOCA cocktail party that was held in a room containing sculptures made from found objects, Neal Manne decided that he could make an artistic contribution to our chambers. Perhaps the contemporary art work that already graced our suite sparked Neal's creativity as well. One day, when he was walking from the courthouse to the parking lot—it was pretty dingy neighborhood at the time—he picked up a hubcap. Inspired by what he saw at MOCA, he then brought the hubcap into work and started stacking things that he found into a kind of tower; hubcaps, tin cans, pieces of aluminum siding, anything that happened to cross his path. He told me that he was creating a valuable piece of art that one day would sell for so much money he would no longer need to practice law.

One day, the MOCA director Pontus Hultén was visiting me in my chambers, and I decided to advance Neal's artistic career by having this renowned curator evaluate his work in progress. Neal was at his desk, immersed in a bench memo, when I introduced Pontus and asked Neal to describe his own sculpture of found objects. After a brief hesitation, Neal told Pontus about the hubcaps and the other detritus he had assembled as his first, but not his last, work of art. Pontus pretended to give it a very serious evaluation, and he then suggested that Neal should probably keep his day job practicing law.

Interestingly, of all my first year cases, the one that was most significant in the long term was one that was not even assigned to me. Though I did not sit on the three judge panel that decided the case, in the end, it was one in which I announced my commitment to enforcing the equality of gays and lesbians in the eyes of the law. It involved a young gay sailor named Dennis Beller. He first enlisted in the Navy in 1960. In 1972, he reenlisted for a third six-year term, and in 1975, the Navy decided "to upgrade his security clearance to permit him access to 'Top Secret' information." While conducting a background check on Beller, the Navy discovered that he "had contact with homosexual groups since entering the Navy."*

---

* *Beller v. Middendorf*, 631 F.2d 788 (9th Cir. 1980).

Beller did not deny that he had begun having gay experiences after he entered the Navy, and he stated that he believed that he was bisexual. An administrative board was convened to look into discharging Beller. The Navy's regulation on homosexuality at the time stated, "Members involved in homosexuality are military liabilities who cannot be tolerated in a military organization ... members involved in homosexual acts are security and reliability risks who discredit themselves and the naval service by their homosexual conduct. Their prompt separation is essential." The Chief of Naval Personnel carried out Beller's discharge in November, 1975.

Beller did not believe that this was fair and sued the Navy. The case traveled through the court system until it finally reached the Ninth Circuit during my first year as a judge. Beller argued that the Navy's policy was a violation of the Fourteenth amendment, which states, "no State shall ... deprive any person of life, liberty or property, without due process of law." The Navy countered that Beller's discharge "was merely one for breach of his enlistment agreement" and that courts were not in a position to make any ruling on the discharge. Beller, the Navy held, could have sought remuneration by sticking to internal administrative or bureaucratic procedure; and moreover, only the Court of Claims could fairly offer any view about the compensation Beller wanted. The Ninth Circuit panel rejected this argument because "the 'primary relief' [sought, reinstatement] was nonmonetary."

I was not on the panel that heard the case. Judge Anthony Kennedy wrote the majority opinion in which he upheld the Navy's right to discharge gays. He wrote, "Upholding the challenged regulations as constitutional is distinct from a statement that they are wise.... [T]he conduct in question is subject to prohibition only to further compelling state interests...." Kennedy believed that the court's hands were tied in dealing with this issue; I could not have disagreed more.

Beller then asked for a hearing *en banc*, in which eleven judges would reconsider the case. But when that request is made, all the active judges vote yes or no to decide whether or not the case should be reheard at all. The nearly unanimous consensus was that we should *not* rehear this case. I was outraged. I voted in favor of rehearing it *en banc* because I believed—not for the first time and not for the last—that the Ninth Circuit was wrong and that Tony Kennedy's opinion was wrong.

Although Stonewall occurred in 1969, and the gay rights movement was taking its first steps, gay rights was not yet a salient legal issue. I suppose that I was ahead of my time, but it was an issue of fundamental rights that I felt strongly about. So I did something that judges just do not do. I wrote a detailed and rigorously argued dissenting opinion to this *en banc* vote, arguing why the court should take the case *en banc* to rehear this. Working with Neal, I argued why I believed the Navy's action was unconstitutional.

It was published in the Federal Reporter like any other opinion and it was styled as a "dissent from the court's rejection of the suggestion for rehearing en banc."* No one had ever seen anything like that before, but it was only the beginning of my crusade. The key case would come a few years later.

The first year set the tone for my seventeen years on the court: find talented clerks who worked hard and had fun, take on unpopular views if they are the right things to do, and accept the fact that even though I may have lost my First Amendment rights, that loss brought with it monumental responsibilities.

---

* 647 F.2d 80 (9th Cir. 1981).

Bill Norris in chambers

25

FROM BORK TO KENNEDY

In the summer of 1987, I got a call from Neal Manne. Neal was now working as Chief of Staff for Republican Senator Arlen Specter from Pennsylvania. Specter was playing a critical role on the Senate Judiciary Committee, which was going to hold the hearings on Judge Robert Bork's nomination to the United States Supreme Court. In order to help prepare Specter for the confirmation hearings, Neal was studying Judge Bork's opinions and other writings. He just wanted to pick my brain about Bork, he said, and if I came up with anything useful on the guy, I should give him a call. Such a request from Neal was not uncommon; we had often discussed issues before the committee, and I had asked him to help smooth the nomination of the extraordinarily intelligent Alex Kozinski to the Ninth Circuit several years before. I told Neal I would think about it and would let him know if I came up with anything of interest.

President Reagan had nominated Robert Bork on July 1, 1987, and it could be considered either Reagan's third or fourth Supreme Court appointment, depending on how you count: he appointed my fellow Stanford Law alum Sandra Day O'Connor in 1981, and then in '86, after Chief Justice Warren Burger announced his resignation, he moved Justice William Rehnquist to the Chief's seat and appointed Antonin Scalia to what had been Rehnquist's seat.

Scalia and Bork had been the top two contenders for the '86 nomination, and Reagan's biographer Lou Cannon argues, in *President Reagan: The Role of a Lifetime*, that they both would have been confirmed had the sequence of their nominations been reversed. The assertion is based on this political equation: Democrats took the Senate in the '86 midterms, about four months after the Scalia confirmation, giving them the power to block judicial appointments. Ted Kennedy, however, one of the organizers of the Bork defeat, would not have been able to block the nomination of Scalia, the first Italian American appointed to the Court.

But the Reagan White House was weakened already by the time that Bork was nominated. Lewis Powell resigned from the Supreme Court at the same time that the Iran-Contra affair came to light. This was the scandal in which the Reagan Administration was found to have secretly sold arms to Iran in order to funnel aid to the Contras in Nicaragua. It was a mess, and the scandal was just starting to break during very important congressional hearings on the matter.

Add to that the fact that Bork was an outspoken opponent of not just abortion—that seemed an inevitable position for a Reagan appointee—but even contraception. He criticized the 1965 *Griswold v. Connecticut* ruling that said contraceptives should be available under a presumed right to privacy. So that made him an even tougher sell to replace the pro-*Roe* Justice Powell, especially given that Reagan's previous two appointments had also been to replace pro-*Roe* justices, Potter Stewart and Warren Burger. Also going against Bork was the fact that he had been Solicitor General under Nixon and carried out Nixon's order to fire Watergate Special Prosecutor Archibald Cox in the "Saturday Night Massacre."

When Bork became the nominee, Senator Kennedy was outraged. He had disliked Bork since the time that Bork fired Cox. As soon as he heard that Bork would be the nominee, Kennedy spoke on the Senate floor and said, "Robert Bork's America is a land in which women would be forced into back alley abortions, blacks would sit at segregated lunch counters, rogue police could break down citizens' doors in midnight raids, school children could not be taught about evolution, writers and artists could be censored at the whim of government, and the doors of the federal courts would be shut on the fingers of millions of citizens for whom the judiciary is—and is often the only—protector of the individual rights that are at the heart of democracy."

He may have been over the top with this speech, but he certainly sounded the alarm, and that was exactly what he intended. The opposition to Bork from women's groups, civil liberties groups and civil rights groups was getting organized.

Already in the early days of July, such national figures as Ben Hooks, Coretta Scott King, and then-presidential candidate Rep. Richard Gephardt began making strong statements against Bork. Given that so much of the controversy around Bork had to do with his alleged stance against civil rights legislation, southern senators—and especially southern Democratic senators—were a crucial constituency in the Senate fight. Reagan apparently did not see the blowback coming. He spent twenty-four days on vacation in California in mid-August and into September.

It was against this backdrop that I got the call from Neal Manne. On a plane ride in mid-August between L.A. and San Francisco, I struggled with what I thought about Robert Bork. I had supported the appointment of strong conservatives to the federal courts before, such as Alex Kozinski, but where Kozinski was a maverick who followed where his keen intellect took him, Bork was, if scholarly, quite doctrinaire. I decided that the issue I would most want to hear Bork discuss involved a case from my past, *Bolling v. Sharpe*. Bork subscribed to an "originalist" legal philosophy which held that judges should hew as closely as possible to the original intent of the Constitution's framers. In keeping with that view, Bork took the position that the Fifth Amendment's due process clause was strictly procedural, placing limits on the processes and procedures by which the government could deprive someone of life or liberty, and did not add any substantive rights, such as property rights or equal protection. Substantive due process as a way to protect property rights arose in the 1920s and 1930s as conservative courts sought ways to restrain government regulation. It was widely rejected during the New Deal. But as liberal judges began to breathe new life into personal rights during the years of the Warren Court, conservatives charged that some of those rights, such as the right to privacy, amounted to substantive due process. The Warren Court, however, had explicitly relied on the Due Process Clause to protect a substantive right only once, in *Bolling v. Sharpe*. If Bork dismissed substantive due process as a completely invalid concept, then he would have to explain what he would have done differently in *Bolling*. And that would not be easy, because *Bolling* is the case that mandated the desegregation of the schools in the District of Columbia.

Bolling was a companion case to *Brown v. Board of Education*, and was decided on the same day. *Brown*, of course, was the landmark Supreme Court ruling that struck down segregation in public schools. The *Brown* decision focused on the fact that "separate but equal" public schools are always separate, but are inherently unequal. The Court used the Equal Protection Clause of the Fourteenth Amendment to find that it was unconstitutional for states (including state political entities like public school boards) to maintain segregated schools.

Bolling dealt with the companion issue of segregation in D.C.'s public schools. It was obvious the outcome had to be the same—segregation was unconstitutional—but it was unclear how the Court would get there. After all, the Fourteenth Amendment, which was the basis of the ruling in *Brown*, did not apply to D.C., which was not a state. The Fourteenth Amendment is explicitly a limitation only on what states may do, not what the federal government may do. As a result, *Bolling* was decided on an entirely different point of law.

The Warren court decided unanimously that even though the Fourteenth Amendment does not apply to the District of Columbia, that amendment's notion of Equal Protection is included within the guarantee of Due Process in the Fifth Amendment, which applies to the federal government. In this way the same equal protection standard that applied to states to prohibit the segregated Kansas schools in *Brown* also applied to the federal government when it prohibited the segregated D.C. schools in *Bolling*. As the Court concluded: "Racial segregation in the public schools of the District of Columbia is a denial of the due process of law guaranteed by the 5th Amendment."

Brown and *Bolling* were decided the year before I arrived in D.C. to begin my clerkship with Justice Douglas, but remained on the docket so the Court could reconvene to discuss how to effectively implement the decisions, and this was still going on during my clerkship. The case stayed with me, and I researched it again in my preparation for my own nomination hearing. Still, I could never have imagined the significance that the *Bolling* case would come to have over thirty years after I first encountered it.

When I landed back in Los Angeles, I called Neal Manne. I told him that I had been thinking about all this and realized that Judge Bork's rejection of "substantive due process," combined with the outcome of the old Supreme Court case in *Bolling*, could put him in a dilemma, and the way he resolved that dilemma would give a strong indication of the type of Justice he would become.

My former law clerk grasped the point immediately. We always could communicate in shorthand, and his mind worked quickly. If, as Judge Bork had proclaimed, the entire concept of substantive due process was wrong, then the holding in *Bolling* was wrong, and the D.C. schools would have remained segregated despite *Brown v. Board of Education*—which was an unfathomable idea. Judge Bork would be forced to make a difficult and revealing choice between ideological consistency and a widely revered civil rights landmark. Manne was impressed by this argument and said he would discuss the point with Senator Specter.

The stakes were high. When the committee hearings began, neither side had enough votes to feel secure. Never before had a confirmation hearing provoked such intense public interest, and never before had a nominee faced such detailed questioning. Senator Specter played a critical role. He was the most independent Republican on the committee and also a graduate of Yale law school and a former prosecutor. He knew what it took to cross-examine a witness. On September 16, the second day of the Senate confirmation hearings, Specter raised the issue of *Bolling v. Sharpe*. He challenged Bork to explain how the court could have desegregated the D.C. schools if substantive due process had not been available as the jurisprudential tool.

"How can you justify *Bolling v. Sharpe* applying the due process clause to the stopping of segregation?" Senator Specter asked the nominee.

"I do not know that anybody ever has," Bork replied. "I think that has been a case that left people puzzled, and I have been told that some Justices on the Supreme Court felt very queasy afterward about *Bolling v. Sharpe....*" When Specter pressed him further, Bork answered, "I think that constitutionally that is a troublesome case...."

"Final question," the Senator thundered. "Do you accept *Bolling v. Sharpe* or not?"

"I have not thought of a rationale for it," Bork answered.

Much has been said about the effectiveness of Senator Specter's examination of Judge Bork. In his 1992 book *Matter of Principle*, former Judiciary Committee chief counsel Mark Gittenstein wrote that Specter's line of questioning on *Bolling* "truly rattled Bork," calling it "devastating." Gittenstein noted that Manne had prepared the Senator to pursue the issue with Bork after having been alerted to the point by an "unidentified federal judge." In his 1989 book *Battle for Justice: How the Bork Nomination Shook America*, Ethan Bonner reported that when Judge Bork gave that non-answer to Senator Specter's question, "Al Kamen, who was reporting on the hearing for the *Washington Post*, felt his heartbeat pick up. Bork was saying that he could not justify the decision to desegregate the D.C. school system thirty-three years earlier. Here was a story." As Bonner described it, the exchange was "a bombshell."

After a short break in the hearings, during which time Bork met with his advisors who told him that he had to return to the issue and try to extricate himself, Bork tried to clarify and supplement his answer. "My doubts about the substantive due process of *Bolling v. Sharpe* does not mean that I would ever dream of overruling *Bolling v. Sharpe*, as you suggested.... And furthermore I should make it clear, as I have said repeatedly, segregation is not only unlawful but immoral," he pleaded with both the Senate Judiciary Committee and the national television audience. It did not get him out of the predicament that he had created.

The day after Specter's confrontation with Bork, the *Washington Post* ran an article under the headline: "Senators Question Bork's Consistency; Nominee Sees No Constitutional Basis for D.C. Integration Ruling." "Bork's comments on the District school-desegregation case caused an uproar among his opponents, who seized on it to question his likely stands on future civil rights cases," reporters Edward Walsh and Al Kamen wrote in the *Post*. "In a statement, the Leadership Conference on Civil Rights called Bork's statement 'astonishing and disturbing' and said that his assurances that he would not seek to overturn *Bolling v. Sharpe* 'is of little comfort.'"

Senator Specter soon announced his opposition to Bork's nomination; he was the first Republican to do so and the dam burst. On October 6, the Judiciary Committee rejected Judge Bork's nomination by a 9 to 5 vote. After twelve days and more than thirty hours of testimony from Bork himself, the Senate voted 58-42—the widest margin in U.S. history—to reject his nomination to the U.S. Supreme Court.

Senator Specter, who spent most of his career struggling to maintain a delicate balance within his own party and who was fiercely criticized for having opposed Judge Bork's nomination, claimed afterwards that he had not set a trap for the judge. In his book, *Passion for Truth*, Specter described Neal Manne's role and their discussions about *Bolling*, noting that the case "posed a potential preparation trap for Bork's approach." Senator Specter insisted that he had not sprung the case on Judge Bork. "I laid out the issue in advance for the judge, to avoid any suggestion that I was trying to trap him."

I did not find out until much later what actually happened. Neal Manne told me, and now that both Judge Bork and Senator Specter have died, he says, "I am free to describe what happened. I was at the 'courtesy call' meeting between Judge Bork and Senator Specter, which was the only in-person discussion they had before the hearings. Specter and I very explicitly and extensively discussed how to set up and raise the *Bolling* issue, and anticipated that it would catch Bork off guard. I wrote the questions for Specter. Contrary to what Senator Specter claimed ever after, he never mentioned the case or the issue to Judge Bork or his handlers prior to the hearings, and intended that it would catch the nominee completely off guard." It is easy to understand why Senator Specter later claimed that he had not intentionally trapped Judge Bork, but harder to understand why Judge Bork never contradicted this. Maybe because the details no longer mattered to him after his nomination was rejected. Or perhaps he could not admit that he had come undone during Senator Specter's questioning of him about *Bolling v. Sharpe*. We will never know.

Democrats claimed victory, and President Reagan set about the task of finding a new nominee. Given the polarizing nature of the confirmation hearings, the President's next candidate would have to be a moderate; he needed someone who could coast through the confirmation process un-assailed. President Reagan picked Douglas Ginsburg, another D.C. federal appeals court judge, but after it was revealed that Ginsburg had smoked marijuana on more than one occasion, the former Harvard Law professor withdrew his nomination.

It was not long before I received another phone call from Washington. This time the call came from Bob Tuttle, an old friend from Southern California who was serving as Reagan's White House personnel director. It was not unusual for Tuttle to call me in my chambers to ask about judicial nominees or potential political appointments, and that afternoon he had a list of five names that constituted the short-list for Reagan's next Supreme Court nominee. "Remember, Bill," he said as he pronounced the names of one Republican after another. "We're talking about ours, not yours."

My first reaction was one of surprise. I asked my old friend why Anthony Kennedy was not on that list. Kennedy had been my colleague on the Ninth Circuit bench for seven years, and while I disagreed with him on pretty much everything—from the constitutional right of lesbian sailors to serve on submarines to the right of Hell's Angels to be free from "no knock" searches of their meth labs—I respected his jurisprudence. Moreover, I knew that Reagan had to have known him from Sacramento. I suggested my Ninth Circuit colleague to the White House personnel director, and not three days later, Kennedy's name appeared in the *New York Times*.

After Kennedy's confirmation—which, by the way, caused no waves—Tuttle called and told me the backstory. Immediately after I had suggested Judge Kennedy, he had called William French Smith, who had served as Reagan's first Attorney General. When Smith confirmed what I had told Tuttle about Judge Kennedy, he had gone straight to his boss, Howard Baker, who had left the Senate to serve as the President's Chief of Staff. Soon thereafter, Senator Baker recommended to President Reagan that he nominate Judge Kennedy to the Supreme Court.

I suspect that most Americans share my view that the country is better off having Justice Kennedy on the U.S. Supreme Court rather than Robert Bork. History sometimes turns on small events. Two fortuitous telephone calls that I had in 1986—a call with a former law clerk that supplied Senator Specter with a question for which Judge Bork had no answer, and a call with a friend at the White House that produced a new name for consideration—opened the door to Justice Kennedy's nomination to the seat that Judge Bork did not fill.

Judges of the U.S. Court of Appeals for the Ninth Circuit, 1986 (outtake photo)

Top row from left: O'Scannlain, Kozinski, Kennedy, Canby, Farris, Tang, Pregerson, Wiggins, Beezer, Poole (arms up)

Middle row from left: Alarcon, Brunetti, Schroeder, Thompson, Hall, Reinhardt, Nelson, Fletcher, Norris, Hug, Noonan

Seated from left: Wallace, Goodwin, Merrill, Browning, Ferguson, Boochever, Anderson, Sneed

26

THE *WATKINS* CASE AND THE BIRTH OF GAY RIGHTS

After I had been on the bench for seven years, my dear friend Andy Kaufman, who clerked for Justice Frankfurter when I clerked for Douglas and who had been a professor at Harvard Law since 1965, called me. "Bill, get on the phone and make an offer to Einer Elhauge," he said. Andy had never been so "presumptuous" in all the years of our friendship, so I paid close attention. He went on to describe an exceptional student who was first in his class at Harvard. He said that Einer had the most extraordinary legal mind he had encountered in a very long time and would be sought after by many other judges, but that he was interested in the Ninth Circuit and in working for me. I talked to Einer and hired him in an instant.

The timing could not have been better. Einer became the principal law clerk in 1988 to work on a case that made me prouder than any other: *Watkins v. United States Army.*[*] This was also known as my "gays-in-the-military" case, and it was both my most celebrated case and the most reviled opinion I ever wrote.

The first day that Einer arrived in my office, I assigned him a case that I could not wait to sink my teeth into. The case involved Perry Watkins, a black man from Tacoma, Washington, who first enlisted in the Army in 1968, when he was nineteen. In his original induction papers and in all his reenlistment papers from 1970 until 1979, he was candid about his homosexuality. Watkins was an exemplary soldier with an exemplary military record, described by his superiors as "one of our most respected and trusted soldiers both by his superiors and his subordinates." He was such an outstanding soldier that even when his sexual orientation was re-

---

[*] 847 F.2d 1329 (9th Cir. 1988).

peatedly looked into by the military, it was repeatedly found to be irrelevant to the quality of his service. But in 1980 he failed a security clearance review that could have resulted in his promotion to sergeant first class.

In January of '81, the Department of Defense issued two new regulations that were meant to clearly exclude gays from the Army and withstand the inevitable court challenge to that policy. One prohibited the reenlistment of any soldier or officer "who desired bodily contact between persons of the same sex ... with the intent to obtain or give sexual gratification." The second regulation required that anyone who fell in that category be discharged from the Army: "Homosexual personnel, irrespective of sex, should not be permitted to serve in any branch of the Armed Forces in any capacity, and prompt separation of homosexuals from the Armed Forces is mandatory."[*]

Watkins, represented by the ACLU, brought a suit against the Army in February of '81, challenging the denial of his security clearance. Many constitutional violations were alleged, but in October '82, Judge Barbara Jacobs Rothstein of the U.S. District Court for the Western District of Washington ruled for Watkins on the narrow grounds that the Army had violated their own procedural regulations. As the Army had by that time taken steps to discharge Watkins and deny his reenlistment, the trial court prohibited the Army from doing so. In '83, a three-judge panel of the Ninth Circuit Court of Appeals reversed those decisions, and sent the case back to the trial court so that the constitutional issues could be decided.[†] The trial court found no constitutional violations. Watkins was "separated from the service" when his term expired in 1984.

Watkins appealed, and in 1987 a new Ninth Circuit panel heard the case again. This is when I became involved. I had been hoping to have the opportunity to grapple with the issue of gay rights ever since the infamous ruling in *Bowers v. Hardwick*, which came down from the Supreme Court in 1986. Also known as the Georgia Sodomy Law case, it was a terrible decision. It held that Georgia's law criminalizing sodomy did not violate substantive due process. The facts of the case involved the police entering the home of an Atlanta man because he did not appear in court after being arrested for public drinking. They found him engaging in consensual oral sex with another man. They arrested him and charged him with sodomy.

---

[*] AR 601-280 and AR 635-200 (1981).

[†] *Watkins v. United States Army*, 541 F. Supp. 249 (W.D. Wash. 1982), and *Watkins v. United States Army*, 721 F. 2d 687 (9th Cir. 1983).

In a very close 5–4 ruling, Justice Byron White wrote for the Court that the Georgia law was in fact *not* a violation of the right to privacy; oral and anal sex between homosexuals was a criminal act. Chief Justice Burger, in his outrageous concurring opinion, wrote, "To hold that the act of homosexual sodomy is somehow protected as a fundamental right would be to cast aside millennia of moral teaching."

After the decision came down, I attended a dinner party at the home of a prominent L.A. attorney and contemporary art collector, Alan Hergott, who implored me to do something about this awful decision. We both knew well enough that the Supreme Court had the last word, but I could not resist asking Justice White about his opinion when I saw him at the Ninth Circuit Judicial Conference that summer. He said that it was not that big a deal since the decision only affected Georgia. I could not believe my ears and was determined to do what I could to change the legal situation for gays should the opportunity arise.

Back then, to be gay was to be a criminal. The breathtaking injustice of this was for me comparable to the injustice of racism, in which an immutable fact of an individual's life became something to be prosecuted or a reason for the denial of basic human rights.

So when the *Watkins* case arrived on my desk, I dove into studying *Bowers*, which was the controlling case at that time. I found a footnote in the decision that startled me. It was the eighth and last footnote and said, "Respondent does not defend the judgment below based on the Ninth Amendment, the Equal Protection Clause, or the Eighth Amendment."

This meant that the Court never dealt with the issue of equal protection because no such claim had been presented by the appellant. I put the decision down on Einer's desk and said, "See that footnote Einer? We are going to drive a truck through that footnote!"

When Einer and I worked on *Watkins* together, he was instrumental in articulating a very important aspect of what was wrong with the Army's attempt to use *Bowers* to justify its regulations. He pointed out that the Army was not banning sodomy, it was banning homosexuality. If you were heterosexual, got drunk and engaged in sodomy, you would not be excluded from the service or denied reenlistment. This was a discrimination based on status, not on conduct, and that became pivotal as we worked on the opinion.

I began drafting a majority opinion for the three-judge panel. The two other judges were both appointed by Jimmy Carter: Bill Canby and Steve Reinhardt. It was a tough opinion to write not only because I had to distinguish it from *Bowers,* but because establishing that a new group deserves heightened protection under the Equal Protection Clause is one of the great labors in constitutional law.

In addition to Einer, another of my clerks, Evan Caminker, joined the team. Both went on to clerk for Justice Brennan, so I had some awesome intellectual firepower working with me on this case. After Einer and Evan went on to clerk at the Supreme Court, the great young lawyer and writer Eddie Lazarus picked up where they left off. Eddie came to me from Yale Law School and was already a gifted writer—in fact he had already written a book, *Black Hills/White Justice*, that was published a few years later. Sitting together at the computer, my clerks and I wrote draft after draft for what eventually became a sixty-page opinion. Every word was thought through, every paragraph reviewed countless times, and we must have written thirty drafts just to get it perfect, just to make sure that "it sang."

My clerks and I picked apart the case. It was clear to me that the Army had overstepped and that Watkins deserved to be reinstated. I focused on the status of gays and lesbians and not their sexual conduct. We had to establish that gays and lesbians were a "suspect class" under the Equal Protection Clause, which would mean that government regulations that treated gays and lesbians differently were suspect, and the government's justifications for those regulations would receive heightened scrutiny. We focused on two points. First, gays and lesbians had suffered a history of purposeful discrimination that by making them the object of pernicious and sustained hostility deprived them of the political power to protect themselves in the legislative process. Second, sexual orientation is an immutable trait, that is, it is so central to a person's identity that it would be abhorrent for government to penalize a person for refusing to change it.

Perry Watkins had no choice about being gay. He could not change it, and in my opinion I wrote, "Although the causes of homosexuality are not fully understood, scientific research indicates that we have little control over our sexual orientation, and sexual orientation, once acquired, is largely impervious to change." And here is where I pushed my argument in very much the same way as I did when confronted with the Teamster's case: I flipped the subject of the sentence to see how logical or consistent the argument would then be. "Scientific proof aside," I wrote, "it seems appropriate to ask whether heterosexuals feel capable of changing their sexual orientation."

Once we established that gays and lesbians were entitled to heightened protection under the Equal Protection Clause, we had to turn to the Army's regulations to see if they were necessary to promote a compelling governmental interest. The Army asserted that it had a compelling interest in maintaining morale and discipline, which would be disrupted if heterosexual and homosexual soldiers served together. But the courts had already ruled in cases involving race that the existence of hostility and tension between protected groups does not allow the military to exclude or segregate one of those groups.

The Army also asserted that homosexual activity would undermine military discipline in various ways, from engendering disruptive emotional relationships to making soldiers more susceptible to blackmail. The problem was that the regulations did not just prohibit the acts that caused the disruption. And indeed heterosexual activity that caused the same disruption was not prohibited. The primary focus of the regulations was not on the disruption caused by sexual acts of homosexual soldiers but rather their identity, their status. The Army was not penalizing Sergeant Watkins for engaging in particular acts that they found disruptive, but for being who he was.

I concluded that the "Army's regulations violate the constitutional guarantee of equal protection of the laws because they discriminate against persons of homosexual orientation, a suspect class, and because the regulations are not necessary to promote any governmental interest."

We worked very hard to satisfy Bill Canby's questions and to respond to Steve Reinhardt's issues. Ultimately, Bill Canby joined in my opinion; I do not want to take all the credit for it, Bill was really with me, and when he responded favorably with some constructive suggestions to the opinion, I felt very comfortable integrating them into our drafts.

My old friend Steve Reinhardt dissented. Steve was pretty open about why he thought it was important that the Ninth Circuit not decide that case the way Bill Canby and I wanted to decide it. The task was whether we could distinguish this from *Bowers v. Hardwick*, and clearly we did. But Steve was thinking ahead. He was worried that the case might then end up in the Supreme Court, which was not exactly sympathetic to the rights of gay people and might then reverse our decision. I absolutely disagreed with him even thinking that way. I said, "Oh, come on Steve, just do your job. Do what you think is right, and don't worry about that."

In his dissent, Reinhardt said that he agreed that the military's policies violated the Constitution—one would have thought that would have been enough—but he said that given *Bowers*, he could not vote in favor of a policy that in effect challenged it. He wrote, "Were I free to apply my own view of the meaning of the Constitution and in that light to pass upon the validity of the Army's regulations, I too would conclude that the Army may not refuse to enlist homosexuals." But he said he was not. He had to abide by the Supreme Court precedent set in the *Bowers* case—which we all now know would eventually be overturned. Nonetheless, Steve stuck to his position.

We published the decision in February 1988 and it was big news. The *Los Angeles Times* wrote, "By striking down Army regulations barring homosexuals from military service, the U.S. Court of Appeals for the Ninth Circuit has tried to vindicate both the rights of homosexuals and the widely accepted view that sexual orientation, like the color of ones' skin, is fixed at birth." The article went on to say, "Though the decision strikes a blow for perhaps the most maligned minority in our society, it may not survive." The headline for the *New York Times* editorial was, "A Wise Court Salutes Tolerance."

Cass Sunstein, law professor at the University of Chicago, wrote in the *University of Chicago Law Review* in 1988 a learned article entitled "Sexual Orientation and the Constitution: A Note on the Relationship Between Due Process and Sexual Orientation." He analyzed our decision and praised it as effusively as a legal scholar would permit himself to do. After explaining the connection between *Bowers* and the *Watkins* case, and dismissing Reinhardt's arguments, he concluded:

> The conclusion of the *Watkins* court also contains a large and often overlooked lesson about the relationship between the Due Process and Equal Protection Clauses. The Due Process Clause is backward-looking; a large part of its reach is defined by reference to tradition. The clause is closely associated with, even if not limited to, the view that the role of the Court is to protect against ill considered or short-term departures from time-honored practices. The Equal Protection Clause, by contrast, is grounded in a norm of equality that operates largely as a critique of traditional practices. The *Watkins* decision provides reason to believe that constitutional protection against discrimination on the basis of sexual orientation will ultimately take place under the Equal Protection Clause.*

As Professor Sunstein demonstrates, the choice to base the *Watkins* decision on the Equal Protection Clause rather than substantive due process was not based merely on the legal technicality that the *Bowers* court left that particular door open. Equal protection is the more natural doctrine to use to address status-based discrimination. Moreover, moving the debate over gay rights from a discussion solely about the unenumerated constitutional right to sexual privacy towards a more complex discussion that includes the explicit constitutional command of equal protection of the laws gives the right a stronger jurisprudential and political basis.

---

* Cass R. Sunstein, "Sexual Orientation and the Constitution," 55 *University of Chicago Law Review* 1161, 1179 (1988).

That was not the end of this case. Another year had passed and at this point I had a new law clerk working on the *Watkins* case, Vik Amar. With all the controversy swirling about the *Watkins* decision, I circulated a memo suggesting that the full Court rehear the case *en banc*. In May 1989, the *Watkins* case was scheduled to be heard by an eleven-member *en banc* panel of the Ninth Circuit. By the luck of the draw, both Bill Canby and I were selected for the panel. Steve Reinhart was not on this one. The panel had to rule on whether to reinstate Perry Watkins to the Army.

The panel reheard the case but it withdrew our judgment! Instead it found that he should be reinstated on the incredibly recondite and technical grounds of "equitable estoppel."* The general idea was that because the Army knew for many years that Watkins was gay and yet promoted him and allowed him to reenlist, they could not thereafter change their mind and not allow him to reenlist just because he was gay. I could not believe that Judge Harry Pregerson would go in that direction, but that was what he wrote in his opinion reinstating Watkins to the Army, which would "simply require the Army to continue what it has repeatedly done for fourteen years with only positive results: reenlist a single solider with an exceptionally outstanding record."

I thought that the majority's opinion made no sense at all. Equitable estoppel is a doctrine ordinarily used in cases involving private parties. It can be applied against the government, and especially the military, only very rarely. In my opinion—and Judge Canby and I both held to our original analysis—there was absolutely no authority at all to support that line of reasoning. But as a strategy to keep it away from the Supreme Court, it worked. I can just see the Supreme Court looking at that Harry Pregerson opinion, shaking their heads, saying, "Huh?! Estoppel?! Forget it! That's a precedent that's going to be of no value to anybody." In the end, Watkins received a retroactive promotion to sergeant first class, $135,000 in retroactive pay, full retirement benefits, and an honorable discharge.

It was quite a case, and one that continued to resonate throughout my life. Right after the *Watkins* case, I was in the San Francisco courthouse, alone in that big marble hall, when a woman who worked on our staff appeared and walked toward me. As she got pretty close to me, I could see the tears in her eyes. She had just read the *Watkins* opinion. And while we had known each other in passing for years, this was a very different kind of encounter. She looked at me, clearly moved but having a tough time speaking. She managed to say how grateful she was for this work.

---

* *Watkins v. United States Army*, 875 F.2d 699 (9th Cir. 1989) (en banc).

Around the same time the Lambda Legal Defense Fund—a group of lawyers who worked in the field of gay rights—asked me if I would accept their award. As a sitting judge, I of course had to decline. Eight years later, when I had retired from the bench, I accepted their award with appreciation.

The case would appear in unexpected places. I was watching a movie on TV that was based on Tony Kushner's Pulitzer Prize winning play about AIDS and gay life, "Angels in America." In one scene two gay men were arguing about a legal case that was in the courts. My wife Jane (by then I had married the love of my life) perked up immediately, "They're talking about *your* case, Bill!" she said. Indeed, they were.

Then fast forward to our son David's graduation day at Columbia University. Tony Kushner was the commencement speaker and gave a wonderful speech which was both profound and humorous. At the end of the ceremony, there was a mob scene and we could not find David. I said to Jane that I will go find him, and as I walked around I walked right towards Tony Kushner. With the little bit of chutzpah that I have learned from Jane, I walked right up to him and introduced myself and explained my connection to the case in his play. I told him how much I appreciated how he referred to that case in his masterpiece.

Throughout the years after *Watkins*, there were many more cases involving gay rights. The AIDS epidemic claimed the life of Perry Watkins in 1996, two years shy of his fiftieth birthday. Much to my dismay, President Clinton signed the Don't Ask, Don't Tell bill that only reinforced how unjustly marginalized gay men and women were in the armed forces—indeed in society.

But slowly things began to change. And I could see the harbingers of that change, year after year, in conversations with my law clerks. Eventually, they all studied the *Watkins* case in law school and even those who did not knew about its importance. I would hear from them about their reactions to the case and their appreciation for working with a judge who had a part in it. One of my law clerks, Michelle Anderson, who is bisexual, told me eloquently how important the *Watkins* case was for her and how my involvement in it was one of the reasons that she had been so eager to clerk for me. Michelle has become a distinguished law professor, one of the leading scholars of the law of rape and sexual assault, and also, for the last ten years, dean of the CUNY School of Law. Under her leadership, CUNY has become renowned for its programs in public interest law and clinical law training, as well as the diversity of its student body and faculty.

This all culminated during an interview with Tobias Wolff, who was to be one of my very last clerks. Tobias had come out as a gay man several years earlier—indeed, he was just a boy when *Watkins* was decided—but during the interview we spoke about the importance of the *Watkins* case in his life. It was not a surprise that over the years he channeled his considerable intellect to work for gay rights and was one of the people who advised President Obama on the repeal of Don't Ask, Don't Tell.

Today, I look back on that groundbreaking opinion as being one of my proudest moments—one that was created with the help of extremely talented law clerks and the additional insights from my colleague Judge Bill Canby. The legal reasoning in that opinion has since become the norm in gay rights cases, and looking back, I have to say it established a milestone. My involvement in that case was one of the greatest privileges I have ever had as a judge. The conservative columnist Pat Buchanan called for my impeachment. The *New York Times* called me a great American and a courageous judge. I cannot say that what I did took courage. After all, I had Article III status and could withstand all the criticism. I was just happy to do something to address a fundamental injustice in our society.

In 2003, six years after I had retired from the bench, Justice Kennedy wrote the landmark opinion for the court in *Lawrence v. Texas*, which overturned *Bowers v. Hardwick*. I was pleased that my old colleague from the Ninth Circuit would have signed his name to that opinion. It may have been long overdue, but was clearly worth the wait.

Wedding of Bill Norris and Jane Jelenko, February 17, 1991

Back row: Don Norris, Barbara Norris, Bill and Jane, Kim Norris, Alison Norris
Front row: Semantha Norris, Seabree Blanchard, Nathan Norris, David Jelenko

27

Completing My J-Turns

I recruited extraordinarily intelligent, interesting, funny, and fully engaged young men and women as my law clerks year after year. And year after year, I watched as they embarked on remarkable careers: some clerked for the Supreme Court before moving on, others went into public service, prestigious law firms, government and the not-for-profit sector. Several became judges; others became respected law professors and law school deans. I developed traditions with them: we would always visit MOCA whenever there were interesting exhibits there. If they were athletes—and many were—there would be tennis tournaments, and I would be sure to take them skiing, whether or not they had ever skied before.

My first time on skis was at Sun Valley, Idaho, as a guest of Victor Palmieri. Victor was working for the Janss Investment Corporation, which had purchased the resort in 1964. The company had become an important client of Tuttle & Taylor's real estate department, and I occasionally did some litigation work for them. Victor invited a large group of business colleagues and friends up to the resort for a ski weekend. Some were fantastic skiers and others were novices; I was one of the novices along with my T&T colleague Graham Tebbe. We could barely get down the mountain! But after just a few hours of instruction—with lots of falling and hilarity—we managed our way down the slope, and I became hooked.

Skiing became a very important part of my life and the life of my family. I decided that it would be a great sport for all the kids; it became the glue that brought us together as a family. We began in Sun Valley, where all the kids learned how to ski, then we started going regularly first to Mammoth and then to Deer Valley, where Jane and I purchased a home.

Once I became a judge, I was sure to take my clerks skiing for at least one weekend. Some had no idea what they were doing, but also eventually became hooked. Others were pretty good on the slopes and just looked forward to our time together. Skiing offered not just a nice break for all of us but gave us some new points of reference once we were back in the office. One important skiing technique is to "complete the J-turn," which means that you want to finish your turn with your ski tips pointing back up the slope before turning the other way. It became a handy metaphor when my clerks would struggle with their legal writing. I would tell them that they had to "complete the J turn" when their argument was almost, but not quite, there.

It took very special young men and women to clerk for the Ninth Circuit generally and for me in particular. How did I find this exceptional group of clerks? First of all, I went about it by fully engaging my existing clerks in the recruiting process. They did the initial screening and the early interviews of the candidates. Not only did that mean that they would have another notch of experience on their belts before they left—this one for spotting legal talent—but they understood who I was and the way that I liked to work, so they could find young people with a complementary metabolism.

Gradually I developed a pretty good reputation, so I would get an impressive number of applications from law students who wanted to clerk for me, sometimes up to 250 in any given year. My law clerks would divide all the applications into three piles. The first would be the résumés of those who did not have a chance. The second would be the worthy applicants who might possibly be approached in the unlikely occasion that the others did not pan out. And then there was the third pile of outstanding candidates, from which they needed to winnow out the limited number we would invite for an interview in my chambers.

But the law students were not the only ones competing; we judges were competing for the top clerks as well. We would all look at the brilliant students who came from Harvard, Yale, Stanford, or the like. We also took into account their undergraduate record. But I was after more than what could be found in a paper record. I wanted to meet them, spend some time with them, and see how they responded to my questions not just substantively but also in other, less easy to quantify ways.

One important quality was the capacity to leave your ego at the door. What I meant by this was that my clerks had to have some healthy detachment from their work product, so that they could see it critically and respond well to criticism. When I worked with a law clerk, or a colleague or a partner, I wanted an exchange in which they were not just defending their own position—any more than I was. I wanted them to have the capacity to be ruthless in looking at their own opinions and their own drafts, as they were of someone else's draft. It was one of the reasons that I wanted them to call me Bill, so that we were all on equal footing.

When I started attracting Supreme Court clerks to join our practice at Tuttle & Taylor, we were able to up our game dramatically. To be a destination law firm for a former clerk in the Supreme Court enhanced the prestige of the firm so that clients began to look at the firm differently. As a judge, I also had my eyes on the Supreme Court. This time, I wanted to become a "feeder judge" to the Supreme Court, so that the best potential law clerks would be interested in working for me. During my years on the Ninth Circuit, I had great success in placing my clerks in the Supreme Court. In fact, Abner Mikva, at the time the Chief Judge on the D.C. Circuit, and I had a friendly rivalry to see who could place the most clerks!

For example, when Eddie Lazarus applied to be my clerk in 1982, it was immediately after Einer Elhauge had moved from my chambers to clerk at the Supreme Court. He was the first of many of my clerks to take that next step. Eddie had hoped for a slot in Ab Mikva's chambers, but did not get it at the first moment of opportunity. So I struck! I called him immediately and I offered him a job. He asked me if he could sleep on it and I told him absolutely not. He then asked if he could have an hour to talk with his father—who was himself a very accomplished attorney in D.C. I gave him that much. He called back and accepted, and later told me that "it was the best decision he ever made."

As was obvious from my approach with Eddie, I had an extremely aggressive timetable when it came to hiring my clerks: I did not give them much time to decide. Ann Alpers applied for clerkships in January, right after her Stanford winter break. I was the first person who called her and made her an offer on the spot. I told her that I wanted to know even before twenty-four hours had elapsed. She said that it was the easiest job offer she ever received and accepted. Once more, even without knowing that it would be this way, when she started work I had the ideal combination of clerk and case. Together we worked on a big and highly publicized case, *Newton v. NBC.*

In October 1980, NBC Nightly News aired a three-and-a-half-minute story called "Wayne Newton and the Law" about the famed entertainer Wayne Newton. In the segment, NBC journalists investigated Newton's ties to Guido Penosi and the Gambino Mafia family, alleging that Penosi may have helped Newton buy the Aladdin Hotel in Las Vegas for $85 million, becoming a hidden partner in the hotel deal in the process. Newton denied these allegations and noted that Penosi was merely a long-time family friend. Penosi, by contrast, claimed that he knew no one with the name Wayne Newton. The segment triggered a decade long legal battle that fundamentally challenged the First Amendment right to freedom of the press.

Seven months after the program aired, Wayne Newton filed a defamation suit against NBC and the journalists involved in the investigation into the Aladdin Hotel deal. He argued that the initial broadcast—and two others that aired after it—drew false and malicious connections between Newton and the mafia. The initial trial lasted thirty-seven days, and a federal jury in Las Vegas overwhelmingly supported Newton's claims. At first, the jury awarded Newton an astronomical $19.3 million as compensation, including $5 million in punitive damages. However, following a lengthy series of negotiations, that amount was lowered to $5,275,000 in 1989—still a huge sum.

Almost immediately, NBC appealed the decision to the Ninth Circuit. The famous First Amendment lawyer Floyd Abrams represented the network, as he had at trial. I heard the case with Judges Alfred T. Goodwin and Dorothy W. Nelson, took the lead in the questioning, and eventually wrote the unanimous decision.

In the New York Times v. Sullivan decision, the Supreme Court noted that in a libel case there is a difference between a public figure and the rest of us. A statement about a public figure is libel only if it is false, disparaging, and made with "actual malice." Actual malice is present only if the speaker knew the statement was false, or "subjectively entertained serious doubt as to the truth of his statement." For Wayne Newton to show he was libeled by NBC, he would have to show NBC broadcast a falsehood knowing it was false, or at least recklessly broadcasting the falsehood while entertaining serious doubts about its veracity.

There were two essential elements that we judges needed to assess: the first was if all the facts that NBC presented in their story were true, and the second was whether the location of the trial could have been a factor in the jury's decision. After all, the first trial had been tried in Las Vegas, the jurors were from Las Vegas, and the courthouse was on Wayne Newton Blvd. It is safe to say that someone who did not live in Las Vegas might consider the venue at least worth a second look.

The Newton case is different from the cases I have discussed before because so much of the disagreement between the parties concerned the facts rather than the law. In reviewing issues of fact, an appellate court like mine can operate on a spectrum ranging from only a cursory analysis of the lower court's procedures and findings of fact all the way to what took place in this case: an intense, meticulous reconsideration of all the facts and the evidence. Ordinarily we would give substantial deference to the findings of fact of the lower court and jury. But this was a libel case, and the First Amendment protection of free speech arguably requires greater scrutiny of a local jury potentially seeking to protect a local hero.

I wanted to be ready in case we as a panel of judges decided to independently review the facts, so I asked Ann Alpers to work on the whole record, sifting through all of the evidence. We needed to be ready at oral argument to ask counsel precisely which facts showed NBC knew parts of their broadcast were false, and determining a person's state of mind in such a situation is enormously complex. I did not read the entire record—though Ann certainly did—and when there was an area that she thought demanded some special attention, we would talk about it.

Here is where the interplay between the temperament of the clerks and the nature of the case could create a special synergy. For some cases, the clerks and I would engage in combat—in crafting our arguments we were claiming new legal territory and needed to aggressively fight over every inch of progress. This was the process with Einer Elhauge and Evan Caminker in the *Watkins* case; we really engaged in pitched intellectual battles on the arguments of the case. At certain points we were all fighting with each other! Not in a personal way, of course, but in highly charged intellectual confrontations, only because the case demanded arguments that were bullet proof, and the only way to establish the strength of those arguments was to subject them to an intellectual battery of tests.

Other cases require the delicacy, precision, and skill of a neurosurgeon, and that is what Ann brought to the Wayne Newton case. This was a case that required meticulous analysis as she underwent the delicate process of reviewing every aspect of its record. The case rested on evidence and credibility determinations because there were disagreements that often raised questions about the various witnesses' testimony. We had to review the evidence carefully first to properly question the attorneys at oral argument, and then to draw our own conclusions. Ann's phenomenal research gave my questioning at oral argument a level of precision and acuity that provided valuable information for writing my opinion.

After we three judges retired to our chambers to deliberate, we unanimously decided to reverse the judgment against NBC. On August 30, 1990, we released the fifty-one-page opinion that Ann and I wrote, and it is one of my favorites: "The media should not fear that its journalists' professional judgments will be second-guessed by juries without benefit of careful independent review." We found that Newton failed to prove malice. Throughout their investigation, NBC News reports had neither deliberately lied nor recklessly disregarded the truth. As such, they should not be held accountable for any misinterpretations that were drawn from the information presented in the segment. Following the 3–0 reversal of the judgment against NBC in 1990, Michael Gartner, the president of NBC News at the time, applauded the decision as "a sound victory for investigative journalism."*

Floyd Abrams wrote about the case in his book *Speaking Freely: Trials of the First Amendment*. He described some of the give and take during the arguments and wrote: "Judge Norris summarized the entire series of questions and the answers I had given by stating that in the First Amendment area, perhaps the approach that should be taken was to give less deference to a jury's determination of credibility, and more to other evidence, so as to guard against local jury bias and to ensure the prosecution of First Amendment rights." Here we return to the issue of the trial being held in Las Vegas. I made it plain to both attorneys that the concern of the court was more about the fairness of the trial of NBC in Las Vegas in front of a jury who loved their "hometown hero." After all, Las Vegas even celebrated a Wayne Newton Day!

When Floyd Abrams' book came out, I sent Ann a copy with the inscription, "Ann, in Chapter 4, Norris should be changed to Alpers. I miss you. Let's talk soon, Bill."

My life was changing during this time. Merry and I had decided to part, although I still remained very much a part of my stepchildren's lives, and I was single for a little while. My daughter Kim decided that I should meet a young woman named Jane Jelenko who was a superstar at the huge professional services firm KPMG. Kim had worked there as a consultant and moved on, but kept the friendship. Jane had astonishing success. She was a Barnard-educated New Yorker, the daughter of Polish Holocaust survivors—whose miraculous story of survival is one that requires another book—but they had died when she was just a teenager. Jane was the first woman consulting partner at KPMG. She was divorced and a single mother of an eight-year-old son named David. Jane and Kim would have lunch every now and then, and one day Jane was complaining because she missed the intellectual stimulation she had experienced at Barnard. She was so busy, she said, she could not find the time to take two weeks off to attend the Aspen Institute Executive Program, something she had long wanted to do.

And Kim said, "Well, I'm going to introduce you to my father. He has moderated some of the programs there." Kim arranged for the three of us to have dinner downtown—it was not a date! But in five minutes Kim backed off, Jane and I started talking, and the rest is history. We had our

---

* http://www.nytimes.com/1990/08/31/us/wayne-newton-s-libel-award-against-nbc-is-overturned.html

first date a week from that dinner at a particularly romantic restaurant recommended by my multi-talented law clerk Ann.

People can talk about soul mates, about the other half, about a marriage made in heaven, and this is what I have discovered with Jane. But I think that the best word to describe our marriage is "bashert," a Yiddish word that Jane, who was raised as a Modern-Orthodox Jew, taught me. It is one of those beautifully resonant and flexible words that encompasses so much—it refers to a fortuitous event, it refers to "meant to be," it means fate, but for me, it means the miracle of Jane in my life.

Jane introduced me to her world: Shabbat dinners, ballet and modern dance, Zionism (we've visited Israel five times), her various corporate boards, including Cathay Bank where she is the lone woman on the all-male board of directors. I rather enjoyed playing the role of "the dutiful spouse" for a change. Especially since I was the spouse of Jane. But I introduced her to my world as well: my children, the world of MOCA, skiing, and of course the life of a judge.

While we were courting in 1991, I invited her to an *en banc* hearing for a complicated white-collar crime case, *Hollinger v. Titan Capital Corp.*

I loved these white-collar crime cases. In 1984, I changed the minds of my panel in *Paulsen v. Commissioner of the Internal Revenue*—a case that eventually made its way to the Supreme Court. In July 1976, Commerce Savings and Loan Association of Tacoma, Washington, merged into Citizens Federal Savings and Loan Association of Seattle. Harold and Marie Paulsen were stock holders in Commerce and wanted to exchange their stock in Commerce for an interest in Citizens as a tax-free reorganization. They ran into trouble with the IRS because they did not report on their 1976 federal income tax return the $152,706 gain that they realized. They argued that since the merger created a tax-free reorganization, they did not have to.

The IRS disagreed.

Other federal circuit courts considering similar mergers had sided with the taxpayers, not the IRS. When the case reached the Ninth Circuit, I was the third member of the panel to hear the arguments in Seattle. The other two judges were from Reno and San Francisco and both arrived in Seattle believing that the Commissioner of Internal Revenue should lose the case.

The case turned on whether the Paulsens' exchange of their guaranty stock in Commerce for their passbook savings accounts and certificates of deposit in Citizens was an exchange of equity for equity or equity for debt. Only if the exchange was equity for equity would the merger qualify as a tax-free reorganization. In the end, we concluded that the Commerce stockholders did not retain a continuing proprietary interest when they received mutual share accounts in Citizens in exchange for their Commerce

Guaranty stock. Thus they did not receive equity. Three circuits had found otherwise, but when I looked at the details of the exchange, I said, "That's OK, they are wrong." After oral argument, my two colleagues agreed with me.

Not only did my panel ultimately agree with me, so did the Supreme Court when the case reached them a year later. The Chief Justice, William Rehnquist, wrote the opinion. When we saw each other at the Ninth Circuit Judicial Conference later that year, he remembered my opinion and gave me a pat on the back for it.

Hollinger was another case where previous courts had reached a result I thought unsound. The facts of the case were that Emil Wilkowski, a securities salesman, embezzled money entrusted to him by four clients. Wilkowski worked as a representative of Painter, a financial counseling firm, and sold the investment products of Titan, a securities company, as its registered representative. He received funds from various customers to invest—which he did, but only for some. Sometimes, however, Wilkowski instructed Titan to make the checks payable to him personally, and astonishingly, they did! Rather than investing these funds, Wilkowski diverted them for his own use. He used Titan stationery to generate bogus receipts and financial statements that indicated that the stolen funds had been used to purchase securities and mutual funds through Titan. A central wrinkle to the case was that eleven years before Wilkowski worked for Titan, he had been involved in some other fraudulent activities. The plaintiffs believed that Titan should have known this and disclosed that fact to them.

Ultimately, Wilkowski's activities were discovered, and he was convicted of criminal securities fraud and grand theft. The investors sought to recover their losses from Painter and Titan in a civil action for alleged violations of federal securities and state laws. The district court granted summary judgment to both defendants, which plaintiffs appealed. The case before us asked: were Titan and Painter responsible for Wilkowski's actions?

I was assigned to the three judge panel that originally handled the case. In the conference after oral argument, we decided that under pre-existing case law, a broker-dealer was not required to inform investors of every negative fact it knew about its registered representatives. After looking carefully at the evidence, we decided that Titan may have made an error in judgment in failing to disclose Wilkowski's conviction to his clients. But we agreed that while a fair-minded jury might reasonably find that the failure to disclose the conviction constituted negligence, a fair-minded jury could not find that Titan had acted recklessly.

I was assigned the opinion. The catch was that the case law in the Ninth Circuit was unsettled on this point. I thought that the best reading of the statute was that recklessness was required to find a violation, and there was a Supreme Court case that agreed with me. But some older Ninth Circuit cases applied a test, the "flexible duty" test, that was much closer to a negligence standard than to a recklessness standard. I circulated a draft opinion to my other two panel members, acknowledging that while it followed prior Ninth Circuit law as required, I was unhappy with it because I believed that the prior decisions were wrong. I then asked my panel members to join me in doing something unusual—to call for a vote by all twenty-seven judges of the Ninth Circuit to take the case *en banc*, so that it would be heard again before a panel of eleven judges. By deciding the case *en banc*, we could decisively overrule the suspect past cases, and make the law in the circuit consistent. The *en banc* vote was successful and I happened to be drawn to sit on the new panel of eleven judges.

I thought that it would be interesting for Jane to actually watch this unfold. Jane came to the courthouse in Pasadena and sat in the public box. She was struck by the tableau of eleven robed judges on the bench—two more than at the Supreme Court. She was also struck by the fact that the attorney for the plaintiff got no more than a few sentences out of his oral argument, when some of the other judges and I started pelting him with questions. There was a very lively discussion back and forth and the attorneys never got back to their prepared remarks. It was exhilarating but also a bit surprising to her. How on earth could the lawyers explain their argument, she thought, when we did not let them get a word in edgewise? In fact, later on she told me that she wondered if it was not a little bit rude of me to disrupt the lawyers' arguments. Could I have been just performing for her?

I reassured her that I was not putting anyone in an awkward position because I wanted to impress her! This was strictly business for me. I explained that the lawyers' arguments were already presented in their briefs, and oral argument is the time for the judges to work through whatever issues might be troubling them. It was an essential part of the process, and in fact, lawyers loved the give and take. I loved it when I was lawyer, and I still loved it as a judge.

After the *en banc* argument, the *en banc* panel voted to change the pre-existing Ninth Circuit law. I was asked to write the new Ninth Circuit landmark opinion in *Titan*. The Supreme Court declined to hear the case, so my opinion stands.

A year later, Jane and I married. It was then, and will always be, bashert.

28

PROTESTING INJUSTICE:
SENTENCING GUIDELINES AND THE DEATH PENALTY

Our justice system has to cope with what could be seen as philosophical questions. What does it mean to be guilty? How do we assess the evidence? Should the defendant's previous brushes with the law be a factor when we determine his guilt or innocence for a particular crime? These may be philosophical questions, but they were also very practical ones. Let the punishment fit the crime is an old cliché, but is a very real consideration for victims, for perpetrators, and for those of us in the justice system. Penalties for crimes can range from payment of damages to serving jail time, but there is one sentence that I will always consider a blot on our country's moral stature—death.

The two most memorable criminal cases from my time on the bench, for me, involved injustices in punishment that I tried to rectify. One case asked which factors that a judge relies upon in determining a sentence need to be proved beyond a reasonable doubt in order for a sentence to be fundamentally fair. The other demonstrated that the system that we have developed for imposing the death penalty cannot be fairly operated at all.

United States v. Restrepo was argued before an *en banc* panel of the Ninth Circuit on January 17, 1991.* The case itself involved the relatively new guidelines for sentencing in the federal courts, which I nicknamed "Steve Breyer's guidelines." The reason for this was that the future Supreme Court Justice served on the United States Sentencing Commission from 1985 to 1989 and was one of the authors of those guidelines. Whenever we talked from then on, I would tease him about the impact of

---

"his" guidelines, because the two of us amiably disagreed about what their effects would be. I believed that they represented an historic break from the practice of endowing trial judges with the virtually unfettered discretion to sentence up to the statutory maximum. Under the guidelines, judicial discretion is all but eliminated. This seemed to me to be a grossly unfair requirement that would inevitably lead to defendants receiving harsher sentences. My prediction was certainly borne out by the facts in *Restrepo*.

Dario Restrepo was indicted on two counts of distribution of cocaine (counts I and II). His co-defendant, Judith DeMaldonado, also was charged with distribution of cocaine in count II. Additionally, she was indicted for two incidents of possession of cocaine with intent to distribute (counts III and IV). DeMaldonado pled guilty to counts II, III, and IV and agreed to testify against Restrepo in exchange for a lighter sentence. At trial, DeMaldonado testified that Restrepo provided all the cocaine that she had sold, and an additional amount of cocaine that she had turned over to the police. Restrepo was convicted of counts I and II.

At Restrepo's sentencing hearing, Maldonado, the only witness, repeated her testimony from the trial. The court then found that all the drugs involved in the charges against DeMaldonado in counts III and IV and the additional drugs she turned over to the police were part of a common scheme in which Restrepo was a participant. Relying on this finding, the court added all those drugs to the quantity of drugs involved in the charges against Restrepo (counts I and II), for the purpose of fixing the base offense level of Restrepo's sentence. As a result, the court adopted the guideline range of forty-one to fifty-one months imprisonment specified in the federal sentencing guidelines. The court then sentenced Restrepo to a forty-six month prison term with six years supervised release. Had the district court not aggregated the drugs involved in counts III and IV and the drugs DeMaldonado turned in with the drugs involved in counts I and II, the guideline range for Restrepo's sentence would have been twenty-seven to thirty-three months.

Restrepo appealed to the Ninth Circuit, claiming that his due process rights were violated. While the facts of counts I and II were found beyond a reasonable doubt by the jury verdict, the facts that formed the basis of his enhanced sentence were only determined by the judge at the sentencing hearing using a preponderance of the evidence standard. The original panel upheld the conviction on a 2–1 vote.

Restrepo petitioned to have the case reheard *en banc* to reconsider whether the preponderance of the evidence standard was consistent with due process. The petition was granted, and the *en banc* panel upheld his conviction, but I dissented.

Congress explicitly made each act of selling or possessing cocaine a separate crime. Due process requires that each element of a crime be established beyond a reasonable doubt. The prosecutor could have charged Restrepo with possession of the drugs involved in counts III and IV, tried to prove the case beyond a reasonable doubt, and achieve the same sentence. Instead, the prosecutor proved part of the case, and tried to get the enhanced sentence through the back door of proving additional crimes at the sentencing hearing under a much easier standard of proof. This seemed to me to violate due process, and I argued that the federal sentencing guidelines should be interpreted to require that additional crimes used to enhance a sentence be established by a stricter standard than a mere preponderance of the evidence.

Beyond the narrow issue of the use of evidence of additional crimes was the larger change the sentencing guidelines made to the long tradition of judicial discretion in sentencing. For all aspects of sentencing, "[t]he [g]uidelines have replaced unfettered judicial discretion with an elaborate factfinding process that structures judicial decisionmaking." I argued that this elaborate factfinding process gives rise to a liberty interest that requires due process protection under *Matthews v. Eldridge*, the cornerstone case of our due process doctrine. This would require that facts used for sentencing be judged under a higher standard than preponderance of the evidence whenever those facts were used to enhance a sentence beyond the base sentence for that offense.

I acknowledged in closing my dissenting opinion that "I am asking our circuit to break ranks with virtually all of our sister circuits. With all due respect to them, I believe their opinions are generally infected with the same faulty analysis that infects the majority's opinion in this case.... There are signs, however, that the dam is finally cracking, signs of an emerging awareness of the truly profound implications of the changes the Guidelines have wrought. I had hoped that our court in this case would have chosen to lead rather than follow."*

Although the Supreme Court denied certiorari review in *Restrepo* in 1992, the Court revisited these issues in later cases. In a line of cases decided under the Sixth Amendment's guarantee of a jury trial, the Court has reformed sentencing in the direction I suggested in my *Restrepo* dissent, and indeed found in 2005 that the mandatory application of the federal sentencing guidelines violated the Sixth Amendment.†

---

* *United States v. Restrepo*, 946 F.2d 654 (9th Cir. 1991) (en banc) (Norris, J., dissenting).

† *United States v. Booker*, 543 U.S. 220 (2005).

I still have a photograph of my clerks from that year: Bill Dodge (now teaching at the UC Davis School of Law), Clark Freshman (now teaching at the UC Hastings College of Law) and Jean Manas. We are wearing baseball caps, a gift to us from Jean who worked on that case with me. The caps are inscribed with the sentence: "Ask about *Restrepo*."

Jean was another one of my extraordinary clerks and a man who was justifiably confident in his abilities. He was born in Turkey, spoke about seven languages, and graduated at the top of his Harvard Law School class. He and Barack Obama competed to be the head of the Law Review; Jean lost the election. I asked him why. "I was too liberal for them," he explained.

Jean was not interested in going to the Supreme Court to clerk, even though I am convinced he would have made it. He wanted to go abroad, to Europe, and do something for the migrant workers coming from other countries. As someone who was born in Turkey, he had a great appreciation for the plight of the "guest workers" who had left their countries to find a new life in Western Europe and were welcomed with horrible exploitation, miserable housing, and often great danger. With his prodigious linguistic ability, he was in a unique position to talk to everyone involved—the workers, the hosts, and the local NGO's addressing the issue.

Jean received some grant money to support a year of this kind of work, and then returned to the U.S. He told me his experience about being over there, and how gratifying he found the work. His challenge was to figure out a way to continue to do it while supporting himself. I pushed him hard on his desire to do something for emerging economies. He assured me that this was exactly the kind of work that he wanted to do. Then I gave him some advice that I do not think he expected.

"Go to Wall Street and get your hands on the levers of power," I told him. "If you can figure out how to influence the movement of capital you could make a real impact. You've got the talent and experience to do things like that."

This piqued his curiosity and he started applying to various investment banks on Wall Street and reported back to me. He had been flooded with offers. Only one firm hesitated because they looked at his résumé and they asked him with more than a touch of arrogance, "What is there on this résumé that indicates that you have the mathematical talents and ability for this job?" He got a little grin on his face as he was wont to do and replied, "Well, I got an 800 on my SATs in math. Will that do it?" They immediately gave him an offer! Eventually he ended up at Goldman Sachs, and went on to become a huge success. He went on to head Mergers & Acquisitions for the Americas for Deutsche Bank before founding the Foros

Group, an independent M&A advisory firm. But when we worked together crafting my dissent in *Restrepo*, he was relentless in tracking down the relevant case law to support our argument. He could make the intuitive leaps that meant that arguing with him about the case expanded the breadth of our arguments.

The vindication of my dissent in *Restrepo* stands in stark contrast to the results of another case that came later—the tragic and troubling case of Robert Alton Harris. This was another situation where I found myself protesting an injustice when a majority of my colleagues as well as the Supreme Court went the other way. During the summer of 1978 in San Diego, Robert Alton Harris and his younger brother gunned down two sixteen-year-old boys and stole their car. The car was meant to be a getaway car when they robbed a San Diego bank. Shortly after the murders and robbery, Harris was arrested. A laundry list of charges was leveled against him, including kidnapping, burglary, auto theft, murder, and bank robbery. He was also mentally unstable, even impaired. This was not an excuse, of course, but a fact. One year later, the San Diego County Superior Court found Harris guilty of kidnapping and murder, crimes punishable by death.

In 1972 the California Supreme Court, in *People v. Anderson,*[*] had ruled the death penalty unconstitutional in California, relying on language in the state constitution, "cruel or unusual punishment," that varied from the language in the United States Constitution, "cruel and unusual punishment." A voter initiative, Proposition 17, reinstated the death penalty in 1973. The California Supreme Court again found the death penalty statute unconstitutional, this time because the statute did not allow defendants to offer mitigating evidence as required by the United States Supreme Court in *Gregg v. Georgia.*[†] However, in 1977, the California state legislature reenacted the death penalty in a form that met the requirements of *Gregg*. Over the following years, trial courts invoked the death penalty in dozens of cases, but the California Supreme Court always vacated the sentence. Political turmoil over the lack of any executions led in 1986 to three justices of the state supreme court, including Chief Justice Rose Bird, losing the election that would have allowed them to remain on the court. The question of whether any crime was punishable by death bitterly split the population of California and the entire country. The Robert Alton Harris case, because of its compelling facts and because it would be the first execution in California since the halt of executions in

---

[*] 6 Cal.3d 628, 493 P.2d 880 (1972).

[†] 428 U.S. 153 (1976).

1972, became the battleground for California's ongoing struggle over the legality of the death penalty.

The case also exacerbated the brewing tension between the Supreme Court and the Ninth Circuit, and within the Ninth Circuit itself. In 1990, the Circuit Court attempted to halt Harris' imminent execution. Judge John Noonan issued the first of many stays—or efforts to suspend further legal proceedings in a trial, sometimes indefinitely. Judge Noonan argued that Harris' traumatic upbringing impeded his judgment, and that he could not be sent to his death because of his mental disorder.

I was not a member of the original panel that heard the case, but as the execution date of April 21, 1992 approached, the conversations within the court became more and more intense. Some of us were determined to do what we could to stay the execution. The legal battle had lasted fourteen years and produced an unprecedented twenty-one separate appeals.

The execution was scheduled for 12:01 AM. The day before, Jane and I had returned from our place in Deer Valley. Our time there had been punctuated by the calls, faxes, and concerns about this case, and I realized that I needed to go back to the office. When I returned, I divided my time between working on a tax opinion and a case that literally involved life and death. The fax machines were constantly humming, with opinions, orders, and information about Robert Alton Harris.

Individual judges or groups of judges could issue stay orders in a situation like this, but we were all running out of time. Over the last hours, the Ninth Circuit issued an unprecedented four orders to stay the execution. The Supreme Court dismissed each one immediately. I issued my own order very late that evening, hoping that there was enough time to stay the execution but not enough time to vacate my order. But the Supreme Court delayed the execution and vacated my order, just as it had vacated the three other orders that were filed by other judges on the Ninth Circuit. Following the four stays of execution, the Supreme Court took an unusual step when it ordered, "No further stays of Robert Alton Harris' execution shall be entered by the federal courts except upon order of this court."*

The coast-to-coast battle delayed the execution until 6:07 AM.

After his pathetic, lavish, childlike, final meal of "Kentucky Fried Chicken, two pizzas without anchovies, Pepsi and jellybeans," Robert Alton Harris was gassed to death in San Quentin State Prison.† Though Harris was the first person put to death in California in twenty-five years,

---

* *Vasquez v. Harris*, 503 U.S. 1000 (1992) (5th order).

† http://articles.latimes.com/1992-04-11/news/mn-140_1_robert-alton-harris

his controversial sentencing, and the subsequent legal battle, highlighted divisions both within the population and throughout the court system, which continue today.

One of my former clerks, Evan Caminker, writing in the *Yale Law Journal* with Erwin Chemerinsky, the husband of my former clerk Catherine Fisk, summed up the legal maneuverings during the last few days before Harris' execution as follows:

> The judicial opinions entered over these few days are shocking. The majority of the Ninth Circuit panel that overturned the district court's temporary restraining order, and the seven Supreme Court Justices who vacated the subsequent stays of execution, ignored or misapplied legal principles without justifying their departures from established law. Their understandable frustration resulting from recent experiences with delayed executions led to a last-minute rush to execution in *this* case. To ensure that the State executed Harris as scheduled, judges sworn to uphold the Constitution failed to exercise their responsibility to exercise detached, considered judgment.[*]

Throughout my life, I have been adamantly opposed to the death penalty. For me it is not just a legal issue; my opposition has been based on moral and practical grounds. How could we as a country interpret and reinterpret the Constitution in such a way that a just punishment was also an officially sanctioned murder? There were some times when the possibility of being nominated to serve as a Justice on the Supreme Court arose, where questions of my position on the death penalty could actually have made a very significant impact.

Once, when Walter Mondale ran for President in 1988, he had put me on his short list of potential nominees. His failed presidential campaign put an end to that possibility. In March, 1993, Justice Byron White announced that he would be retiring from the bench at the end of the term. There was a brief flurry of activity among some of my supporters to advocate for my candidacy to fill the vacancy, though I did not participate. Eddie Lazarus met with several others at the venerable California Club in downtown L.A. to strategize about this and then Eddie drafted a letter to President Clinton on behalf of all the Norris clerks. It concludes: "In sum, if you seek to appoint a Supreme Court Justice who has a lifelong record of commitment to progressive values but who is not an ideologue, who is

---

[*] Evan Caminker and Erwin Chemerinsky, "The Lawless Execution of Robert Alton Harris," 102 *Yale Law Journal* 225, 225-26 (1992) (emphasis in original).

scholarly but not narrowly academic, and who has demonstrated re-markable success in building coalitions across political and social divides, you could do no better than Judge Norris." Although I did not think I was a likely appointment for political reasons, and did not take my boomlet seriously, I was tremendously touched when I found out what my friends had said of me.

Around the same time as this was going on, I happened to be with Justice Scalia in his chambers one day. The Justice teased me and said that I could easily do this Supreme Court job. I replied that it was not for me: Justices' vacations came at an inopportune time for me because I liked to take off during ski season rather than during the summer. I also pointed out that I was too old, and had taken too many controversial positions. Scalia agreed, and said that they were unlikely to make such a bold appointment. Of course we were both right. Clinton appointed Ruth Bader Ginsburg in June 1993. She is a great appointment.

I stepped down from fully active status as a Ninth Circuit Judge in July, 1994 (to enable President Clinton to appoint another judge to the Ninth Circuit), and found myself in the luxurious position of having Senior Status. My family staged a celebration at MOCA. I continued to hear cases, I had law clerks, but the pace of my life on the court slowed and I felt a bit more freedom to express my opinions.

When I was asked to be the commencement speaker for the Loyola College of Law in May 1995, I took the opportunity to discuss the death penalty, because I have always been disappointed in the lack of passion among our Supreme Court Justices on the topic, as well as the refusal to look at the larger context surrounding each individual case.

One of my former clerks, Larry Solum, was the dean of Loyola at the time and is now a professor at Georgetown Law School. Catherine Fisk, another former clerk, was at Loyola as a professor before moving to the UC Irvine School of Law. I told the graduates that they were actually crashing a "Norris chambers' reunion," and that my primary job was not to be a judge, but to run "a farm team for the Loyola law school faculty."

But I quickly went on to more serious matters and spoke about the death penalty. I wanted to describe to them why, despite its unfortunate recent resurgence of popularity, capital punishment was not working in the United States. I did not make a moral argument; these were new lawyers, with lawyers' minds, that had to think wisely and well about seemingly insoluble problems.

First I described the numbers from that year—it pains me to realize that these statistics have only gotten worse today. Back then, there were more than 3,000 inmates under sentence of death in our prisons, and the numbers kept growing. The previous year only thirty-one of those inmates had been executed but during that same year 250 more death sentences were announced. Congress had recently made fifty-eight new crimes punishable by death, and the Supreme Court was spending half of its time on death row cases.

Only ten days before I delivered this speech, the most recent execution in the United States had taken place, this time of a mentally impaired Montana man named Duncan McKenzie, who murdered a Montana school teacher and had spent twenty years on death row. I asked the graduates a basic question: what took so long? Why was it necessary to warehouse Mr. McKenzie for such a long time? I had served on four of the five Ninth Circuit panels that considered the McKenzie case over the years so I knew the case well. And his ultimate death felt to me like a failure.

One of the constitutional claims of McKenzie's lawyers was that the state trial judge had given the jury unreasonable instructions for their deliberation. McKenzie's main defense was that he did not have adequate mental capacity to actually form an intent to kill. The state trial judge told the jury that McKenzie had to prove this lack of intent to kill; he was not innocent until he was proven guilty. He was guilty until he could prove himself incompetent.

These instructions were terrible, because they relieved the prosecution of the burden of proving every element of the crime beyond a reasonable doubt. When the verdict was appealed to the Montana Supreme Court, McKenzie's lawyers argued that the instructions had violated the Due Process Clause of the Fourteenth Amendment. The state court again ruled that the instructions were just fine. The case went to the U.S. Supreme Court and was returned to the Montana court for reconsideration. This time the state agreed that the jury instructions violated due process, but McKenzie was still guilty and should be put to death. They said that the jury instructions were "harmless," even if they violated the U.S. Constitution.

Resolving this question of whether or not unconstitutional jury instructions entitled McKenzie to a new trial took thirteen years. Thirteen years to settle that single issue and seven more to settle other issues. For twenty years McKenzie was on death row—which in itself could be considered as cruel and unusual punishment—only to be ultimately executed. In one of those decisions, a majority of the Ninth Circuit actually supported his execution and said that his long incarceration did not constitute cruel and unusual punishment. I was furious and wrote in my dissent, "In advocating that death row inmates forego opportunities to remedy constitutional violations that they may have suffered at trial and at sentencing in order to avoid suffering the additional constitutional violation of cruel and unusual punishment, the majority gives new meaning to the notion of 'mockery of justice.'"*

His death filled me with despair. I told the law school graduates, "I wonder whether our country, which prizes both human life and due process of law, will ever be able to administer what retired Justice Harry Blackmun called the 'machinery of death' in a way that anyone could possibly say was rational."

When I spoke to these graduates, I had a chance to articulate what was so important to me about capital punishment, but also about the law. I told these young people that I truly believed that lawyers are our democracy's great advisors, critics, commentators, shapers of perspectives and opinions, analysts and leaders. We are the officers of justice and the defenders of our constitutional legacy and the heart of our power is legal reasoning. But legal reasoning goes only so far. Its greatest strength emerges when it is tempered with compassion.

I like to think that my talk made an impression on these young graduates. My former clerks in the audience certainly thought that it did, and I was grateful for that, because much of what I have learned has come from my clerks. Even though we never spoke about it explicitly, when we were writing a brief, or sitting at Shabbat dinner at our home, or skiing together in Deer Valley, or just hanging around my chambers, I could see that they took seriously their responsibility to uphold the promise of liberty and fairness that rest at the center of our legal heritage. These young people reinforced my belief in that promise year after year. Each new class of law students, and each new class of clerks or young associates offers me the hope that perhaps in these young men and women, we will come closer to resolving some of the great social issues of our time—with compassion and justice.

---

* *McKenzie v. Day*, 57 F.3d 1461, 1489 (9th Cir. 1995) (Norris, J., dissenting).

PART V

RECLAIMING MY FIRST AMENDMENT RIGHTS

"The law is also memory; the law also records a long-running conversation, a nation arguing with its conscience."

Barack Obama

Final official judicial portrait of Bill Norris, 1997

29

LEAVING THE JUDICIAL MONASTERY

Being a circuit judge is a dream job: fascinating work, the opportunity to make a contribution to society, and job security for life. Why would anyone want to leave such a powerful job?

These were the points that Jane was making to me over breakfast one morning in 1997 when I told her that I had decided I wanted to retire from the Ninth Circuit. She was surprised. "Are you crazy? People would kill for your job," she said. "What you do is so important. Isn't that where you want to be?"

In truth, I had to tell her that it was not. I had thought about this question a great deal, increasingly now that I was so happily married and my life with Jane was so complete. I had been on the job for seventeen years, and certainly I had loved a great deal of my work there. Nonetheless, throughout those years a part of me always wanted to be back and fully engaged in the game. I wanted to participate in political and civic life in ways that were simply impossible for a sitting judge.

And earlier in 1997, my dear friend and college roommate, Don Stokes, had passed away after a bout with leukemia. Jane and I went back to Princeton for the memorial service to pay tribute to this great man and share our memories with Sybil, their kids and Layman Allen. It was an inspirational yet simple service which reminded me of the Quaker wedding service I had attended for Don and Sybil decades before. I don't know that Don's death played a role in my decision to retire from the bench. But I do know that he was an enormously important figure in my life and, subconsciously, I might have been thinking of him when I chose to embark on a new path.

I had taken Senior status three years earlier, but over that time the voice in my head only got louder. "That is enough," I thought. "I want to

243

go back to my old life. I don't know what that means, exactly, but I want to get involved in community affairs and Democratic politics again." While I was a judge, Jimmy Carter, Ronald Reagan, George Bush, and Bill Clinton had all been president. We were already through Clinton's first term when I made my decision to retire (thereby giving the President an opening for another appointment), and I began thinking about how I might become a political activist again.

I had just completed *Jacobson v. Hughes Aircraft*, a very complicated and challenging case that focused on ERISA, the Employee Retirement Income Security Act of 1974, in which retired employees of Hughes Aircraft objected to the restructuring of their pension fund.

Hughes Aircraft is a huge corporation that set up a defined benefit retirement pension plan (the Contributory Plan) in 1955. This plan required Hughes' employees to contribute a fixed amount, and Hughes to contribute whatever amount more was required to keep the plan solvent. The employees' contributions were automatically deducted from their pay. The plan was well managed over the years, and by 1986, as a result of employer and employee contributions and substantial investment growth, the Contributory Plan's assets exceeded the value of accrued benefits by almost one billion dollars.

In 1987, Hughes stopped making contributions to the overfunded plan, as the terms of the plan allowed. The employees' contributions continued to be deducted from their pay, as the terms of the plan directed. In 1989, the plan was amended to establish an early retirement program for existing employees. Soon thereafter, Hughes again amended the plan to provide that, effective January 1, 1991, new participants would not contribute money to the plan, but would receive fewer benefits. Existing members could continue to contribute at the old level, and receive the old level of benefits, or opt to be treated as new participants. The new arrangement (the Non-Contributory Plan) thus covered all new employees as well as those old employees who opted out of the Contributory Plan. The same pot of money was used to fund both plans.

Five Hughes retirees receiving benefits under the Contributory Plan filed a class action lawsuit claiming the amendments violated ERISA. They claimed that Hughes was using the surplus from the Contributory Plan to fund the new amendments: the early retirement program and the Non-Contributory Plan. But ERISA allows employers to make just such changes to pension plans. The heart of the argument was that billion dollar surplus. The retirees sought to have it divided among themselves rather than used to fund the plan in the future. They argued that Hughes was improperly using plan assets for its own benefit. And they argued that by changing the plan the way they did, Hughes effectively terminated the old plan, and that termination of a plan requires the company to distribute the accumulated surplus to the plan participants.

The district court dismissed the case before discovery or trial, stating that according to the facts alleged in the retirees' complaint, Hughes had not violated ERISA. The retirees appealed.

I suppose that the predictable liberal ruling would side with the 10,000 retirees against the corporate giant and say yes, Hughes violated ERISA. But I just could not be the predictable judge. As far as I was concerned, under federal law it was an open-and-shut case—the company had not violated ERISA. The three judge panel consisted of Betty Fletcher, Harry Pregerson, and me. Betty agreed with me in conference, but Harry did not. I had the writing assignment for the majority opinion. I circulated what I thought was just a run-of-the-mill opinion based upon the language of ERISA. As expected, I got a dissent from Harry but, at least initially, Betty concurred with me. So I amended my opinion a bit to respond to Harry's dissent and circulated that opinion. After I did, Betty changed her mind. Betty and I were often on the same page so I was quite surprised by this. I will never know what caused her to switch, but I ended up turning my majority opinion into a vigorous dissent.

In my view, there was no basis in ERISA, in case law, or in basic logic for the majority's decision that in amending its pension plan, Hughes effectively terminated the plan. If ERISA needed to be changed to restrict amendments to pension plans that are running a large surplus, that need should be addressed by Congress, and not by the Ninth Circuit.

Furthermore, terminating the plan and distributing the surplus could have serious negative consequences for all of the current participants in the Hughes Plan still working towards retirement, because the plan assets could be diminished to the point of putting their ultimate benefits in jeopardy.

I wrote, "Today's decision announces that in the Ninth Circuit there are severe, if vague and ill-defined, restrictions on the discretion of employers charged as plan settlors under ERISA with responsibility for the design of qualified pension plans. Only time can tell what impact these vague and uncertain restrictions will have on employers and their employees."[*]

Hughes, of course, asked the Supreme Court to review the Ninth Circuit ruling. Not long afterwards, I retired from the court.

---

[*] *Jacobson v. Hughes Aircraft Co.*, 105 F.3d 1288, 1312-13 (9th Cir. 1997) (Norris, J., dissenting).

There is a cute ending to this story. A year later, I was in the San Francisco airport and heard someone calling me, "Judge Norris! Judge Norris!" It was my former colleague, Judge Alex Kozinski, who was excited to fill me in on the continuing saga of the Hughes Aircraft case. He told me that his former law clerk, Paul Cappucio, was representing Hughes in its appeal to the Supreme Court. I had gotten to know Paul a little bit, and he was keeping me posted about the case. I knew that the Supreme Court had granted the petition for certiorari and learned that Paul's brief pretty much lifted my arguments from my dissenting opinion. Paul called me immediately after the argument before the Supreme Court and said, "Look, my job was not to screw up your dissent." He also told me that the government had filed an amicus brief on their side because it was a major issue relating to the interpretation of ERISA. When the Deputy Solicitor General got up to argue, Judge Breyer interrupted him immediately and asked, "Does the United States government agree with Judge Norris?"

The answer was, "Yes, your honor." And that was that. The Ninth Circuit decision was unanimously reversed on January 25, 1999. Justice Clarence Thomas wrote the opinion. I will always consider *Jacobson*, which we decided in the Ninth Circuit on January 23, 1997, as my last major opinion, albeit a dissent.

At the end of my judicial career, as at the beginning, my relationship with my clerks was one of my great joys. While I had a solid track record of hiring women law clerks, the years from 1994 to 1997 were remarkable in that all the clerks selected in those years were women with one notable exception. When President Clinton appointed Stephen Breyer to the Supreme Court in 1994, Steve called me and asked me to help him out by taking one of his law clerks whom he had picked to work for him on the First Circuit. l already had a full house of three clerks—all women—for the 1994-1995 year, but I agreed and took on Kevin Russell as a fourth clerk. Kevin went on to clerk for Justice Breyer the next year.

When I made my decision to leave the bench, there were still some smaller cases to complete, but my most important task was to tell my new law clerks—Tobias Wolff, Eric Hecker and John Pottow, who had not even started work yet—that they would be moving to a different judge.

Jane and I were in Deer Valley for a few days when the three new clerks first arrived, so when we returned I called them all into my chambers. "Well, gentlemen, I have some news for you," I said, and then proceeded to explain that I was in the process of making a decision to step down from the bench. This was all very confidential because as a sitting judge I did not want any of this to be revealed to the outside world until it became official. I looked at the stunned faces of the three young men and reassured them that I would take care of them when the time came.

A bit shell-shocked, the three of them walked out of the meeting and went to lunch. "Wait a minute," John Pottow said, breaking the silence, "Did we just get fired?" They all laughed.

I was as committed to these young men as I had been to all my clerks and made sure that they found good places to land, which they did. Tobias worked for Judge Betty Fletcher in Seattle. John Pottow finished up the year with Judge Calabresi, and I secured a clerkship for Eric with Judge Thelton Henderson, a distinguished U.S. District Court Judge in San Francisco. Nonetheless, the next six weeks, we had a lot of work to do finishing up some important final opinions.

The press release was faxed to major media outlets on July 24, 1997. "Senior Circuit Judge William A. Norris announces his resignation from the Federal Bench." The calls flooded in; people with whom I had not spoken for years reached out to congratulate me and find out my plans. I told them all the same thing, "I want to reclaim my First Amendment Rights!" And I meant it!

I had looked around to find my next professional home. The Tuttle & Taylor I knew no longer existed; it fell prey to the dislocations brought on by the expansion of huge national firms into Los Angeles. I liked the idea of finding a firm that might have the same appealing qualities as my old firm had. I thought that I found them in Folger Levin, a prestigious, fifty-attorney San Francisco firm that was founded in 1978. The partners seemed eager to bring me on board.

I packed up my files, took down the art that decorated the walls of my chambers, and sat at my desk for the last time. I began my work there when Jimmy Carter was the President and I was fifty-three years old. I was now seventy, practically still a newlywed in a relationship that had brought me more happiness than I had ever imagined possible. I had accumulated a new family of more than fifty law clerks, gifted and giving men and women, who had gone on to do great things and who continued to reach out and let me know about their lives. I was privileged to write some opinions that will be studied by many future generations of young lawyers, opinions that even may have nudged history along a bit. And now I was off to a new law firm and new chances to reclaim my First Amendment rights. Of course I felt a little sad as I walked down the hall to say goodbye to my old friends.

But I also felt free.

Donald Stokes

30

INDIAN GAMING, PROPOSITIONS, AND PRIVATE PRACTICE

After I retired, I began to work at Folger Levin. Johnny Levin was the son of an old friend of mine who had been very supportive of me when I ran for Attorney General. And Folger was from the Folger coffee family! They were a very small law firm and I was reminded of the early days of Tuttle & Taylor when I joined them. I had some routine cases and helped them out on some of them, but I realized that I was not interested in returning to the life of a trial lawyer. I wanted to do appellate work, but a small firm such as theirs did not have a great deal of appellate work. While it was a perfect transitional spot for me after I left the judicial monastery, I knew that I would not be there for long.

Even though my stay was short, I was involved in a very important case while I worked at Folger Levin. My old friend Ray Fisher had moved to Washington as Associate Attorney General under Attorney General Janet Reno. One afternoon, I got a call from Ray. He told me to expect a call from Governor Gray Davis, who was in a bit of a fix because he needed to do something about the tribal casinos.

A federal statute requires that Indian tribes seeking to offer casino-style gambling must get approval from their state government.* In early

---

* I recognize that there is a controversy over the best term to use to refer to the indigenous peoples of North America. In general, I believe groups should be able to choose their own names and to decide which terms should be considered disfavored. Nationally, there remains no strong consensus among the First Peoples themselves. In California, among the people I interacted with, Indian was the term most used. Four of the five tribal groups most responsible for the passage of Proposition 5 use the word Indian as part of the official title of their tribe. Indian was the term most used in the negotiations I describe, and it is the term used in the applicable statutes and regulations.

1998, at the end of his term, Governor Pete Wilson negotiated a compact with a tribe that was very restrictive about the types and amounts of gambling that could be offered. In response, the Indian tribes of California drafted an initiative designed to ensure they could offer all the gaming they wanted, and qualified it for the ballot. California voters overwhelmingly passed Proposition 5, the "Tribal Government Gaming and Economic Self-Sufficiency Act of 1998." This statutory initiative required the governor to approve any tribal casino proposal. The campaign to qualify and pass Proposition 5 was the most expensive in history at the time—$90 million in total spending. In addition to money spent to qualify and pass the initiative, California Indians spent another $5 million backing political candidates including Governor Gray Davis and Attorney General Bill Lockyer, who both won their elections by very narrow margins.

After Proposition 5 passed, some tribes immediately opened casinos. The Justice Department did not want to engage in any conflict with the Indian tribes of California, but they were obligated under federal law to shut down casinos operating without state approval. Governor Gray Davis was faced with the challenge of reaching an agreement with the tribes that was fair to both those tribes that had jumped the gun, and those who waited. Ray Fisher had spoken to the new Governor and told him to call me because "Bill will get you the compacts." In March, 1999, Gray Davis did call and asked me to help him out. He told me that he wanted to make me his Special Counsel for Tribal Affairs, which was a title that I had never imagined receiving!

For me, this work was intriguing. Everyone knew about Proposition 5, but no one could imagine how it was going to be implemented. The difficulty of obtaining a general agreement consistent with the Justice Department's requirements for the signed covenants only added to the challenge. Davis and I spoke about this for a little while, and then I agreed. Before I knew it, on March 25, 1999, a press release with the headline "Governor Davis Appoints Special Counsel for Tribal Affairs" was circulated. "Judge Norris' judicial experience, commonsense, and willingness to listen will enable my administration to negotiate the compacts in good faith," Governor Davis said in the press release. "His appointment underscores my intentions to treat tribes with the respect and dignity they deserve as sovereign nations."

The first step was for us to appear at a large meeting that he had planned for leaders of all 107 of the state's Indian tribes in April. The meeting was going to be at the auditorium of the Ronald Reagan Office Building in Los Angeles, and this was a command performance for me. It was the first time in history that all of the state's Indian tribes were invited to attend a meeting with the Governor, and the auditorium was packed with men in suits and men and women in formal tribal dress. The meeting opened with appropriate tribal ceremonies, followed by remarks by the Governor and Attorney General Bill Lockyer.

When it was his turn to speak, Governor Davis made it clear to the tribes that he was opposed to gambling as a matter of public policy. He was, however, willing to enter into negotiations with them in deference to the will of the people in California as expressed by their overwhelming vote in favor of Proposition 5. He also made it clear that he wanted reasonable limits on the number of slot machines the tribes could operate to make sure that California would not turn into a gambling magnet like Nevada. Finally, he cautioned the tribes that he was not in favor of the creation of casinos in large cities like Los Angeles, San Francisco, San Diego, and Sacramento.

Not every tribe was operating a casino. Davis told the assembled tribes that he would let the ones that had already started casinos keep them. We had not discussed this before, and I cringed inside when I heard him say that. This policy seemed blatantly unfair to the tribes that were obeying the law and not operating casinos because they did not have signed compacts.

Davis then said that he wanted to limit the number of slot machines in the aggregate in the state of California. Slot machines were a crucial issue because they generate a small fortune. By permitting the law breakers to carry on, he raised the possibility that tribes that followed the rules and waited to start gaming operations would be left with very little room under the cap to install new slot machines. Clearly this did not make any of the tribal leaders happy.

When he introduced me, he told the story about when he and Jerry Brown applied to be associates at Tuttle & Taylor and we hired Jerry Brown and not Gray Davis. He said this in a self-deprecating way, with a bit of a wink towards me. Then he introduced me as his newly appointed Special Counsel for Tribal Affairs and promptly departed with the Attorney General, Bill Lockyer, leaving me with the task of figuring out how to relieve some of the tension and negotiate with 107 separate sovereign nations.

There I was, sitting on the stage with two government lawyers, facing 107 tribal leaders and an army of lawyers. I said to myself, "What have I gotten myself into? How am I supposed to do this? How do you negotiate with 107 sovereign Indian tribes?" I had no idea. One thing became clear was that they were pleased with me as Davis' appointment. This is where my old Ninth Circuit colleague, Judge Bill Canby comes in. He is the leading expert on Indian law, and I was in the majority with him on a very important opinion that he wrote. This news had somehow gotten out among the tribal leaders, so my reputation as someone sympathetic to their cause had preceded me.

There were microphones all over the auditorium, and I looked out on this mass of tribal leaders and lawyers, wondering where I should begin. I remembered the State Board of Education, the Police Commission, and meetings about modern art as we organized MOCA, and knew that I always began working in the same way—by listening—and it would be a good place to start here. "Look, I want you to know that I know very little about Proposition 5," I said. "I know a little about it, I've taken a look at it, and I voted for it, and I must say I didn't read it very carefully. We have to get this negotiation started, so why don't you educate me?"

I encouraged them to start talking to me. I let one after another take the microphone, and listened. In fact, when I finally looked at the details of Proposition 5, I realized that it was a mess. It placed no limits on the number of casinos statewide or the number of gambling machines and tables each casino could operate. It lowered the gambling age to eighteen. It purported to allow the tribes to continue using the video slot machines that the state and federal governments had deemed illegal, without actually changing the state constitution to make those machines legal. Under terms of the initiative, tribal casinos would be self-regulated, governed by a tribal appointed gaming board, so state or local governments were prohibited from any involvement in casino operations. A fund was set up to reimburse local governments for their costs associated with casino operations and gave two percent of the profits to tribes that were not involved in gaming.

Attached to the proposition was a detailed gaming compact that required the Governor's signature. There was absolutely no window for negotiation. It was a completely one-sided compact in which there was no possible leverage for the state. The only input from the state was a signature line for the Governor, and that clearly was not going to happen.

One after another the leaders said the same thing in different ways, but it all boiled down to the fact that the Governor needed to sign the compact. I listened to each one. After a few hours, I got up, thanked them, and said, "Okay, I get it. Now my client, the Governor, was just on the stage, and he said he was not very happy from a public policy standpoint in having a Las Vegas-type casino. But you've got your initiative passed by the voters, with a lot of votes, and I'm going to respect that. But we are going to a have to have some limits."

I told them that I was the Governor's lawyer and that the message that I had received from them was "that I have to go back to my client and tell him something that he's not going to want to hear and that is contrary to what he just laid out." I appealed to their reason, noting that if that was what they wanted me to do, then I would do it. But it would be counterproductive because the Governor would not accept this plan.

"If I were the Governor, I don't think I would either," I continued. "So where do we go from here? "

The room was silent.

I then suggested that we begin to discuss a process for moving forward. "How are we going to do this?" I asked. "Given that all of you are individual Sovereign Nations?" After a fruitless back and forth, I suggested that we stop the meeting and they should go out, talk among themselves, and figure out a manageable process. After they do, they should let me know, and we would start our negotiations. I could not have come up with a better plan.

For the next five months, through the spring and summer, we met with smaller groups of tribes all over the state. They became more engaged in the negotiations, and we were making some progress in our efforts to get the tribes to agree to a uniform compact rather than dozens of separate agreements, each with one nation. Complicating the matter was the fact that there was a challenge to Proposition 5 that was before the California Supreme Court and no one knew what the court was going to decide. In August the California Supreme Court struck down Proposition 5, saying that it was unconstitutional because Proposition 5 was put on the ballot by the tribes as an initiative process statute. Instead, a constitutional amendment was required because the California State Constitution prohibits Las Vegas-type gaming in California.

With this California Supreme Court decision, I had some new leverage, and our negotiations became more serious. We were not going to negotiate individually with all the tribes; we were going to have a common compact that every one of them was going to sign or they could not operate a casino. We were running out of time because the legislature would be in recess in early September. The governor would only sign a compact if the constitution were amended to allow the gaming machines the tribes wanted, which could be achieved by a straight up or down vote on the ballot. But we had to have the approval of the legislature before we could get that amendment on the ballot in the springtime.

I spent a lot of time in Sacramento negotiating and finally worked out an agreement that seemed to have promise. Many tribes had not been operating casinos in violation of federal law, and we had to take care of them. The formula that I worked out for everyone was every tribe that signed a compact would get a minimum of 350 machines, since the slot machines were a critical issue. The tribes that had obeyed the law pointed out that many of the tribes that had already set up their casinos already had a thousand slot machines. I was having a tough time with that, because I basically agreed with them. But I knew that I could not get Gray to go any higher for the total number of machines in operation, and a 350 minimum was the most that would fit. And I thought, "I can't do it. I can't do it." I kept trying, but it looked as if we were at impasse, and we only had two or three days left.

I must say I really pulled a rabbit out of a hat. By this time, there were three or four of their lawyers that I knew well, and we were able to really talk to each other on terms of mutual respect. I could not have all of the tribal lawyers in the room or a hotel meeting room at one time, but talking with those few might allow us to reach an agreement they could share with their clients and the rest of the tribes. The Governor wanted to have an aggregate of about 30,000 machines statewide, and the tribes wanted about 8000 more. We also had to deal with the distribution of these casinos because not every tribe wanted to operate one.

I do not remember the genesis of the idea, but I came up with the solution of giving every tribe the right to 350 machines. If a tribe did not want their machines, they would be transferred into a pool that could be accessed and licensed by other tribes. In essence, tribes without casinos would trade in their right to machines for an ongoing payment, and the tribes with casinos would have the opportunity to add more machines. I took the three or four lawyers with whom I had been working and explained my plan. They immediately understood how it would work and persuaded their clients and other tribes to accept the terms. One of the tribes had an excellent location for a casino in the Sacramento area. The lawyer told me that his client had been operating lawfully, but was only going to be entitled to 350 machines while other tribes might have over a thousand. I knew exactly what he was getting at, so we worked out a formula that would give the tribe some priority for future machines above the 350 minimum.

Then we were faced with the problem of how much they would pay the non-gaming tribes for their allotment of machines. I came up with the strategy that we should take the revenue stream from gaming and divide it up among the non-gaming tribes on a per capita basis. This meant that all of the non-gaming tribes were going to get different amounts of money. It seemed to me to be fair and just.

I got nowhere with it. All I heard was, "Sovereignty!" Even the larger tribes with a couple thousand members wanted the tribes to be treated equally, with equal payments to each tribe. They were adamant in designing the scheme to emphasize the sovereignty of each tribe. I realized that this was unlike any other negotiation that I had experienced. The clock was ticking, and we had to get our plan to the legislature the next morning.

We worked all night, and the negotiating group now included Gray's chief of staff. I went down the corridor in the building in Sacramento where we were working, into the big room where we were going to meet all of the tribes who were there. And someone reviewing the document that we were going to present to the legislature found a mistake. So we had to run back to the offices and make the correction and then move even faster into that room. But by morning we reached an agreement on the entire scheme, and knew what we needed the legislature to put on the ballot.

We finally finished all our negotiations with nearly sixty tribes. Our agreement allowed them to expand current gambling operations into a system that looked a lot like the kind of gambling in Nevada. Video slot machines were legalized, and casino employees were permitted to unionize. The non-gaming tribes each ended up with over a million dollars every year. We also made sure that tribes that were reaping the benefits from large numbers of slot machines gave money to the state for gambling addiction programs.

On March 7, 2000, sixty-five percent of California voters approved Proposition 1A, the Gambling on Tribal Lands Amendment. This time, when I voted on that proposition, I knew exactly what it involved! But this issue was not settled quite yet. If I had still been a Ninth Circuit Judge, I might have had to decide on the validity of Proposition 1A, which was challenged on the grounds that it offers preferential treatment based on ethnicity and was therefore unconstitutional. On December 22, 2003, the Ninth Circuit Court of Appeals upheld Proposition 1A, finding that federal law allows states to grant Indian tribes a monopoly on Nevada-style casinos.

I had a tremendous sense of accomplishment in that work, but also was getting a bit restless at Folger Levin. In 2000, as if he knew that I might be restless, a partner at Akin Gump approached me and asked me to come aboard and only do appellate work. The plan was for me to develop a distinct appellate practice with which all of their offices, even the international ones, could be involved. The ultimate addition to the deal, which made it completely irresistible, was that my former law clerk Eddie Lazarus was a part of the package!

Jane Jelenko and Bill Norris, 1991

31

•

Last Legal Adventures at Akin Gump

For fourteen years, I worked at Akin, Gump, Strauss, Hauer & Feld, a huge law firm that in size and reach and ultimate influence was the polar opposite of Tuttle & Taylor. Originally a Texas firm, founded in 1945 by Robert Strauss and Richard Gump, Akin Gump eventually was home to nearly 800 lawyers all over the world. One might think that in a firm of that legacy, that prestige, and that size, all of their practice areas would have been fully developed. But the beauty of the firm for me was that there was still some uncharted territory for me to explore.

In 2000, I got a call from Channing Johnson, the co-founder of the Los Angeles office of Akin Gump. I had recruited Channing to Tuttle & Taylor out of Harvard Law School in 1975. He was (and is) a marvelous corporate lawyer. At one point, he expressed interest in getting into the enter-tainment industry and asked me to make a connection for him with my friend, Max Palevsky. Max, being his impish self, turned me away, saying that Channing was not crazy enough to be in that business. I had remained in touch with Channing over the years and was intrigued by his suggestion to get together and discuss joining Akin Gump. Channing believed the firm needed a first class appellate group to help elevate it to the top tier of firms in the country. I knew that Eddie Lazarus would be interested in starting an appellate practice with me, so the two of us negotiated a package deal.

Many consider an appellate practice to be the crown jewel of a law firm, a practice devoted to the purity of legal reasoning that can eventually lead lawyers to arguing their cases all the way to the highest court in the land. As a judge, I faced hundreds of appellate lawyers, all of whom were trying to persuade me about a point of law. They were distinct from the litigators—which I was at Tuttle & Taylor—whose job it is to focus on the facts and marshal those facts in the most persuasive possible way so that a jury (or judge) would decide cases in favor of their clients. As appellate lawyers, we are far less concerned about "facts" than we are in exploring the relevant points of law and where interpretation of the law may have been flawed, may require reinterpretation.

Eddie and I were a perfect match. We had an intellectual and generational synergy between us that gave us a strong gravitational pull within that large firm and with the legal community outside the firm. We quickly added another superstar to our team when I reached out to Rex Heinke, a lawyer's lawyer from Gibson Dunn and a boutique appellate firm, who was completing his tenure as president of the Los Angeles County Bar. He would eventually become the leader of our national appellate practice as well as the L.A. litigation group. The national appellate practice grew to twelve lawyers, including a Washington contingent that boasted Tom Goldstein of the famous SCOTUS Blog and Patricia Millet who went on to sit on the D.C. Circuit Court of Appeals. I am told by my colleagues that the initial appeal for them to join the firm was that I was a significant part of the team.

I had barely settled in my new office at Akin Gump in Century City when I received a call from the General Counsel for Suzuki, the large Japanese automobile manufacturer. They had been battling with the magazine *Consumer Reports* over an old story about one of Suzuki's SUVs and had retained two very large law firms in the East to represent them in seeking damages and a reevaluation of their cars. They were appealing a summary judgment that they had lost in federal district court, and were going up to the Ninth Circuit. The General Counsel concluded that it would be in their interest to find a former Ninth Circuit judge to join their team.

This case fell right into the sweet spot of the practice that Eddie and I had been hired to develop, so I agreed that we should talk. Eddie Lazarus' office was right next to mine and I would not think about taking on such case without his intellectual legal horsepower. We met with the representative from Suzuki, and he told us the background of the case.

In 1988, *Consumer Reports* published a story about the Suzuki Samurai and rated it "Not Acceptable" because it could to roll over during accident avoidance tests. Suzuki addressed the problem but could never get *Consumer Reports* to change their ratings. In 1996, the Sixtieth Anniversary issue of *Consumer Reports* was published and they still had not changed the ratings. Suzuki challenged the validity of the *Consumer Reports* Samurai test and, on the heels of the Sixtieth Anniversary issue, brought an action against the publishers of the magazine, an organization called Consumers Union, alleging product disparagement. Consumers

Union made a motion for summary judgment that was granted by the district court, which held that a reasonable jury could not conclude by clear and convincing evidence that CU had acted with actual malice.

Eddie and I had a fantastic time with that case—it was one that we could sink our collective teeth into! We filed our brief on June 25, 2002, and Warren Ferguson, Wallace Tashima, and Susan Graber were on the panel. Wally Tashima wrote the opinion.* The key issue that we focused on was that *Consumer Reports* was actually biased against Suzuki. We argued that a reasonable jury could find by clear and convincing evidence that *Consumer Reports* was actually aware that its statements about the Samurai were false. We pointed out that *Consumer Reports* essentially rigged its testing to produce a predetermined result by modifying its testing course solely for the Suzuki test and repeatedly running extra tests until a rollover could be achieved. We also relied on evidence that *Consumer Reports* personnel urged drivers to try to tip the SUV over, and cheered when one finally did so. We also argued that Consumers Union was in the midst of an aggressive capital campaign, so there was an additional motive to boost its revenues.

Consumers Union challenged our argument and noted that the overwhelming weight of the evidence demonstrated the skill and dedication of its staff in researching and publishing the Samurai story. There could not possibly be any actual malice, it argued, because *Consumer Reports* would never engage in this practice given its long tradition of providing these evaluations of consumer products. It said that we took "a few facts out of context," and pieced them together "in a contrived and inherently implausible fashion without any supporting evidence." It argued that the Ninth Circuit should reject our arguments as conjectural and instead place greater weight on Consumer Union's assertions that it absolutely believed in the truth of its statements.

The court disagreed! It found in our favor concluding that there was sufficient evidence from which a jury could reach the conclusion that Consumers Union was guilty of rigging its tests. They also found that there was sufficient evidence of a financial motive that a jury could have reasonably reached a conclusion of actual malice. In a vote of two to one, the court reversed the lower court's decision, and we won. The case was sent back to the lower court for trial, but Consumers Union settled with Suzuki before the trial could begin.

---

* *Suzuki Motor Corp. v. Consumers Union of United States, Inc.,* 330 F.3d 1127 (9th Cir.), *cert. denied,* 540 U.S. 983 (2003).

260 | LIBERAL OPINIONS

We had a number of fascinating cases over the years and a few of them ended up in the Ninth Circuit.

On occasion, an old friend of Jane's from her college days, Russell Frackman—a top entertainment and intellectual property litigator at Mitchell Silberberg—would bring me in to prepare his team for oral argument before the Ninth Circuit. I had helped out with a case involving the singer Michael Bolton, and in 2000 and 2001, he again asked me to get his team ready for their appeal on behalf of the music recording industry in the very closely watched case against Napster, the P2P file sharing online service. This was the first major case to address the application of copyright laws to peer-to-peer file sharing.

The three judges on the panel were Judges Beezer, Schroeder. and Paez. Russ did an excellent job presenting the primary appellate argument. A fairly young partner from Paul Weiss had a small part arguing on behalf of the music publishers. Apparently, I had grilled the young lawyer so thoroughly in moot court that when it came time for him to make his argument for real, he addressed one of the judges as "Judge Norris." He did this once, and the judge ignored it, but the second time it happened, the judge said, "Counsel, Judge Norris is not here today. But if he *were* here today, he would have something to say about that!" The next day, before my colleagues even began to get to the substance of what had transpired in court, they told me that little vignette. We all had a great laugh about it, and it became something of an inside joke among us.

One of our most important cases was the *City of Hope v. Genentech* appeal in which the plaintiff sought to preserve the unprecedented judgment of $300 million in compensatory damages and $200 million in punitive damages it had won in the lower court. City of Hope sued Genentech for breach of their contract whereby Genentech was to develop, patent, and commercially exploit a secret scientific discovery in return for royalties. The case turned on whether there was a fiduciary relationship which would support the punitive damages award, and if not, whether the jury award of compensatory damages should be set aside. Irell and Manella had taken the City of Hope case on a contingency basis, and like their client, they were highly motivated to win the appeal. There were 18 amicus briefs filed in the case, demonstrating its significance to the intellectual property world and the business of biotechnology. Eventually Eddie became the principal writer of the brief which involved coordinating with an army of lawyers. In the end the fiduciary duty claim was thrown out, but we prevailed on the compensatory damages so our client and our legal colleagues were ecstatic.

I never made any secret about my opinion of capital punishment and what a stain it is on our integrity as a nation. I did what I could as a judge, but had never litigated a case that involved the death penalty—until I joined Akin Gump.

In 1993, Bobby Lee Holmes was convicted of a horrible rape and murder of an elderly woman, who had been beaten, raped and robbed and died a year later of her injuries. At trial in a South Carolina court, Holmes argued that the forensic evidence that placed him at the scene of the crime had been contaminated, and in one instance, planted. He also attempted to introduce evidence that another man named Jimmy McCaw White actually had attacked the women and was responsible for the injuries that led to her death. The trial court refused to admit the exculpatory evidence.

The South Carolina Supreme Court affirmed his conviction and death sentence. Mark McDougall, a lawyer in Akin Gump's Washington D.C. office who does lots of death penalty work and had been part of Holmes' trial team, contacted Eddie Lazarus about taking Holmes' case to the U.S. Supreme Court. I acted as counsel of record, and Eddie, Jeff Kehne, and another attorney named Mike Small filed a petition for certiorari, which was granted.

Mike was another member of our appellate team and already quite a star. He was a former Justice Department and ACLU official with extensive experience in high-profile constitutional and civil rights matters and was a perfect match for this case. We added a Cornell University law professor and veteran death penalty appellate lawyer named John Blume to the team that prepared Holmes' briefs on the merits. We decided that Blume should argue the case before the Supreme Court.

We focused on Jimmy White as the cornerstone of our defense, arguing that he committed the murder for which Holmes was charged. The point of law was that South Carolina's rules of evidence effectively prevented Holmes from presenting evidence of third-party guilt. Our brief to the Supreme Court argued that South Carolina's rules on third-party guilt evidence violated the Sixth Amendment rights of capital defendants.

On January 31, 2006, the Supreme Court found in our client's favor in a unanimous 9–0 decision authored by Justice Alito (his first majority opinion as a member of the Court). The Supreme Court resoundingly agreed with our position. It reversed Holmes' conviction and sentence and remanded for a new trial at which Holmes could present evidence of third-party guilt. The *Holmes* case is also notable because it was the last time that Justice Thomas asked a question at a Supreme Court oral argument until shortly after the death of Justice Scalia, more than ten years later.

In 2009, Eddie was tapped by President Obama to become second in command at the Federal Communications Commission, so he left Akin Gump for Washington. I continued to work at the firm for another five years. Looking back, I feel very proud about my contributions to the

development of Akin Gump. When the firm launched a national advertising campaign showcasing our core values, it chose me as the face of
"Integrity."

My skiing days were over (thanks to a "tib/fib" break caused by an
errant skier on Christmas Day in Deer Valley), so I took up golf with the
same zeal I had devoted to skiing in the past. My kids have all caught the
bug and enjoy playing with their dad at Bel Air Country Club. Jane and I
take several golf trips a year—in the Desert, in Cabo and in our beloved
Deer Valley. We have also enjoyed traveling together to exotic places like
St. Petersburg, Turkey, Kenya and Tanzania, Bhutan and India—places
where a kid from Turtle Creek would never even dream of visiting.

In those final years, one case that was especially dear to my heart
involved Proposition 13. My opposition to that proposition began soon
after it had passed in 1978, when I represented over twenty school
districts in their attempt to have it overturned. Over the years, I continued
to be unhappy with what had unfolded in California because of it.

One day in 2009, I was reading about the California Supreme Court's
decision on Proposition 8,* a proposition that banned gay marriage that
had been approved by California voters the year before. The decision was
highly anticipated, and because I had always been particularly concerned
about the civil rights of gay citizens, I wanted to read the decision itself
very carefully. The Supreme Court of California upheld Prop 8 as constitutional—a terrible result for gay people—but its reasoning gave me an
inspiration. While the question of gay marriage was not ostensibly connected to California tax policy, the arguments that the judges had to
resolve involved some of the same vexing questions that I had dealt with
in the *Amador* case on Prop 13 in 1978: was Proposition 8 an amendment
or a revision of the California Constitution?

The Supreme Court concluded that Prop 8 was an amendment because
it did not affect the structure of state government. I thought that the
decision was correct, even though I did not like the outcome. But what
intrigued me was the analysis in which Chief Justice Ron George sys-
tematically reviewed the various California Supreme Court cases over the
decades and the distinctions between an amendment and a revision.

The case that jumped off the page at me was *Raven*. The California
Supreme Court held that a proposition put on the ballot through the
initiative power restricted the judicial power of the California judiciary,
specifically their power to interpret the constitution with respect to provisions in the constitution protecting criminals. The California Supreme

---

* *Strauss v. Horton*, 46 Cal.4th 364, 207 P.3d 48 (2009).

Court said you *cannot* restrict the interpretive power vested in the judicial branch to that extent in an amendment. That is a revision.

"Wow!" I literally said, "Wow!" It felt to me as though the Chief Justice, who had given speeches deploring California's initiative process in the past, had written his analysis as a personal invitation to me to use it as an opening to actually challenge Prop 13. I raced into the office of my colleague Rex Heinke, who ran the appellate and litigation department in our Los Angeles office. "Rex," I said, "We can finally do something about Prop 13—not in its entirety, but we could now challenge the constitutionality of the two-thirds requirement to raise taxes. As far as I know, it has never been litigated. Here's our case that we go with."

He was extremely skeptical and looked at me as if I had lost my mind. But the more I explained my reasoning, the more he began to see some merits in what I was saying. I focused on one of its four sections—Section 3—that had been very easy to ignore. Sections 1, 2, and 4 of Proposition 13 delineated property taxes and the power of local governments to determine the tax rates. In fact, those sections went to the heart of what triggered Proposition 13: the legitimate concern, even anger, over the high and escalating property taxes in California.

Section 3 had nothing to do with property taxes, nor with how the value of the property is assessed or how the rates should be determined. Section 3 explicitly limits the legislatures' power to tax, which is one of our elected officials' most fundamental powers. Section 3 mandated that there must be a two-thirds majority to increase taxes, which often led to paralysis in the legislature. I wanted to find a way to return power back to the legislature.

As Justice George had noted in the Prop 8 decision, the 1849 California State Constitution made a distinction between an *amendment* to the Constitution and a *revision* of the Constitution. There is no clear line differentiating amending and revising, other than that the process for doing each is different. Put simply, it is easier to *amend* a Constitution than it is to *revise* the Constitution, which requires a much more rigorous process.

In 1911, the state instituted the initiative process, which moved the power to amend the constitution directly to the people, without the intermediaries of their elected officials in the legislature or the governor's office. The issue went back to that basic question: was Proposition 13 an amendment to the California Constitution or a revision? If it were an amendment, then the vote of the people stood. If it were a revision—which is what I believed—then it required the involvement of the legislature because it required a change in the basic plan of the government, a change in its fundamental mode of operation.

Slowly Rex began to see where I was headed and said, "Hmm, let's go." And we got the firm to back us up. We dove into this question and brought in other attorneys. We went back to the time in the seventies when Proposition 13 was first passed. At that point property taxes in California were escalating rapidly, the most vulnerable people and even the middle class were worried about losing their homes, and the state treasury had a surplus. When the property taxes were limited to 1 percent of a property's value and annual increases were severely restricted, it all seemed as if this was a traditional amendment.

This is where Section 3 comes into play, which said, "any change in state statute which results in a taxpayer paying a higher tax" must be approved by two thirds of both houses of the legislature. All of a sudden, as we pointed out in our lawsuit, "legislators opposing a tax increase are given the functional equivalent of more votes than those legislators who favor such proposals." If that does not go the basic issue of government's functioning I do not know what does.

The defendants were officials of the state of California, so the state had to decide if the Attorney General's office should get the case or if they would farm it out to an outside law firm. We were very pleased to learn that the state had hired a very good San Francisco firm to defend the case. What was their position? "We're not going to defend this case. Just hurry up." Apparently, the state would have loved for this issue to be settled, and we suspected they really wanted us to win.

Then we wondered what we were going to do. We needed to have an adversary—an opponent who would defend Section 3. Howard Jarvis, the successful California businessman, unsuccessful political candidate, and very successful architect of Proposition 13 was one of its most passionate defenders. Initially, the Jarvis Tax Institute wanted to do battle with us, but we were hoping for a different adversary, so we opposed them. At this point we withdrew our opposition, and the court allowed the Jarvis folks to intervene as the opponent.

We had our adversary, but we needed our plaintiff. I had talked to some friends who are political leaders, and who were very excited about our idea, and they were going to get us a lot of plaintiffs. They thought that hospitals or schools might serve that purpose. Then a friend of mine had a conversation with Charles Young, who for nearly thirty years was chancellor of UCLA and had been instrumental in its becoming a world-class educational institution. Chuck Young was as disgusted with the effects of Proposition 13 as I was, and interested in serving as the plaintiff in our suit. He and I discussed this, and once he agreed, I did not want anyone else.

Our strategy was two tiered. We attacked the initiative first on the basis of the Section 3. We argued that Section 3 of the initiative, as put on the ballot and approved by the voters, was a revision masquerading as an amendment. Our second challenge was on the constitutionality of the whole initiative process. We argued that the whole proposition process violates the Guarantee Clause of the United States Constitution. The Guarantee Clause says that every state shall have a republican form of government, and a republican form of government, in our history, is very clear in its meaning. It does not mean direct democracy. It means law-making by elected representatives. Now there is a *lot* of law that supports this, that serves as precedent for this all the way back to the beginning of our nation. In fact, the power of a legislative body to vote by majority rule is at the core of our democratic system.

I would like to say that we were successful, but despite our incredibly hard work, our careful strategy, the brilliant legal minds that participated on this case, and Rex Heinke's very skillful oral arguments, we failed: first with the lower court, then with the Second District Court of Appeal in Los Angeles, which denied our appeal, and finally, in November 2012, when the California Supreme Court declined to review our case.

Rex, Eddie and I built a robust and significant appellate practice at the firm. We hired lawyers who institutionalized the work, we took on important cases and often won them, and we had a great time doing it. Even in the midst of all our successes, I never stopped fighting this battle against Proposition 13. Maybe this is the white whale of my legal career, the unattainable quest for justice and victory. I just know that I am right about the importance of defeating this. After all these years, I know that I still have to trust my gut.

32

MY TWENTY-FIRST CENTURY

On July 31, 1995, Jane and I were in Colorado for an Aspen Institute seminar. The "Ideas Festival" had not yet been established—that happened in 2005—but well before they gave the event that famous name, the Institute's mission was to present programs to "foster values-based leadership, encouraging individuals to reflect on the ideals and ideas that define a good society, and to provide a neutral and balanced venue for discussing and acting on critical issues."

I had been invited to participate in the panel discussion on the issue raging at that time about a constitutional amendment requiring a balanced budget. I had co-moderated other programs in Aspen in the past—the signature Executive program with John Nolan and the Justice in Society program with Burt Neuborne—and I was delighted to be included among the experts assembled to discuss and debate this issue. The panel included the great philosopher, Mortimer Adler, who had created the Great Books program at the University of Chicago that was the backbone of the Executive Seminar, and some Conservative think tank representatives who were promoting the constitutional amendment proposal.

During the nineties, conservatives—especially the libertarians—were eager to amend our Constitution to include allowing Congress to prohibit flag burning, term limits, the balanced budget, and even an amendment making it impossible for Congress to create such regulatory agencies as the National Labor Relations Board and the Security and Exchange Commission. I suppose that when I was invited, my hosts had expected me to discuss these current issues from the perspective of a sitting judge. But the more that I thought about it, the more I realized that this was not what I wanted to discuss at all. I was speaking in front of an influential audience and I wanted discuss issues that were, for me, far more fundamental to our democracy than whether or not we should take seriously some reactionary amendments that would never move forward.

The session was crowded. The initial remarks were about constitutional history, specific amendments, and other highly focused investigations of the greatest document in American history. Then it was my turn. I spoke a bit about the nature of the meeting, but then said, "I want to lay on the table for your consideration a set of problems that are not in fashion in today's discussion of constitutional reform. Indeed, I find no discussion of these problems whatsoever in the large book of reading materials the Institute has sent us."

I had recently reacquainted myself with the great Franklin Delano Roosevelt speech on the Economic Bill of Rights that had so captured my interest on that January evening in 1944, when he first delivered it. I remembered sitting in our parent's house in Turtle Creek and tuning in for his State of the Union Address. We were all riveted not only by the brilliance of his analysis but also by how he spoke to all of us who had gone through the Great Depression, as if he truly knew what our families had experienced. He seemed to resonate with our worries and our hopes and our frustrations. It is a wonderful speech, and it does not get a lot of attention.

I began by explaining to my audience that from my perspective, the problems of poverty, race, the growth of the underclass and the simultaneous increase in the concentration of wealth had enormous social impact that should not be ignored in any serious discussion of constitutional reform. The term "the one percent" had not yet entered our national lexicon back then, but clearly the "one percent" was highly represented in our audience. It seemed a crucial audience for this message.

Then I spoke about Roosevelt's speech and his discussion of what he called a second, "economic" Bill of Rights. Roosevelt said that these rights included the right to adequate medical care, the right to a good education, the right of every family to have decent housing. Moreover, these rights should be as guaranteed as our constitutionally protected political and civil rights. I added "our Constitution is a masterpiece when it comes to individual liberty. It is, however, deafeningly silent when it comes to the economic rights Roosevelt laid out." Roosevelt pointed out that our political rights had proved inadequate to the pursuit of happiness because "true individual freedom cannot exist without economic security and independence."

I noted that the great debates of the nineties had revolved around the role of government in promoting distributive justice. Finally, I permitted my exasperation with these arguments to show, when I said that I had grown tired of listening to those who argued that the government is the enemy of economic justice and should be considered the problem not the solution. They are the ones who say that government should get out of the business of trying to regulate the distribution of wealth and income because economic growth is the key to economic justice. And that can only happen with unregulated market forces.

I had thought about this deeply, looked at the United States with its terrible inequality, and the continued struggle to reconcile the seemingly irreconcilable ideals of liberty and equality. I appreciated the fact that a comprehensive Economic Bill of Rights was not realistic any time soon. But I did believe that we could create magnificent social change by simply beginning with the children. At the end of the speech, I suggested that these are the issues that would bring the debate into focus as we spoke about constitutional reform. "Consider whether our Constitution should be amended to define the government's responsibility in providing for the well-being and education of our children—the most politically powerless members of our society."

I suggested that we restrict this Economic Bill of Rights just to the children and have the Constitution recognize that all children, regardless of the happenstance of birth, have the right to adequate nutrition, housing and health care, and a right to a good education.

As I look at my closing remarks today, I am struck by their prescience:

> In my view, the dominant challenge of the twenty-first century will be to demonstrate that economic and racial justice is compatible with a growing and productive market economy. Without economic justice, I believe we will never have racial justice. And without a free and vibrant economy, we cannot have the goods and services essential to the economic well-being of all Americans. So there you have it. How do we strike the proper balance between liberty and equality? We haven't answered the question yet, and it's not likely that we ever will, but we sure better keep trying.

Roosevelt could never have imagined the relevance that his words would have over fifty years later when I invoked them for my speech, nor could I have dreamed of the relevance of my words twenty years later, as I write my book in 2015. In fact, I have lived long enough to see in many of our contemporary debates echoes of the issues and concerns that have been a part of my life for my entire life. Questions of race, of equality, of supporting our citizens through healthcare and education, and of the power of the court system—especially but not only the Supreme Court—to both advance what is the best of us, or reinforce those values that should cause us shame. All this forms the warp and woof of my personal experience but also, I believe, of the American Experience.

Bill Clinton had been president for three years when I gave my speech. Clinton was troubling for me because I could see how the very problems that I highlighted in my speech seemed to have gotten worse during his administration. The tense relationship that he had with Congress had deteriorated after the mid-term elections, when Newt Gingrich seized control of the Congress. Clinton bore some responsibility for the failure of his admirable attempt to change our healthcare system. The widening gap between the haves and the have-nots only became wider with an increasing concentration of wealth and a concomitant growth of an underclass. Clinton had to spend so much time battling for his political survival; I felt that he had lost sight of some of the most important issues of his presidency.

In 1997 I began to wonder if someone might run for President who I would really be excited about, who I would really like to see be the President. I was in a position to be able to help that person. I had supported my fellow Princeton Alum, Bill Bradley, who I think would have been a great President, but it was not meant to be. I had to wait for a transformative figure to emerge—and ten years later he did.

I remember watching Barack Obama's speech in the 2004 convention, and I thought almost from the get go that anyone who would have the courage to make a speech about what a mistake it was to go to war in Iraq was a man who commanded my respect—and interest. I liked everything about him, and I still do. As Jane and I watched, we wondered if this could be the man who might be our first African American President.

I had known about Obama from two of my former law clerks. One of them was Crystal Nix, an elegant, six-foot-three, African American woman, a Princeton undergraduate (she knew Michele Obama when she was there) who clerked for me from 1990 to 1991—she then went on to clerk for both Thurgood Marshall and Sandra Day O'Connor. Before going to law school, she was a reporter for the *New York Times* on the city desk and was an outstanding journalist. Even the hidebound Gray Lady was devastated when she told them she was going to leave to go to Harvard Law School. While there, she and another of my clerks, Jean Manas, were on the Law Review with a guy named Barack Obama.

So when we first saw Obama speak in 2004, we felt a personal thread of a connection to him that extended from two members of our law clerk "family."

In the summer of 2006, Jane and I were driving from L.A. to our vacation home in Deer Valley and listening to Obama read his powerful memoir, *Dreams from My Father*. I think it is one of our greatest books on race and the United States ever written. But he is also very insightful about the law. In one passage he writes, "The study of law can be disappointing at times, a matter of applying narrow rules and arcane procedure to an uncooperative reality; a sort of glorified accounting that serves to regulate the affairs of those who have power—and that all too often seeks to explain, to those who do not, the ultimate wisdom and justness of their condition. But that's not all the law is. The law is also memory; the law also records a long-running conversation, a nation arguing with its conscience."

If he did not have me before, he got me then.

We were attending a Renaissance Weekend in Park City, and talk of politics was intense. Bush's disastrous presidency was nearing an end, and it appeared to many that Hillary Clinton was going to be our candidate. I would have thought so too, but I was not sure that I could support her if Obama decided to run. We had many conversations about this in Deer Valley that summer, and I said to my Hillary supporting friends, "Not so fast, we really need to talk to this guy."

Shortly afterwards, we were invited to his book signing party in Los Angeles at the home of John and Kimberly Emerson, and I had my first experience meeting him. You could get near to him, you could talk to him, and he treated everyone with a deference and interest that was compelling. I liked the way he responded to people, I liked the way he thought, and I liked his personality. I also liked what I heard from some of my other law clerks, such as Eddie Lazarus, who also knew him. They were impressed.

Then, in early February 2007, I received a telephone call from our future President. He said, "I'm going to pull the trigger, Judge, are you going to be aboard?" I gave him an emphatic yes. "That's great," Obama said. "I just wanted to be sure that you would support me before I do this."

On February 10, 2007, in Springfield, Illinois, he announced that he was running for President in another great speech. "Each and every time, a new generation has risen up and done what's needed to be done," he said. "Today we are called once more, and it is time for our generation to answer that call."

Immediately after that speech, we attended his first fundraiser in Los Angeles, which was held at the gracious home of Michael and Mattie Lawson, previously owned by Muhammad Ali. As an A-list interior designer, Mattie had created a stunning home and had gotten to know the Obamas, another highly accomplished African American couple in Chicago. This was his first fundraising event in the campaign anywhere in California, and it set a tone for what happened afterwards: many Hillary supporters realized that they had another option.

Jane and I brought the great actor Leonard Nimoy and his wife Susan, who lived down the street and were good friends of ours. There were many people we knew who were there, and I cut through the crowd to introduce Leonard to Obama. I thought that the two of them meeting would be a terrific photograph and I was ready to take it! Obama remembered that meeting when Leonard died eight years later, on February 27, 2015. The official White House statement said, "In 2007, I had the chance to meet Leonard in person. It was only logical to greet him with the Vulcan salute, the universal sign for 'Live long and prosper.'" And after 83 years on this planet—and on his visits to many others—it's clear Leonard Nimoy did just that. Michelle and I join his family, friends, and countless fans who miss him so dearly today."

It was another behind the scenes moment for Jane and me—another small footnote in history in which I had the privilege of being a part.

I signed on with great enthusiasm for Obama's campaign, and I would spend time calling people to gain their support. What a joy it was to have reclaimed my First Amendment rights! I would get names and phone numbers from campaign headquarters in Chicago, and sometimes I would call lawyers, other times just regular citizens. I told the people in charge of the phone bank that the one place I most wanted to call was Turtle Creek, Pennsylvania.

They got me the phone numbers and the names to call. It had been a long time since I had been a member of that community, but some folks still remembered me. What was most meaningful for me was that I was able to make a difference not because I was a lawyer or a judge, nor because I had gone to Princeton or Stanford, but because I had graduated from Turtle Creek High School and was going to bat for Barack Obama. When he won the election, Jane and I were on one of our great trips—this time to India and Bhutan—but even from that great distance the impact of this election was felt. I felt a surge of pride, not just for this young idealistic man who broke through every imaginable barrier by the sheer strength of his intelligence and his determination, but also for the men and women of our country, who transcended a history of prejudice to vote for this young African American man.

From the time that I wrote my senior thesis at Princeton, over half a century before Obama became President, I knew that the healthcare system in our country was broken. Back then, Harry Truman had tried and failed to institute a universal health care system. At last, we had a President who was committed to try to fix it. In his efforts with the Affordable Care Act, I saw two areas that were most meaningful to me— the law and health care—converge in ways that were both exhilarating and disturbing. I marveled at the fact that my President was able to accomplish something that should have been done decades ago and provide some sort of coverage for nearly everyone. It was far from perfect, but it was a valuable beginning.

But then I watched that very same law, that fundamental human right as far as I was concerned, come under attack and reach the Supreme Court—frighteningly, as I write this, it is happening again. No case law could possibly offer any kind of a precedent for invalidating the act, and yet the Supreme Court took it on. I had often heard discussions about so called "judicial activism." One could not serve on the Ninth Circuit when I did, and not hear that we were "out of step" or "judicial activists." I found these suggestions absolutely off base.

The courts are not "steps" that progress neatly from one to another, with the ninth one being a different height, or at an inconsistent angle. The Ninth Circuit is composed of many individual judges; only a few are responsible for any single opinion. I can think of dozens of opinions when judges appointed by Republicans would write opinions that liberals would applaud. And other judges, who were considered to be flaming liberals would be on a side that could be held up by any conservative as a model. I remember contemplating these issues even when I clerked for Justice Douglas, because he too would recoil at the notion of something called "judicial activism." If the result is something people like, then they are happy with it. If they do not like the opinion, he said, then the accusation of "judicial activism" is leveled.

On June 28, 2012 the Supreme Court issued a 5–4 decision on the constitutionality of the Affordable Care Act. The central question was whether Congress could legitimately authorize its requirement that most Americans obtain insurance or pay a penalty by its power to levy taxes. Chief Justice Roberts wrote, "Because the Constitution permits such a tax, it is not our role to forbid it or to pass upon its wisdom or fairness." But the Court rejected the argument that the law's "individual mandate" was actually justified by Congress' power to regulate interstate commerce, and it also limited the expansion of Medicaid, finding that Congress exceeded its Spending Clause authority by coercing states into participation in the Medicaid expansion by threatening to revoke all of their Medicaid funding if they declined.

I believed that the combination of the individual mandate and the Medicaid expansion was an obvious and appropriate way of guaranteeing something closer to universal health care coverage, an important issue for the wellbeing of so many people. I did not think the existing case law required the Court to strike down the Medicaid expansion. But whatever the Court decided on these new and complex issues, it was bound to develop new law, and so lead some, on one side or the other, to see judicial activism. For myself, I was mostly just relieved that the core of the Act, the individual mandate, survived.

I was disappointed to read Justice Kennedy's dissent: "The values that should have determined our course today are caution, minimalism, and the understanding that the Federal Government is one of limited powers. But the Court's ruling undermines those values at every turn. In the name of restraint, it overreaches. In the name of constitutional avoidance, it creates new constitutional questions. In the name of cooperative federalism, it undermines state sovereignty."

But for my conversation with Bob Tuttle, Tony Kennedy might not have been on the short list of Supreme Court nominees and thus not have become a Supreme Court Justice. When I spoke to Tuttle, I did not know what Kennedy's "judicial philosophy" was. He always appeared a middle of the road jurist in line with the Justice he would replace, Lewis Powell. Kennedy's vote on the healthcare act came as a surprise. I concluded that Kennedy is a libertarian—in the sense that he wants the government to be hands off in what happens in the private lives of an individual, in the bedroom, or when praying in public school. On these issues, we agree. But when it comes to the way that government allocates its resources, its power to provide for social or economic justice, that is where we part company. I have always been put off by social and political philosophy that advocates a kind of social Darwinism, a survival of the fittest.

Survival of the fittest. Was that how we thought our society should work, coming from Turtle Creek, PA? Were those of us who managed to achieve some measure of success in our lives, those of us who emerged from the hard scrabble world of the Depression and the war, were we the ones who somehow *deserved* it because we were the fittest? What a pernicious and destructive model to superimpose on the promise that resides in every single American.

I need only go back to my growing up, go back to my family and my gifted brother George, and use them as the perfect examples of how wrong and dangerous this line of reasoning is. Timing. Luck. Happenstance. These are the qualities that gave me the opportunities that George never enjoyed. Was he bitter? Of course not. Was I grateful? Absolutely.

When I gave my speech at the Aspen Institute those many years ago, and invoked FDR, I knew that I could be seen as being somehow old fashioned or out of step. Liberal opinions have always been a part of my life: As a kid working as a journalist; in the Navy serving my country and eventually getting a first class education, courtesy of the GI Bill; as a clerk to William O. Douglas in the highest court of the land; as a young lawyer, juggling all the balls of the law and my political engagement; as a judge, crafting opinions that were not always liberal, but always informed by hard work and balanced judgment. To live and to see the day when gay rights include the right to marry, when the Affordable Care Act is law, when an African American man is the President, is to have the fundamental areas of injustice that have defined my personal and professional values move closer to a resolution.

During my privileged and engaged life, I never lost sight that with great rights come enormous responsibilities. That recognition is part of my DNA, and it all began in Turtle Creek.

LAFLA award ceremony, 2013: Ray Fisher, Bill Norris and Neal Manne

EPILOGUE

At the end of July in 2013, I received a letter from Paul Salvaty, the President of the Los Angeles Legal Aid Foundation board, inviting me to "accept LAFLA's Maynard Toll Award for Distinguished Public Service at our fifteenth Annual Access to Justice Dinner." I had known about the dinner and known a bit about Maynard Toll, the crusading lawyer and civil rights activist. I also knew that the dinner was always a major fundraising event to sustain their work in providing high quality free legal services throughout the city of Los Angeles—in community offices and courthouse domestic violence clinics and Self Help legal centers. But, quite honestly, Jane and I had not attended those dinners and I was not exactly sure what they involved.

The letter then explained that the award that they wanted to bestow on me was "to honor members of the bar whose exemplary records of public service and commitment to legal services for the poor are in the best traditions of the legal profession."

Exemplary record...

Public Service...

Commitment to the poor...

Best traditions of the legal profession.

I was eighty-six years old. I had enjoyed a remarkable life with the kinds of privileges and blessings—in family, in education, in opportunity, and in friends—that were bounteous by any standard. I could not even speak when I handed the letter to Jane and she read what it said. She looked up and our eyes met and held each other for a moment. Her face broke into one of her classic Jane radiant smiles, filled with pride and love. I realized that this was a big deal. We also realized that on the date they proposed for the event, we would be in Argentina, on a long planned tango vacation there. But that was resolved when LAFLA agreed to move the date.

My biggest worry then was what could I possibly say in my acceptance speech?

It is difficult for me to explain how consuming this concern was. That damn speech very nearly led me to decide at several points that maybe this was just not meant to be. Perhaps I could bow out gracefully. But that was so utterly uncharacteristic of me and a non-starter for Jane. Clearly for the last eight decades I was not a quitter; all I had to do was figure out what to say. The challenge was to somehow manage to focus my remarks not on my so-called "exemplary record," but on something bigger, perhaps something that had motivated me. Racism and inequality? Human rights for all including the LGBT community? The responsibilities of the courts in securing the promise of our Constitution? Maybe a walk down memory lane, talking about Justice Douglas excoriating the whole notion of so called "judicial activism"? Jane and I talked about it endlessly and the more we talked, the clearer she became that there was only one approach that would work.

She was, as always, correct.

Two dear friends—my former law partner Ray Fisher and my former law clerk Neal Manne—had both agreed to speak at the event, which was held at the Beverly Hilton Hotel on December 3, 2013. I put on a dark Armani suit and Jane looked stunning in a blue dress. When we walked into the ballroom of the Beverly Hilton, the crowds who had gathered there—close to a thousand people—took me aback. Some faces in that crowd I recognized from various parts of my career: from the days with Pat Brown, from Tuttle & Taylor, from Stanford Law, from my run for Attorney General, from MOCA, from the Ninth Circuit, and from Akin Gump.

When we got to our table my whole family was there along with Nigel Lythgoe, a producer friend who along with his son had recently traveled with us to Argentina. Never before in my life had so many important people in my life been gathered under one roof.

My son Don, who was a Stanford lawyer in private practice in Los Angeles, attended with his daughter Semantha, an athlete, artist and NYU graduate. His son Nathan was in New York, where he had embarked on studies towards getting his Ph.D. in History. Barbara, who as a child would gather her friends to quiz me on the First Amendment, now lived in Hawaii and could not attend because of her health. My youngest child Alison was there—her delicate build belied her exceptional athleticism, especially as a tennis player. She knows more about marketing in the tech world than any of us, and has worked in it for years. Kim, who was responsible for bringing Jane into my life, tragically lost her much too young husband to lung cancer; she created the Lung Cancer Foundation of

America to raise funds to support research in combatting this terrible disease. Our son David and Karina, both lawyers in L.A.'s entertainment industry, were newlyweds and much to our happiness had just moved back to L.A. from New York. I looked around the table and was so thankful they came to share this moment with me.

How nice to still be alive for the experience! On each place setting was a thick program that both described the event and the great work of the Legal Aid Society. It was also filled with paid ads from people in my life, some of whom were not able to attend. Audrey Irmas, our dear friend and MOCA board member, was an important philanthropist and a great supporter of legal aid services for the poor. She had the inside cover tribute. Ann Alpers, who had clerked for me brilliantly from 1989-1990 and worked on the Wayne Newton NBC case, had corralled my law clerks for their own tribute page. She later told me that this was the easiest money she had ever raised!

I looked at the thick program and read the lineup. Gary Blasi from UCLA was going to receive the Lifetime Achievement Award, then I was going to receive the Maynard Toll Award, Steptoe & Johnson would receive the Pro Bono Service Award, and the Corporate Achievement Award was going to an organization called JAMS, The Resolution Experts. It was going to be a big, emotional night.

The lights dimmed and Paul Salvaty went to the microphone and thanked everyone for attending. He welcomed the board members and the honored guests and spoke about Maynard Toll and what the award and the dinner meant. He then described some of my work, but said that he would leave most of that to the two guests who had agreed to make remarks: Judge Raymond C. Fisher from the United States Court of Appeals for the Ninth Circuit, and Neal Manne, the managing partner of Susman Godfrey.

As Ray walked up to the microphone, I remembered our first meeting when I was at Tuttle & Taylor. When we met, I knew—trusting my gut, as always—that Ray would not only be an exemplary lawyer, but twelve years my junior, he was likely to also become a good friend. When Bill Clinton installed him as Associate Attorney General of the United States in 1998, I was asked to speak about Ray at the event and said that I had to admit, "I feel a little like the proud father watching his son leave home to serve his country. I take a special pleasure in this feeling because I am one of the few people who can still get away with expressions of paternal affection for Ray Fisher."

And there he was. A distinguished man and now both a grandfather and a Ninth Circuit Judge standing at the microphone and looking down at me and at the crowd in front of him. He is a wonderful speaker, dignified and thoughtful. He asked the question that I imagine a few people in the crowd might have been wondering: "How was—and is—Bill particularly special?" Ray described me in a matter-of-fact-way, pointing out that what drives me is the desire to "bring about real world results."

He went through my career and highlighted many of its aspects that had given me the most pride: my work on the State Board of Education, my work in helping to recruit and elect Wilson Riles to be the first African American elected to any statewide office when he became California State Superintendent of Public Instruction, and Tom Bradley who became the first African American mayor of Los Angeles. Ray talked about my run for California Attorney General, the founding of MOCA, and my seventeen years on the Ninth Circuit. Then he spent some time discussing my *Watkins* opinion and described how important that decision was.

I listened and it was as if a movie were running through my head with his remarks as the narration. I could see all the moments and people he described. I could remember the sting of losing the Attorney General race and the thrill of the moment when it all came together for MOCA. And I thought of all the people he mentioned, from Justice Douglas to Governor Pat Brown, from Wilson Riles to Sergeant Watkins, and all the law clerks and young associates who worked behind the scenes to help me be a whole lot smarter and more successful than I could ever have been on my own.

After he finished his speech and the applause died down, one of those law clerks came up to the podium. Neal Manne was now the managing partner of the Houston law firm of Susman Godfrey and a brilliant commercial litigator. He was neither from the Ivy League nor Stanford but the University of Texas, both as an undergraduate and from the law school. But when I first interviewed him I knew that he was a world-class intellect and a brilliant young lawyer. He was quicksilver smart but irreverent. He began his speech that night by saying that when he arrived in my chambers "there was a clear division of responsibility. My co-clerks did excellent legal work. I made Bill laugh."

He was right about that. He did make me laugh when he clerked for me, he has made me laugh during the following decades of our friendship. He certainly made the crowd laugh during his remarks. He pointed out that my conservative colleague on the Ninth Circuit, Judge Anthony Kennedy, provided me with plenty to do during my first year on the bench: "Bill spent the year disagreeing with and dissenting from everything that came out of the chambers of Judge Anthony Kennedy."

Good Texan that he is, Neal is a natural storyteller and quite a gifted writer, so his speech was a great yarn. He focused on the Bork hearings because Neal was Senator Arlen Specter's chief of staff at the time. He described for the crowd the "secret role of a particular Ninth Circuit judge in Judge Bork's demise and Justice Kennedy's ascent to the court."

I knew both stories pretty well, for heaven's sake I *lived* them, but listening to Neal gave them a freshness that was as if I were listening to them for the first time. He had everyone in that room eating out of his hand. He then wound up his talk by offering some morals to the story. I will quote a few of them here, not to be immodest, but to show Neal's facility with a closing argument:

First, always take Bill Norris' phone calls, even when you are busy. Second, don't take it personally if Bill writes a lengthy and incendiary dissent from your one sentence denial of a rehearing *en banc*, he may help get you to the Supreme Court one day. Third, Bill has ten new ideas every morning before breakfast and yes, most of them are nutty, but the good ones, boy they are really good. Some have changed the course of history. Fourth, Bill has a brilliant legal mind and a brilliant sense of practical politics, which is a powerful combination. Finally, Bill has always been and remains deeply engaged in the world around him, always enthusiastically scheming to achieve good as he sees it.

And then Neal closed in a way that moved me nearly to tears. "I know how proud you are, even fifty-eight years later, to describe yourself as a William O. Douglas clerk," he said. "I speak for all of your former law clerks in saying we are just as proud to call ourselves William A. Norris clerks."

And then it was my turn.

That evening has a magical quality for me still. All that was said, everyone who was there. I felt in some ways as if I was moving in slow motion up to the podium, now that the time had come to deliver the speech over which I had agonized. Jane walked me to the stage and gracefully slipped into the wings. I would like to say that I began my speech without a hitch. But I did not. I was overwhelmed and the sheer emotion of the whole evening disorganized me. I went off my prepared remarks to try to extemporaneously say a few words, and I became hopelessly lost. Even from my days in Turtle Creek, when I was Jack Frost in the first grade play and choked, I appreciated that memorization and going off script were not my strengths.

Jane came to the rescue. She walked out onto the stage, and gently refocused me to my prepared remarks, the speech that the two of us had crafted that expressed exactly what I had wanted to say. With her standing nearby, I looked down and began to read. And the words took over.

I said that I was turning eighty-six this year and "It's natural to look back and ponder what my legacy will be." But then, those who may have expected a public meditation on what I had thought of my own legacy, might have been disappointed, because I changed course. My remarks were not going to be about me: they were going to be about "some of my heroes who opened doors for me and gave me the confidence to walk through them. So it is to their legacy of public service that I want to pay tribute tonight." I could feel something palpable in the atmosphere of the room change. There was a little ripple of surprise, of curiosity, of the unexpected.

I spoke about Turtle Creek and my parents who did not have more than an eighth grade education. I said that my first hero was Franklin Roosevelt, who signed the GI Bill of Rights and made an education possible for me, in a way that wasn't possible for my very gifted oldest brother George. I next mentioned Warren Christopher, who not only was responsible for getting me into Tuttle & Taylor, but also into Adlai Stevenson's campaign office "thereby launching me into a lifetime of public service combined with the practice of law." Of course I thanked Ed Tuttle and Bob Taylor for giving me the freedom to "get engaged in public service while practicing the law in their firm."

Pat Brown was the next person, the next hero I thanked for appointing me to the State Board of Education that led to so much else in my civic life in California. I was so grateful to Tom Bradley who appointed me his first President of the Los Angeles Police Commission and who trusted me to lend the power of the Mayor's office to the creation of MOCA. I thanked Sam Williams, a prominent lawyer who recommended my appointment to the Ninth Circuit and used his persuasive powers to talk me into abandoning my life as an activist lawyer to become a monastic judge.

I then pointed out that in reflecting on the impact that all these people had on my life in the law and in public service, I also realized that when it comes to my legacy, it "lies in the accomplishments of all those I have been privileged to work with." I mentioned Ray Fisher and Neal Manne, but also all my other Tuttle & Taylor colleagues and my extended family of more than fifty law clerks, over twenty of whom went on to serve in the Supreme Court. I gave a special expression of gratitude to my former law clerk Eddie Lazarus, who with Rex Heinke established Akin Gump's appellate practice. I said that "it has been my privilege to have worked with all of you and I am certain that my most enduring legacy is in the impact that all of you are now having and will have for years to come."

Finally, I thanked Jane, "my loving wife, soul mate, editor, and tango partner" and my children and grandchildren, "who give the word legacy its most compelling meaning."

And then I was done.

I looked up and there was that moment of complete silence that comes when people are hanging on to every word and not quite sure they want it to be over. All of a sudden, the applause shook the hall. People were standing up, some complete strangers were wiping tears from their eyes, and I looked over at Jane who smiled with the kind of pride that showed me that I had done a good job. Together we descended the stairs into the mass of friends and family and colleagues and perfect strangers who reached out, grabbed my hand, patted me on the back, expressed their congratulations and yes, their gratitude.

Because in the end, that is what the gift of my life has taught me: there is no accomplishment, no failure, no achievement, and no decision that is ever in a vacuum, that ever comes without touching another life. Sometimes, one has the honor of being able to touch many lives. Sometimes, one has the special joy of touching the life of one person in particular—a child, a spouse, a friend, a bashert soul mate.

And the miracle of my life, of the long and happy journey from Turtle Creek to that magical evening in the Beverly Hilton Hotel, were all the other lives that have made mine not only rich and wonderful, but actually possible. My family and friends, my teachers and mentors, my colleagues and clerks, some still alive, many long gone, were all somehow gathered that evening, in fact and in memory. I realized that night, that to have been able to live the life of an unapologetic liberal, during some of the most interesting and demanding times in our history, in public service and the law, was one of the greatest privileges I could have ever imagined.

* * * * *

Bill Norris and his grandchildren,
Semantha and Nathan Norris, 1999

ACKNOWLEDGMENTS

This memoir was a labor of love, but it would never have been possible if not for the support and collaboration from many people who believed in this project even more than I did. It took some persuading from my wife, Jane Jelenko, who for many years insisted that I had a story worth telling. By the time I agreed to take it on, many of the details of my life had been relegated to the deep recesses of my memory. Thankfully, we had a great place to start—an oral history conducted a few years earlier by Bradley Williams, Ph.D., then Director of the Ninth Judicial Circuit Historical Society, and arranged by my friend Marc Seltzer.

With the transcript in hand, we reached out to Marianne Szegedy-Maszak, a wonderful writer in Washington D.C. Her background and talents as an investigative journalist were perfect for this project, but it was her warmth and understanding of my values, my priorities and frankly, my demanding personality, that made our collaboration such a joy. Marianne spoke to many people who are important to my story who gave of their time generously including Eddie Lazarus, Neal Manne, Ann Alpers, Einer Elhague, Jean Manas, Maria Acebal, Tobias Wolff and Gloria Lujan. I also want to thank those who helped jog my memory and check my facts—Kitty Hagen, Layman Allen, Ray Fisher, Eli Chernow, Rex Henke, Cathy Catterson, Michael Small, Johanna Shargel, Danny Waldman, Russell Frackman and Michelle Anderson.

When the first draft was done, many of my friends and family came over to read it aloud with me, a truly awesome experience. I thank my readers Susan Loewenberg (who also introduced us to Marianne), Ranee Katzenstein, Paul Stern, Jill and John Bauman, Don Norris, Kim Norris, Alison Norris, David Jelenko and Karina Yamada Jelenko. David also provided astute legal advice for which I am grateful.

Special thanks to Eddie Lazarus for his wonderful Foreword and for his friendship all these years. I also appreciate the advice and support of many old and new friends through this process—Bert Deixler, Annie Gilbar, Daniel Weiss, Rachel Moore, Erwin Chemerinsky, Catherine Fisk and John Emerson. I am so grateful for your generous offers of help.

It was Rene Balcer who made the serendipitous connection to our publisher, Quid Pro Books. Many thanks to Rene and Carolyn Hsu for their support and friendship.

I would like to thank Alan Childress from Quid Pro Books for appreciating this project and immediately understanding that a judge who has lived through many interesting times—and decisions—might be able to write something more than an opinion. And I have Alan to thank for suggesting that we work with John Stick, one of my first law clerks and retired professor from Tulane Law School, as our editor. His care and meticulous work went far beyond anything I could have expected, and the book is all the better for his input.

Finally, I must thank Jane, my wife, who urged me to write the book, but it could not have been written without her. Her sharp editorial sense, her ability to fill in some of the memories that may have receded for me, and her passionate commitment to this work has made this as much her book as it is mine. I will never be able to thank her for making this dream, as so many others, come true.

W.A.N.

Los Angeles, California
July 2016

APPENDIX

LAW CLERKS TO JUDGE WILLIAM A. NORRIS

LAST NAME, FIRST NAME	YEAR	SCHOOL
1. Manne, Neal	1980-1981	Texas
2. Stick, John	1980-1981	UCLA
3. Waldman, Daniel	1980-1981	Columbia
4. Heldman , Julie	1981-1982	UCLA
5. Levinson, Michael	1981-1982	Stanford
6. Richardson, Susan	1981-1982	Boalt Hall
7. Blacklock, Bonnie	1982-1983	Texas
8. Samuels, Jocelyn	1982-1983	Columbia
9. Simpson, John	1982-1983	Harvard
10. Hahn, Richard	1983-1984	Columbia
11. Noblin, James Robert	1983-1984	Harvard
12. Phillips, Gregory D.	1983-1984	Stanford
13. Cheston, Sheila	1984-1985	Columbia
14. Solum, Lawrence	1984-1985	Harvard
15. Zacharia, Karen	1984-1985	Stanford
16. McConnell, Stephen	1985-1986	Chicago
17. Miller, Scott D.	1985-1986	Columbia
18. Warnke, Stephen	1985-1986	Harvard
19. Caminker, Evan	1986-1987	Yale
20. Elhauge, Einer	1986-1987	Harvard
21. Teitelbaum, David	1986-1987	Columbia
22. Crouter, Mary	1987-1988	Yale
23. Fisk, Catherine	1987-1988	Boalt Hall
24. Lazarus, Edward	1987-1988	Yale
25. Amar, Vikram	1988-1989	Yale
26. Hay, Bruce	1988-1989	Harvard
27. Keeny, Virginia	1988-1989	Stanford
28. Alpers, Ann	1989-1990	Stanford
29. Feder, Meir	1989-1990	Harvard
30. Landsman, Lisa	1989-1990	Boalt Hall
31. Marder, Nancy	1989-1990	Yale
32. Araiza, William	1990-1991	Yale
33. Helyar Meyer, Linda	1990-1991	Boalt Hall
34. Nix-Hines, Crystal	1990-1991	Harvard
35. Dodge, William	1991-1992	Yale
36. Freshman, Clark	1991-1992	Stanford
37. Manas, Jean	1991-1992	Harvard

38.	Chander, Anupam	1992-1993	Yale
39.	Ehrlich, Miles	1992-1993	Yale
40.	Forman, James	1992-1993	Yale
41.	Tucher, Alison	1992-1993	Stanford
42.	Fitzpatrick, Michael	1993-1994	Stanford
43.	Jones, Carla	1993-1994	Yale
44.	Kang, Jerry	1993-1994	Harvard
45.	Rowe, Gary	1993-1994	Yale
46.	Acebal, Maria	1994-1995	Yale
47.	Anderson, Michelle	1994-1995	Yale
48.	Grossman, Joanna	1994-1995	Stanford
49.	Russell, Kevin	1994-1995	Yale
50.	Green, Julie	1995-1996	Harvard
51.	Katzenstein, Ranee	1995-1996	Stanford
52.	Wang, Cecillia	1995-1996	Yale
53.	Bircoll, Alexis	1996-1997	Stanford
54.	Lee, Sandra	1996-1997	Stanford
55.	Lhamon, Catherine	1996-1997	Yale
56.	Hecker, Eric	1997	Michigan
57.	Pottow, John	1997	Harvard
58.	Wolff, Tobias	1997	Yale

Visit us at *www.quidprobooks.com.*

CPSIA information can be obtained
at www.ICGtesting.com
Printed in the USA
FFOW02n1259091116
29213FF